SO-AIB-441

DATE DUE			
Jun7 '82			

WITHDRAWN

ECONOMIC REGULATION AND THE PUBLIC INTEREST

The Federal Trade Commission
in Theory and Practice

ECONOMIC REGULATION AND THE PUBLIC INTEREST

The Federal Trade Commission
in Theory and Practice

ALAN STONE

CARL A. RUDISILL LIBRARY
LENOIR RHYNE COLLEGE

Cornell University Press

ITHACA AND LONDON

353.008
Sx7e
120619
Ma.1982

Copyright © 1977 by Cornell University

All rights reserved. Except for brief quotations in a review, this book, or parts thereof, must not be reproduced in any form without permission in writing from the publisher. For information address Cornell University Press, 124 Roberts Place, Ithaca, New York 14850.

First published 1977 by Cornell University Press.
Published in the United Kingdom by Cornell University Press Ltd., 2-4 Brook Street, London W1Y 1AA.

International Standard Book Number 0-8014-1066-5
Library of Congress Catalog Card Number 76-25645
Printed in the United States of America by York Composition Co., Inc.
Librarians: Library of Congress cataloging information appears on the last page of the book.

FOR

Leslie, Bill, and Ralph

Contents

Contents

Preface

While it is common to categorize writings on social action according to radical, liberal, and conservative traditions, an even more fundamental distinction exists. On the one hand, there is a tradition, particularly strong in America, which seeks to explain behavior on the basis of the actors' personal characteristics. This mode of analysis cuts across the spectrum from left to right, and its most frequent form is the "discovery" of a conspiracy of malevolent men. Whether the alleged conspiracy is Communist or Wall Street, the focus is on the personal qualities of the actors. A variant of the "malevolent" theme is the finding of a conspiracy of incompetence. Again the personal qualities of the actors form the major focus of inquiry and lead inevitably to the remedy—throw out the incompetents and boodlers, replace them with competent persons dedicated to the public interest, and all will be well. The numerous Nader reports, of which the 1969 study of the Federal Trade Commission (F.T.C.) was a prototype, are modern examples of this tradition. The fact that things never do turn out to be quite so rosy when "reformers" replace the incumbents at the examined institutions undermines the position of this school. But instead of examining underlying premises, a new generation of muckrakers re-examines agency personnel and comes to the same conclusions as the earlier ones.

In contrast to the tradition that seeks explanations of social action in personal characteristics is the social theory tradition. While readily conceding that individuals' personal characteristics do make a difference, analysts of this persuasion examine the underlying characteristics of institutions, laws, and social arrangements to explain social action and development. This tradition too is embraced by writers across the spectrum of political opinion; among its most famous adherents are Adam Smith, Karl Marx, Emile Durkheim, and Max Weber. Marx's theoretical structure has heavily influenced this book. The concepts of contradiction and conflict both between classes and between factions within classes underpin my analysis. Max Weber's exposition of the relationship between rationality and capitalism is a striking reflection of the Marxian concept that a society's superstructure is determined by its economic structure and has also heavily influenced my analysis. One of the major works on the F.T.C.'s genesis, Gabriel Kolko's brilliant *Triumph of Conservatism,* is in the social theory tradition, and while I disagree with some if its interpretations, the work also exercised an enormous influence on my orientation.

Of even greater consequence in developing my attitude toward regulatory conduct was the cumulative impression made by eight years as an attorney with the F.T.C. Contrary to the impression created by occasional anecdotal "evidence" offered by Ralph Nader's investigators, I found most of the F.T.C.'s employees to be decent, hard-working, attentive to their tasks, and sufficiently competent. Certainly there were a few notorious cases of incompetence and indolence, but these were rare exceptions. Yet I could fully agree with the finding of Nader's investigators that the agency's performance, measured by the goals of protecting the consumer and preserving competition, was inadequate. The discrepancy between this widely shared conclusion and my own lack of an adequate explanation for the agency's conduct and performance led to this study.

In the course of developing this work, I have been aided by many persons, but four of them have been of major importance in forcing me to rethink the arguments made and positions taken. James E. Anderson (University of Houston), Michael Levy (Rutgers University), Theodore J. Lowi (Cornell University), and my wife, Celeste Stone, read and reread the manuscript, continually making suggestions for improvement. In addition, my wife typed the entire manuscript. I am also grateful to Kenneth Prewitt and Herbert J. Storing, both of the University of Chicago, for reading an earlier version and making constructive suggestions. Franklin Edwards and Robert P. Shay (Columbia University) made very useful comments on the section dealing with truth-in-lending legislation. I would also like to thank Laquita Stidham and Liz Jurica for typing major portions of the revised manuscript and the Editorial Department of Cornell University Press for their detailed and perceptive work. Finally, thanks are also due to many F.T.C. personnel for aid in obtaining documents and clarifying factual matters. The Commission's secretary, Charles A. Tobin, was helpful beyond the call of duty in this respect. None of them is necessarily in agreement with the views I have set forth here.

ALAN STONE

Houston, Texas

PART ONE

REGULATION AND
CAPITALISM

CHAPTER 1

Introduction: The Political
Contradictions of Capitalism

Modern capitalist enterprise has been beset since its inception by a fundamental contradiction that has found its reflection in the realm of public policy. On the one hand, the enterprise wants to increase its sales and profits at the expense of its rivals; on the other hand, it wants to maintain its profit and sales position against the encroachments of rivals and thus to assure its own stability. Adam Smith was one of the first important commentators to note this contradiction, observing that individuals have a strong incentive to grow through vigorous competition, yet that "people of the same trade seldom meet together, even for merriment and diversion, but the conversation ends in a conspiracy against the public, or in some contrivance to raise prices."[1] The contradiction manifests itself when a firm acts collusively at one moment to fix prices in order to promote stability and at another cuts prices in order to gain additional custom at the expense of rivals. The conduct of business enterprises cannot be understood without an appreciation of this basic contradiction.

A firm's decision to court or avoid competition at any given time depends on its immediate circumstances. A firm that has a considerable proportion of a market but is beset by hungry rivals is apt to favor stability over competition. Judge Elbert Gary, for example, while chief policy maker of the United States Steel Corporation at a time when the firm was losing part of its market share to smaller rivals, wrote to the Attorney General, "We are perfectly satisfied to limit the amount of our business to our proportion of capacity and to do everything possible we can to promote the interests of our competitors."[2] Another firm's strategy might be one of intense competition; or a firm might adopt an ambiguous strategy, incorporating goals of both competition and stability during the same period.

Business enterprises—individually, collectively, even universally— may seek to restrict competitive conduct not only by voluntary action but also through governmental action or law.[3] Formal trade associations as well as the numerous informal collusive arrangements for which firms have been under attack by prosecuting agencies represent voluntary action designed to influence competition. Indeed, the growth of trade associations is ascribed to "the general movement away from cut-throat competition and the increasing desire for more regularity, continuity and stability in business."[4] There is a serious deficiency in voluntary action, however: sanctions against violation are frequently either nonexistent or ineffective. But a government authority, with its lawful monopoly of force, can effectively impose sanctions. Adam Smith was among the first to recognize this fact when he attributed government-imposed restraints on certain imports to "the monopolizing spirit of merchants and manufacturers."[5]

Government intervention in the competitive process forms the major focus of this book, but for the moment it is sufficient to indicate some ways in which it has been employed to the benefit of some segments of the business community. Public policy is, of course, not just government intervention on behalf of affected business interests. As I shall later attempt to show, it is far more. But at this stage it is necessary only to show that some important kinds of public policy were very much desired by business interests for their effect on the competitive process. Studies of nineteenth-century railroad regulation illustrate the point. They have tended to show that the leaders in the battle for state regulation were local businessmen intent on avoiding rate structures that discriminated against them relative to competitors in other locales selling to the same markets. Moreover, the railroads themselves were not averse to state regulation, since discrimination often involved lowering rates below a level that they felt would yield a fair return. Federal regulation of railroad rates was favored by most railroad executives because their firms were thereby precluded by law from engaging in rate wars or acceding to a shipper's demand for an "unreasonable" discount.[6]

Indeed, a veritable cottage industry of historical studies has sought to show that regulatory legislation, especially that enacted during the Progressive Era, amounts to nothing more than attempts by business interests to have the government meliorate competition and help them attain a stability they could not achieve voluntarily. In accordance with this theory—known as the Kolko hypothesis—big bankers favored the Federal Reserve Act because it would dampen interest rate competition; timber interests supported forest conservation because it would preserve the resource that yielded their profit; meat packers favored federal quality standards and inspection because they would prevent smaller packers from producing and selling low-quality products that would result in the general banning of American meat from important European markets; and established drug firms favored food and drug legislation because it would prevent quacks from degrading drugs in consumers' minds, leading them to be wary of drugs of any kind. Finally, it has been claimed that the Federal Trade Commission's birth and the enactment of the statutes it was originally designed to administer are primarily attributable to business' desire to suppress competition.[7]

While these studies serve as a necessary corrective to the once popular view that the enactment of legislation to restrict competition constituted "reform" that came about as a result of popular pressure, great scandals, and the work of muckrakers and public-spirited leaders over the opposition of the business community, they too present only a part of the picture.[8] First, the Kolko view ignores the other side of the contradiction; when the Clayton Act and Federal Trade Commission Act became law, the Sherman Act, which outlawed monopolization and collusive price fixing, was not cast aside. Rather, it coexisted with the new legislation designed in part to restrict methods of competition. Indeed, the new agency could, and did early in its career, employ its powers against collusive practices as well as against practices that restricted competition.[9] Further, the Wilson administration, which promoted the F.T.C. and Clayton acts, rejected an attempt by business groups to curtail the Sherman Act's prohibitions against collusive arrangements.[10] Second, the Kolko hypothesis does not explain the strong support given to legislation that restricted competition by persons generally regarded as hostile to very large business. Louis Brandeis, no friend of big business, joined many big businessmen in supporting the enactment of the Federal Trade Commission Act—but, as we shall later see, his reasons were entirely different from theirs. Third, this theory fails to provide a nexus between the forces favoring enactment of a statute and the question of

its administration: how could those supporting a particular piece of
legislation make reasonably sure that the statute would be administered
in accordance with their desires? Finally, is the Kolko hypothesis
time-bound to Progressive Era legislation and perhaps a few other
subsequent pieces of legislation?

In examining the Federal Trade Commission, its administration,
and its subsequent statutory responsibilities, I shall seek to show that
the agency's actions as well as its successes and failures are in large
part attributable to a central contradiction in the conduct of both
business and government. Yes: like the firms that fix prices and yet
cut prices, the F.T.C. renders some decisions that restrict competition
and others that advance it. Before we examine how and why this is so,
however, that ambiguous word "competition" should be defined
more clearly.

Competition

Judicial and administrative decisions, the proclamations of political
actors, and much popular literature all employ the word "competition" in at least two senses, referring either to the number of firms in
a given market (the structural sense) or to the behavior of firms in a
market (the conduct sense). The assumption of interrelatedness stems
from elementary price theory, according to which firms in a structurally "purely competitive" market behave in a more competitive
manner (conduct) than does a firm in a monopolistic (single-seller)
market. Prices will be lower, and so on. But in the real world pure
competition—defined as a market in which there are (1) many small
sellers offering (2) homogeneous products (identical both physically
and in the minds of consumers) to (3) many buyers with perfect
knowledge in a market characterized by (4) free entry and exit and
(5) independent decisions individually arrived at—is almost nonexistent. Instances of pure monopoly are equally rare.[11] While many
policy makers and popular writers recognize that the real world is not
purely competitive, they often make two unsupported assumptions:
that pure competition is the most desirable structural state, and that
the relationship between structure and conduct is close to linear—
that is, the closer a structure is to pure competition, the more conduct
will resemble pure competition. Yet these assumptions have been
subjected to a wealth of criticism.[12] There are, of course, relationships between structure and conduct, but they are more complex and

various than the models employed in elementary price theory suggest. We shall turn to these relationships in the course of this book.

How, then, do firms compete and, conversely, prevent market competition through either voluntary arrangements or public policy? Firms are expected to compete in price. Yet price competition, insofar as it means reducing prices to gain custom at the expense of rivals, is often impossible or nearly impossible, for barring a decisive cost breakthrough on the part of one firm, any price can be met by rivals. Knowing this, a firm will ordinarily be loath to reduce prices in order to compete with rivals, although it may be compelled to do so in the face of reduced aggregate demand for its product or because of the pressures of interproduct competition. The many convictions that have been obtained under Section I of the Sherman Act for conspiracy to fix prices are testimony both to the attempt to end price competition and to the contradictory pressure to compete. For why should firms enter into an agreement or conspiracy not to compete in price if identical prices are automatically arrived at?

The two major means by which enterprises compete in the face of the tendency toward uniformity are price concessions to selected customers or markets, often given surreptitiously, and the broad range of practices lumped together under the rubric "nonprice competition." We shall examine the first of these practices later in the context of price discrimination;[13] let us now consider nonprice competition. In a general way, a firm engages in nonprice competition in order to differentiate its product from those of its rivals. In turn, product differentiation—the establishment of a separate identity for a firm's product in the minds of customers—allows the firm to establish prices different from those of its rivals. To the extent that nonprice practices are standardized or forbidden, opportunities for nonprice competition are foreclosed. To take two extreme hypothetical examples, if advertising of products were entirely forbidden or limited to a list of contents, much nonprice competition would be eliminated. Similarly, if all brands of a given product class had to contain precisely the same ingredients, another facet of nonprice competition would be removed. Such thoroughgoing restrictiveness is, of course, extremely uncommon. Yet, as we shall see, considerable limitation is imposed on nonprice competition both voluntarily within an industry and by public regulation, reflecting, once again, the fundamental contradiction between competition and stability. As I shall suggest later, the compromise that results from this contradiction may be one important cause of the apparent ineffectiveness of much trade regulation.

Nonprice competition is much too valuable to forgo entirely, however. Businessmen tend to prefer nonprice appeal for several reasons, the most important of which is

> that consumer good will based upon non-price factors tends to be more lasting than that depending simply upon price appeal. The manufacturer whose sole selling argument is price must continue to undersell his competitors indefinitely. Should they meet his offer, his advantage is gone. On the other hand, if he had in some way succeeded in creating a demand among buyers for his products because of their quality, or appearance, or packaging, or through the effective use of trade marks or advertising, his position in the market becomes more secure.[14]

This statement should be qualified in several ways. First, forms of nonprice competition that involve quantification are open to the same kinds of objection as price competition. Length of warranty or speed of delivery can be stated in quantitative terms and can be readily imitated by a competitor;[15] if automobile firm A offers a 20,000-mile guarantee, so can automobile firm B. Similarly, if chocolate bar A maintains its price but reduces its weight, chocolate bar B can follow suit. Competition therefore tends to gravitate toward those forms of nonprice competition that are not readily susceptible to quantification, such as advertising, style, and design. But such forms of nonprice competition have their own peculiar dynamic that reflects the contradiction between competition and stability. Take advertising, for example. All other things being equal, the advertising budget of a firm in any given industry will be approximately proportional to its volume of sales—although the ratio may vary from industry to industry. The smaller firm eager to increase its market share will then tend to counter the quantitative superiority of the larger firms with qualitative exaggeration. Even though larger firms can imitate such exaggeration, the smaller firm, from its perspective, has less to lose and more to gain by it.

Such exaggeration may overstep the boundaries of puffery into the area of deceit and falsity. Moreover, the gross exaggerations of smaller firms desperately eager to increase their market shares may reach such a point of transparent deception that consumers react adversely to the entire product class. Thus, as we shall later see in detail, the outrageous claims of patent medicine purveyors engendered such distrust of pharmaceuticals generally that sales of all such products were threatened.

One method of curtailing the market instability that can result from competition through advertising is to outlaw deception, thereby preventing dissemination of the sort of blatant claims that could greatly affect market structure or create consumer doubts about the whole product line and thus threaten established producers' sales and profits. Again, such a prohibition may be effected either by voluntary action of the enterprises or by public policy, and will reflect the fundamental tension between the drive to compete and the drive for stability. Compromise and hesitation in statutory standards, however, can lead to evasion of the prohibition by a firm whose hunger for an increased market share exceeds the threat imposed by it. Moreover, as Max Weber observed, "Those who continuously operate in the market have a far greater rational knowledge of the market and interest situation than the legislators and enforcement officers whose interest is only formal. . . . It is those private interested parties who are in a position to distort the intended meaning of a legal norm to the point of turning it into its very opposite."[16]

The struggle to restrict aspects of competition in the face of the relative lack of statutory and administrative efficacy causes a gradual shift in emphasis from legislation designed generally to correct abuses to legislation aimed more specifically at creating standards.[17] In the case of the Federal Trade Commission, the original goal of thwarting "unfair methods of competition" has been supplemented by more recent legislation imposing standards in such matters as wool labeling and food-package claims. At the same time, resistance to measures restricting competition has created weaknesses in the new statute, and consequently in its administration. Clearly, however, the direction of both public policy and voluntary arrangements among enterprises has been toward the imposition of standards, whether in symbols, dimensions, content, grades, service, or performance. Often the impetus toward standardization does not stem from the immediate purpose of restricting competition, although that may be the effect. "Standardization means economy at nearly all points of the process of supplying goods, and at the same time it means certainty and expedition at nearly all points in the business operations involved in meeting current wants."[18] But standardization, especially at a high level, can also impose burdensome costs on marginal producers, effectively driving them from business.[19] Setting high standards can, in addition, lessen the possibility of consumer resistance to a product or class of products and thereby prevent the declines in sales and profits that might result from shoddy quality or unsafe products. As we shall see when we examine the Wheeler-Lea Amendment to the Federal Trade Commission Act, the scandal of deaths attributable to the consumption of quack medicines and the consequent threat of a widespread fear of drugs generally prompted pharmaceutical manufacturers to support legislation designed to raise standards.

For these reasons trade associations have voluntarily sought to impose standards on member firms. In at least one instance, the announced principal purpose of standardization was to prevent "uncontrolled competition in sizes, models, and capacities."[20] Voluntarily adopted standards may be readily abandoned, as we saw earlier, or some members of an industry may refuse to accede to standards approved by the majority.[21] Accordingly, government support and sanction have been enlisted in the cause of standards. The Department of Agriculture first recommended standards for consumer goods in 1917, and the Department of Commerce established a commercial Standards Unit for the voluntary establishment of standards under government imprimatur in 1927.[22] But the F.T.C. has played a more significant role in the development of standards through its trade practice procedures. As early as 1919 the Commission established the "procedure of holding conferences with industry for the purpose of eliminating unfair methods of competition as well as trade abuses existing therein." Rules that in effect establish standards with greater or lesser specificity have come out of such proceedings. The rules, which do not carry the force of law for individual firms, are supposed to cover specific industries as diverse as the ripe olive industry and the wet ground mica industry. The rules covering the silk industry illustrate the sort of standards that are established at the behest of industry members: these rules define such trade terms as "pure silk," "silk noil," "waste silk," and declare that it shall be an unfair trade practice to use such terms other than as defined.[23]

The voluntary standards under federal imprimatur are, however, affected by the basic contradiction discussed earlier, with the result that the F.T.C. has devoted most of its efforts to prosecuting individual transgressors and entering cease-and-desist orders against them. But this technique, reflecting an uneasy compromise between the need for stability and the need to compete, has been, as we shall see, ineffective, with the result that pressures for more efficient sanctions and more specific standards are generated—and resisted—within the business community. The story of the Federal Trade Commission, the statutes it administers, and the agency's performance is, then, in part a reflection of the fundamental contradiction between stability and competition. Yet the direction of legislation and administration is inexorably toward the elimination of competition. It would be wrong to conclude that competition is entirely stifled, however; rather, its "emphasis shifts from those aspects of the transaction which are regulated to others which are free of control,"[24] and the basic contradiction remains. At the same time, the tension mirrored in each new statute—in its loopholes and exceptions—will often mean that some in the marketplace can readily circumvent the statute's announced intentions.

While the clash between competition and stability is the contradiction that is central to an understanding of the Federal Trade Commission, it is by no means the only one. Other statutes administered by the F.T.C. reflect other conflicts. Several of these statutes are the result of attempts by one group of businessmen to curtail the competitive opportunities of another group. The Robinson-Patman Act, restricting price discrimination and related practices, exemplifies this conflict, as do many of the so-called labeling acts. Conflict between business and other groups in American society has led, especially since the mid-1960s, to the enactment of much consumer legislation, some of which is administered by the F.T.C. In the face of concentrated demand for such new legislation, business groups have usually reacted carefully, employing a strategy of seeking modifications to proposed legislation after an initial phase of outright opposition. The strategy has been generally successful.

When we look at public policy toward business in the United States as a whole, we see a complex picture: policies embodying the ideal of competition; policies reflecting the need for stability; and policies enshrining, as the F.T.C. Act does, both parts of the contradiction; policies that reflect the attempts of one business group to limit the competitive opportunities of another business group; and, finally, actions by nonbusiness groups designed to limit the activities of business groups.

Of the maze of statutes, one stands out as the embodiment of the principle of competition. The rest chip away at this statute by restricting competition in one fashion or another. We turn now to the Sherman Act.[25]

The Sherman Act

An examination of the legislative debates preceding passage of the Sherman Act in 1890 shows that the major underlying purpose of the law was to preclude "artificial" enhancement of prices through cartel arrangements or monopoly. Thus, Senator John Sherman asserted, in the debate on the first form of the bill, that the first section (defining the wrong) "declares the principle of the common law against combinations, trusts, etc. to affect the value of articles necessary to human life."[26] When asked at what evils the bill was directly aimed, Senator Sherman replied that the target was "increased" selling prices of articles.[27]

Earlier forms of the bill were phrased in terms of outlawing cartel and monopoly arrangements that raised the price of goods to the consumer. In general, the participants in the congressional debate considered this the major substantive function of the bill. A tenable argument could be made that the sole purpose of the Sherman Act was to prevent artificial enhancement of prices. For example, when asked whether an agreement by farmers not to buy cotton bagging was an unlawful combination, Senator Sherman replied that there was "nothing in the bill to prevent a refusal by anybody to buy anything. *All* that it forbids is . . . combinations to advance the price of the necessaries of life."[28] Congress may have had other vague or nefarious intentions in passing the Sherman Act, but the one explicit purpose was the prevention of artificial increases in prices.

Senator Sherman asserted that the bill did not announce a new principle of law, but simply incorporated old common law principles in a national law. The common law of England favored "low" prices, even above free prices.[29] Congress' conception of the effects of monopoly was part of the then conventional wisdom and enjoyed a long history in legal and economic thinking. Adam Smith succinctly proclaimed the cardinal principle of this doctrine: "The price of monopoly is upon every occasion the highest which can be got. The natural price, or the price of free competition, on the contrary, is the lowest which can be taken, not upon every occasion indeed, but for any considerable time together."[30]

The common law monopoly principles mentioned by Senator Sherman were in accordance with Smithian doctrine and were clearly intended to prevent artificially high prices.[31] A monopoly established as a result of vigorous competition and efficient operation was not to Congress a legal monopoly. Such a monopolist "has not done anything but compete with his adversaries in trade . . . to furnish the commodity for the lowest price."[32] The extent to which public outcry against the trusts was a factor in the Sherman Act's genesis and ultimate passage is debatable. There is no doubt, however, that the public's principal objection to the trusts was their ability to raise prices.[33]

In the legislative debates on the Sherman Act, there is no trace of the notion that the existence of many small units is an objective of antitrust policy, or that competition should be anything but free. Regulations about "unfair competition" with the common law purpose of preventing appropriation of the fruits of another's labor were regarded as having virtually nothing to do with the maintenance of competition or the prevention of monopoly.[34]

Yet even the strongest legislative commitment ever given to the principle of free competition was not given without reluctance. Many of the stern enforcement instruments proposed for inclusion in the act—the suspension of tariffs on articles involved in violation of the law, special forms of taxation, government seizure, forfeiture and sale of violators' goods, forfeiture of corporate charters, restrictions on the right to ship goods in interstate commerce—were not even seriously debated.[35] Instead, the act's enforcement instruments were limited to criminal penalties, damages, and injunctive directives. The germ of resistance to the principle of competition was to flower with the enactment of the Federal Trade Commission Act.

CHAPTER 2

The Origins of the F.T.C.

Before the late 1950s, when the onslaught of revisionist studies of the Progressive Era began, the burst of legislative activity during that era was simply explained. It was seen as the result of popular pressure, a great scandal, or the work of either muckrakers or public-spirited political leaders over the opposition of the business community. According to this view, the Supreme Court had effectively scuttled the Sherman Act in 1911 by declaring, in the famous Standard Oil and American Tobacco cases, that only unreasonable—not all—restraints of trade were unlawful. In order to strengthen competition and prevent monopoly, the Federal Trade Commission and Clayton acts were passed. As one of the leading proponents of the traditional view puts it, "Both the Federal Trade Commission Act and the Clayton Antitrust Act were long overdue. They represented the firm belief that the Sherman Act had failed and that further federal legislation was necessary if monopoly was to be prevented."[1] The decision to enforce the new antitrust legislation through a commission was the result of the great administrative success of the Interstate Commerce Commission.

The revisionist theory of Progressive Era legislation takes an almost diametrically opposite point of view. While the conventional theory argues that the F.T.C. and Clayton laws were enacted in order to promote the competitive process, the revisionist hypothesis, which received its finest exposition in Gabriel Kolko's *Triumph of Conservatism*, is that the statutes were designed to promote stability by restricting competition. The revisionist theory urges that the regulatory legislation enacted during the Progressive Era was actively supported by important business leaders, who sought to have their activities regulated in order to meliorate competition and attain a stability they could not achieve voluntarily.[2]

In reviewing the evidence I shall seek to show that both sides are right. Strong as the revisionists' case may be, it is incomplete. It ignores the opposition to regulation on the part of many business groups—the National Association of Manufacturers, for example—and the wavering back and forth between support and rejection on the part of others precisely because they feared restrictions on competition.[3] Moreover, while it focuses on big-business support for the 1914 legislation, it ignores the reasons that small-business spokesmen hostile to bigness also supported the legislation. Louis Brandeis often acted as a spokesman for small business because of his view that "unrestricted competition, with its abuses and excesses, leads to monopoly, because these abuses prevent competition from functioning properly as a regulator of business."[4] Brandeis' views did not, it should be added, prevent other spokesmen for this group from opposing the new statutes or from wavering between support and rejection.

The 1914 statutes reflected the internal contradiction between competition and stability. President Woodrow Wilson, while clearly dipping his toe in the water by supporting the new trade commission, did so with caution and would have no part of "a bold program of administrative control" that would severely curtail business rivalry.[5] As we shall see, both the F.T.C. Act's language and its remedies constituted a victory and a compromise for the proponents of both stability and competition. Further, the F.T.C., contrary to the exaggerated claims of the Naderites and other exuberant critics,[6] has responded to its mandate in precisely the contradictory manner one might have anticipated. As critics have pointed out, it has devoted a great portion of its efforts to restraining smaller firms. But what the critics have overlooked is that since its birth the Commission has continuously entered orders forbidding price fixing and other cartel practices against such giants as the manufacturers of cement, steel, rubber tires, and antibiotics, among others.

A closer examination of the contending forces and the concerns that led to enactment of the F.T.C. and Clayton acts is the first step toward explaining the Commission's contradictory application of the principal statutes it administers. We begin with the topic most notoriously debated in connection with new legislation—the "trusts."

While the term technically refers to a specific form of business arrangement, it came to refer generally to the problems of industrial concentration and the absolute growth of large firms.[7] Strangely, both traditionalists and revisionists find evidence to bolster their hypotheses. We shall now see why.

The American Political Economy, 1890–1914

One of the major arguments advanced by the revisionists in seeking to show that the growth of trusts was not the major impetus behind enactment of the F.T.C. and Clayton acts is that in virtually every sector, the large corporations were in fact losing part of their market shares to smaller competitors. The larger firms therefore desired to stabilize market structure by restricting competition. Thus, the argument concludes, fear of trusts could not have been the real reason for the new legislation; rather it was the drive for stability.

The revisionists begin their analysis by noting that between 1904 and 1909 the number of manufacturing concerns increased by 24.2 percent. "Of the nine manufacturing industries with a product value of $500 million and up in 1909, only one, the iron and steel industry, had less than 1,000 establishments, and the exception had 446. In the thirty-nine industries with products valued at $100–$500 million, only three had less than one hundred establishments."[8] Important industrial markets were, moreover, becoming less concentrated.

After the great merger wave of 1897–1902, the newly consolidated firms were unable to hold on to the share of the market gained through consolidation. Congress knew this when the F.T.C. bill was debated. Senator John Weeks, in one of the more informed speeches during the debate, inserted Bureau of Corporations statistics showing that Standard Oil's share of the market for refined oil dropped rapidly from 1899 to 1906. In 1904, for the first time, its market share was less than 50 percent. Standard's American production of petroleum also declined to about 11–12 percent of the market by 1906. Other figures introduced into the record by Weeks showed that U.S. Steel's share of the steel-products market declined substantially from 1902 to 1912. Weeks concluded that the very large companies were not growing at the expense of smaller firms; rather, the small firms were growing at the expense of the larger ones. Weeks selected steel and petroleum as examples because, in the popular mind, those industries were prototypes of the trusts.[9] Kolko has shown that the same process of deconcentration was occurring in the automobile, agricultural implements, telephone, copper, meat packing, and other important industries during the period after the first merger wave. The primary causes of the deconcentration trend were the ease with which these industries could be entered, technological innovation (particularly by new entrants), and changing consumer tastes.[10]

The reports filed by the Bureau of Corporations, the F.T.C.'s predecessor agency and the principal source of information for both the President and Congress on matters of industrial economics, did not indicate any alarming trends in concentration or conduct before 1914. A report on the beef industry—popularly viewed as one of the most pernicious trusts—observed in 1905 that in preceding years the profits made by packers were very reasonable. Swift, for example, never made profits exceeding 2 percent of sales in the period 1902–1904. The report concluded that economies of scale accrue to large packers as a result of their size, and that consumers were able to purchase beef more cheaply from large packers than from local or small-scale concerns. Finally, the Bureau noted that entry into the meatpacking industry by viable competitors was easy.[11]

In its 1911 report on the steel industry, the Bureau of Corporations noted that the market share of U.S. Steel, the industry leader, materially diminished in the period 1901–1910, a fact that attested to the presence of increasingly strong independent producers. Again, the profits of U.S. Steel during these years could hardly be called excessive. Finally, the report reveals no evidence of the use of abusive trade tactics.[12]

In the case of farm machinery—another industry that has often been singled out as an example of a trust—Bureau of Corporations reported in 1913 that while International Harvester, the industry leader, had held a near monopolistic position at the turn of the century, its share of the market had slipped considerably by 1911. Of great significance was the fact that International Harvester's share was lowest in the newer lines of agricultural machinery; for example, it accounted for only 37 percent of all disk harrows—then a major innovation in farming—sold in 1911. Further, many old concerns were expanding into the agricultural machinery business, and others were planning an early entry into the industry. International Harvester's profits were not excessive, averaging 8.47 percent of net assets in the years 1902–1911. Finally, the report noted, the company's success was due in no small part to its efficiency and its ability to produce machines more cheaply than competitors could.[13]

As Tables 1–6 show, the percentage of total output accounted for by the largest firms in many industries declined in this period. The figures are approximate, but they do show trends over time.

Table 1. Percentage of total U.S. output of motor vehicles produced by major manufacturers, 1904–1921

Manufacturers	1904	1909	1911	1921
General Motors	28	22	17.1	11.8
Ford	9	9	19.2	55.4
Others	63	69	63.7	32.7

Figures in Tables 1–6 are derived from J. Fred Weston, *The Role of Mergers in the Growth of Large Firms* (Berkeley: University of California Press, 1961), pp. 39–41.

Table 2. Percentage of total U.S. output of steel ingots and castings produced by major manufacturers, 1901 and 1920

Manufacturers	1901	1920
U.S. Steel	61.6	39.9
Republic Steel	3.6	2.5
Bethlehem Steel	1.6	5.7
Jones & Laughlin	7.1	3.1
Others	26.1	48.8

Table 3. Percentage of total U.S. output of electrical machinery, apparatus, and supplies produced by major manufacturers, 1904–1919

Manufacturers	1904	1909	1919
General Electric	28	23	23
Westinghouse	12	13	14
Others	60	64	63

Table 4. Percentage of total U.S. meatpacking output (wholesale) produced by major firms, 1904–1929

Manufacturers	1904	1909	1929
Swift	19.0	9.5	10.2
Armour	11.8	10.3	13.2
Cudahy	4.3	2.1	2.3
Others	64.9	78.1	74.3

Table 5. Percentage of total U.S. output of rubber tires and inner tubes produced by major manufacturers, 1904–1919

Manufacturers	1904	1909	1919
U.S. Rubber	22.2	19.6	19.8
B. F. Goodrich	—	—	12.4
Goodyear	—	2.2	14.9
Firestone	—	—	8.0
Others	77.8	78.2	44.9

Table 6. Percentage of total U.S. output of tin products produced by major manufacturers, 1901–1914

Manufacturers	1901	1904	1914
American Can	85	60	52
Continental Can	—	—	17
Others	15	40	31

A plausible case can, then, be made for the proposition that leading firms had a great interest in promoting legislation that would restrict competitive methods threatening their market shares. But why would such legislation also be supported by persons whose dislike of large firms was almost virulent? The Bureau of Corporations reports on the steel and farm machinery industries offer a partial explanation for their fear of large firms. Despite U.S. Steel's decline in market share, the Bureau still concluded that the company controlled two-thirds of the country's production of crude steel and between one-half and four-fifths of the principal rolled products. Moreover, without the benefit of hindsight, the Bureau concluded that the firm's control over iron ore resources virtually assured it of continuing dominance in the industry.[14] And the International Harvester Company was accused by the commissioner of maintaining a position of dominance in its industry in part by engaging in objectionable competitive methods, including the acquisition of rivals.[15]

But it was an earlier investigation by the Bureau of Corporations— the famous 1906 oil investigation[16]—that supplied most of the ammunition for the antagonists of big business. In this report the Bureau accused Standard Oil of habitually receiving secret transportation rates and of other "unjust" discrimination. Standard's leading position in the industry was attributed to the fact that it paid much lower rates than competitors. Thus, while the revisionist view sees restrictions on competition as a method of promoting stability, the conventional view perceives "unfair competition" as a method by which larger firms could and did destroy the competitive process. But, with some exceptions, those who held the conventional view at the beginning of the twentieth century did not want to destroy the trusts; rather, they desired to restrict the power of large corporations to engage in certain forms of conduct so as to maintain competition. Both the revisionist and the conventional viewpoints are correct, therefore, but each misses a significant part of the picture.

Restricting the Trusts

Probably no work was more influential or articulate in setting forth the argument in favor of new legislation restricting certain forms of competition than *The Control of Trusts* by economists John B. and John M. Clark.[17] John B. Clark, perhaps the foremost American economist of his day, was a founder and president of the American Economic Association. His views were extremely important to policy makers, and he was a co-architect in preparing specific legislation on trade regulation matters in 1913 for the influential National Civic Federation for transmission to key congressional and executive branch figures.[18]

In essence, the Clarks argued that the central political-economic problem in America was how to "preserve the good that is in [the trusts] and cast away the bad."[19] The good consisted in largeness of scale, with its attendant increase in efficiency and access to resources to improve production methods. The bad lay in the fact that as large-scale firms approached a monopoly position, invention declined and prices approached monopoly levels. The Clarks' solution was to restrict the ability of trusts to employ "unfair practices" against their smaller competitors. Local price cutting, exclusive dealing, and similar practices were cited as the most common of such unfair practices that ought to be outlawed. Moreover, a new law proscribing such practices by the trusts was necessary since, by the time the Sherman Act could be enforced against a would-be monopolist who used such practices, smaller competitors would have fallen by the wayside. If such practices were made illegal, competition would be based on efficiency and quality. The Clarks were confident that, in battle under such terms, the "overgrown" trust would not be so efficient as one of more manageable size.[20]

If this argument was correct, and if it influenced the shape of the F.T.C. and Clayton acts, why, one might ask, were the provisions not limited to corporations with more than a certain sum in assets or sales? Why, in a word, were the trusts not made the explicit targets of the new laws? Indeed, Senator Francis G. Newlands, one of the principal actors in this drama, wanted in 1911 to confine new legislation to the 300–500 largest corporations.[21] The Clarks proposed instead legislation that would outlaw "unfair competition" generally and be administered by a commission. They argued that when a smaller firm employs such a tactic as price discrimination, the "cutthroat competition" spreads to the larger firms, which are better able to use it and to withstand the ensuing losses. The inevitable result was that smaller firms either were driven out of business or sought refuge in absorption by larger firms. If certain methods of competition were entirely prohibited, therefore, the probability would increase that over time there would be a larger number of firms competing in an industry. Therefore, concluded the Clarks, let us have an administrative body that will ensure that competition is "tolerant" and not "unfair."[22]

The Clarks' theoretical framework for legislation that would both restrict and promote competition provided the basis for widespread support from a diversity of interests across the ideological spectrum. In 1908, for example, Andrew Carnegie said he favored government control to solve the problem of fierce price competition in the steel industry; in 1911 George W. Perkins, a partner in J. P. Morgan and Company, proposed a federal business court or commission to place limits upon the legality of business action; the U.S. Chamber of Commerce informed the President that it favored a strong trade commission; and steel industry executives approved the strengthened form of the Trade Commission bill.[23] Many trade associations joined the call for a new commission,[24] and strong support came from such figures as Louis Brandeis and Robert M. La Follette—both viewed as antagonistic to big business—as well as from top officials of the Bureau of Corporations, which had filed the reports critical of the conduct of big business.[25]

Opponents of the new legislation and those who wavered included such business groups as the National Association of Manufacturers, the Illinois Manufacturers Association, the New York Chamber of Commerce, several other eastern commercial organizations, and many small businessmen who were wary of anything that smacked of cooperation between government and big business.[26] And they were joined by legislators ranging from conservatives sympathetic to business interests to progressives with an antipathy to big business. The progressive Senator William E. Borah argued that if Congress feared trusts and monopolies, it should simply pass legislation breaking them up. In the words of Senator Knut Nelson, "If you restrain that little matter of unfair competition, as you call it, what then? You still leave the trust intact . . . to prey upon the public. . . . Now what good does that do?"[27]

Behind the various arguments made by opponents of the new legislation lay fear that the F.T.C. and Clayton acts would greatly restrict competition. Senator Porter J. McCumber succinctly summarized the antipathy to restriction when he said, "In the antitrust law we proceed upon the theory that it is no part of our legislative duty to protect competing businesses against each other, but simply to protect the people against the combination of any business interests." Now, he noted, Congress intended to put a limit on competition.[28] But, as the legislative history shows, McCumber and other opponents spoke for a small minority, albeit a highly articulate one.

The F.T.C. Act: Prelude to the Legislative History

The story of the Federal Trade Commission began in 1903, when Congress created a Bureau of Corporations within the new Department of Commerce and Labor.[29] Its function was to investigate possible abuses by industrial corporations engaged in interstate commerce and to make public reports on the findings of its investigations. Some of these reports, as we have already seen, raised the issue of unfair competition in concrete, dramatic form. But the Bureau's inability to rectify the conditions it disclosed inexorably contributed to the movement for a new, vigorous agency.

Senator Newlands first proposed the idea of a business court or commission in 1911. In his initial thinking on the subject, he wanted, "on the one hand . . . the benefit of the combination of great capital in the enterprises of the country, and, on the other hand, we would be able so to regulate them as to protect the country from the abuses which up to this time existed."[30] In July 1912, after consulting with and receiving support from businessmen, most notably Perkins of J. P. Morgan, Newlands originated a bill to create an Interstate Trade Commission (renamed the Federal Trade Commission shortly before passage of the final bill, to avoid confusion with the Interstate Commerce Commission). Nothing became of Newlands' initial attempt, but the ground was laid for subsequent enactment. Big-business support for such a commission had been growing since 1908.[31] Experience with the Interstate Commerce Commission had demonstrated that a regulatory agency could serve as a buffer between the public and industry, and that government intervention could preclude such intensive competitive devices as rate wars. For these reasons, Elbert H. Gary of U.S. Steel, who had previously sought industry-wide price fixing, favored the Interstate Trade Commission bill, as did spokesmen for various retail federations and manufacturing trade associations.[32]

In his enthusiasm for an interstate trade commission, the attorney representing the Yellow Pine Manufacturers Association said, "The old fashioned cutthroat competition is a relic of the dark ages. Men engaged in competitive lines should have an opportunity of cooperating to a certain extent. Of course, there is danger in this, and there is just the very need of a Commission so that the danger line is not crossed."[33] In other words, he sought a commission that would soften and attenuate competition.

As we previously noted, other associations favored the bill too. A poll of the membership of the U.S. Chamber of Commerce showed a decisive majority in favor of a trade commission.[34] Senator Newlands cited approval of a trade commission by the Illinois Manufacturers Association, the Ohio Manufacturers Association, and the American Vehicle Association; they all favored the provision of the act outlawing unfair competition.[35]

The National Civic Federation (N.C.F.), an elite club dominated by big businessmen, among them Samuel Insull, Andrew Carnegie, various J. P. Morgan partners, Cyrus McCormick, and Judge Elbert Gary, proposed a bill that differed from the final F.T.C. Act in only one significant respect. The N.C.F. bill called for federal licensing of corporations, a provision that was missing from the F.T.C. Act. Seth Low, N.C.F.'s president, testified, on the basis of preliminary returns of a questionnaire sent to 30,000 businessmen, that American businessmen favored, by almost 3 to 1, "an interstate trade commission with powers not unlike those now enjoyed by the Interstate Commerce Commission." Senator Newlands was himself a member of the N.C.F. and worked closely with its officials. His bill was not an N.C.F. bill, although he and the Federation sought the same objectives.[36]

The first version of the Trade Commission bill, introduced in the House by Harry Covington, did not contain the central substantive provision of the final version: Section 5, outlawing "unfair methods of competition." The principal substantive provision (Section 11) of the Covington bill stated "that when in the course of any investigation made under this Act, the Commission shall obtain information concerning any unfair competition or practice in commerce not necessarily constituting a violation of law by the Corporation investigated, it shall make report thereof to the President, to aid him in making recommendations to Congress for legislation . . . and the information so obtained and the report thereof shall be made public by the commission."[37] Thus adverse publicity and guidance were to be the major weapons of the Commission as it was first contemplated.

Before we examine the way the principal substantive provision was changed to one declaring "that unfair methods of competition in commerce are . . . unlawful," it should be noted that the change is not so significant as a first impression might indicate. The original procedural portion of Section 5 permitted three bites of the apple before any sanctions would be imposed on a violator. First, on finding a violation, the Commission would issue a cease-and-desist order. Second, if the Commission concluded, on the basis of new facts, that there had been a violation of this order, it would have to apply to the Court of Appeals for enforcement. If the Court of Appeals were satisfied that a violation had in fact occurred, it could enter its enforcement order. Finally, a third violation, after the entry of the court's order, would have to be found before penalties could be assessed.[38] The first cease-and-desist order of the Commission became, in effect, guidance to businessmen not to engage in a certain form of competition.

The major reason that antitrust proposals did not languish in 1914 as they had done in 1912, but were eventually enacted into law, was that new legislation in this area had become part of President Woodrow Wilson's program. Before 1914 Wilson had generally favored revision of the Sherman Act. But an event in 1913 forced him to be more explicit in his wishes. In that year Attorney General James C. McReynolds, angered by actions of the "tobacco trust," proposed a graduated tax so high that it would have seriously weakened the trust's successor firms. After its introduction in Congress by Senator Gilbert M. Hitchcock of Nebraska drew horrified responses by many in the business community, Wilson sought to evade responsibility for the McReynolds plan and assured the public that he was not contemplating any serious plan for the destruction of big business.[39]

Wilson's views, in essence, were that a "safe and sensible" agency—not a "dangerous experiment"—should be created to define unfair methods of competition. In the words of his most eminent biographer, Arthur Link, the new legislation's purpose would be "an attempt to rewrite the rules of the business game in order to restore and maintain competition, without, however, trying to destroy big business per se or launching the government upon a bold program of administrative control."[40] Though Wilson initially favored legislation specifying certain practices as unfair, he later became converted, after discussions with businessmen and students of legislation, to George Rublee's plan to create a commission with the power to declare unfair competition unlawful; the number and variety of unfair methods of competition were simply too great to be delineated in a single piece of legislation. As Link observes, Wilson's developing views were in substantial accord with those of many businessmen who were groping for new concepts of regulation and who desired a commission that would act as a friend, guide, and protector of the business community.[41] The final structures of the F.T.C. and Clayton acts, however, developed only slowly in 1914.

Legislative History

On January 20, 1914, President Wilson addressed a joint session of Congress about forthcoming trade legislation. After the usual oratory about the growth of trusts that in those days preceded every proposal on a commercial subject, he said: ". . . we desire the laws we are now about to pass to be the bulwarks and safeguards of industry against the forces who have disturbed it. . . . And the businessmen of the Country desire something more than that the menace of legal process in these matters be made explicit and intelligible. They desire the advice, the definite guidance and information which can be supplied by an administrative body, an interstate trade commission."[42] Such a commission was to serve to provide "information and publicity, as a clearing house for the facts by which both the public mind and managers of great business undertakings should be guided, and as an instrumentality for doing justice to business."[43] The purpose of the new proposals was to achieve business rationality. The President noted that nothing hampers business like uncertainty. But he did not, at that point, indicate the substance of his proposals.

Administration bills were introduced by Congressmen Henry Clayton and Harry Covington and by Senator Newlands. The Covington bill reached the floor first and, as we saw earlier, did not contain the provision outlawing unfair methods of competition. Congressman Covington, the principal defender of the bill on the floor, noted that requiring corporations to file annual and special reports with the Commission was especially important, since the Commission's circulation of such information would be "one of the surest means . . . to an elevated business standard and a better business stability."[44] Congressman Frederick Stevens of Minnesota, ranking minority member of the House Committee on Interstate and Foreign Commerce, supported the bill, declaring that "establishment of a trade Commission of some sort has been generally acceptable to the business world" and noting that the 1912 Republican platform had supported the idea of a trade commission and that many foreign countries regulated the methods by which trade might be conducted.[45]

Stevens clearly linked the rationale of the Covington bill with the purpose of the provision in the final bill outlawing unfair methods of competition. He stated: "We all realize that there must be a few irresponsible, greedy, unscrupulous and capable men who will use [certain business methods] for their own selfish ends. This necessarily compels their competitors to adopt somewhat similar means in order to maintain themselves. So that unless some higher power like the government intervenes and protects and encourages the good citizens, oppression and disaster necessarily result."[46] Underneath the emotive language of this statement lay the two basic ideas that there should be restraint on competition and that it should be effected by government intervention.

On June 5, 1914, the Covington bill passed the House of Representatives. By the time the Newlands version reached the floor of the Senate, the bill had been changed in committee to include, as Section 5, the provision making unfair competition unlawful. The reason for the change was revealed in a 1926 article by George Rublee, a New Hampshire Republican lawyer who subsequently became an F.T.C. commissioner. Rublee had at one time been associated in the practice of law with Victor Morawetz, a major railroad attorney, and later became a partner in Covington & Burling, a Washington law firm that represented major corporate interests. At the request of Congressman Raymond Stevens of New Hampshire, Rublee, who at the time was a member of a special committee on Trade Commission legislation of the U.S. Chamber of Commerce, planned and drafted the version of the Trade Commission bill that conferred power on the Commission to order a stop to unfair competition. In early June, Stevens, Rublee, and others held a conference with President Wilson during which the President became convinced that the bill should contain language making unfair competition unlawful. Wilson then told Newlands that he wanted the Section 5 provision.[47]

Rublee and Stevens intended the words "unfair methods of competition" to mean competitive methods not embraced by any previous law; they did not intend them to cover conduct already forbidden by the Sherman Act. Rublee said, "I do not think it occurred to anyone at the time that a voluntary combination or contract putting an end to competition could be regarded as a method of competition."[48] Indeed, there is evidence that some of the leaders in the fight for passage of the Federal Trade Commission bill, including Brandeis, were hostile to the goals of the Sherman Act. For example, Congressman Raymond Stevens sponsored a "fair trade" bill drafted by Rublee that would have enabled manufacturers to fix the prices at which commodities could be sold to consumers. Unless some such legislation were passed, this practice would clearly contravene the Sherman Act's prohibition against price fixing. Nevertheless, the language of the F.T.C. Act clearly invites the construction that price fixing is an unfair method of competition. What, indeed, could be more unfair than a clear-cut violation of the Sherman Act? And the F.T.C. from its inception had no hesitation in attacking price-fixing conspiracies and other anticompetitive practices while, at the same time, attacking vigorous competitive practices.[49]

While the new legislation's principal supporters had a great deal of difficulty in defining unfair methods of competition, a theory of the legislation can be patched together from some of their statements. The first notion to consider is the so-called incipiency doctrine, according to which the F.T.C. could stop a practice that *might* lead to monopoly if the practice continued over a period of time. If monopoly could result, argued Senator Henry Hollis, a leading proponent, such practices ought to be stopped early, long before they could enable the perpetrator to become a monopolist.

The next problem, then, was to ascertain what competitive practices could ultimately lead to such results. While the act's theorists felt they knew of several such practices—price discrimination and exclusive dealing, for example—they refused to be pinned down on a definition of unfair methods of competition. Senator Albert Cummins went so far as to say that it never could be defined. Others defined it by using an equally vague term; Senator Newlands, for example, asserted at various times during the legislative debate that the function of the legislation was to "civilize competition" or establish "fair competition" in accordance with the "moral law," while Senator Cummins urged those who sought guidelines to look to the "civilized sense of mankind" or "the improving and developing sense of the country with respect to matters of commerce."[50]

They refused to compile a list of practices because they believed that unfair competitors could always invent new unfair methods to employ against their rivals. Accordingly, they deliberately sought a vague definition. But, as we shall see in the next section, the amorphousness of their conception had important consequences.

Unfair Methods of Competition

One study of the phrase "unfair methods of competition" prepared shortly after passage of the F.T.C. Act found so many and such divergent definitions that the phrase was judged virtually meaningless.[51] Another, more recent study finds virtue in the vagueness, since "whether a method of competition is unfair must be gleaned from the facts of the case, not from the application of any abstract standard of another statute. Section 5 of the Federal Trade Commission Act is its own measure of right and wrong; it is a concept of continuing redefinition."[52] The first study expounds with great clarity the legal confusions and contradictions in the attempted definitions of unfair competition but ignores a political synthesis that may arise from the definitions; the second evades the obvious point that something must have been meant by the phrase.

An examination of the works of contemporary scholars, legislative debates, and other relevant materials will aid us in discovering what "unfair methods of competition" was intended to mean. Despite the tendency of many of the contemporary definitions to be tautological and to define unfairness by describing certain conduct as unfair, a reasonably accurate conception of unfairness and the substantive implications of the use of the term can be spelled out.

The phrase "unfair competition," as it was employed in the Federal Trade Commission Act, was not intended to have the meaning it has in common law; it was intended to be a new term. Senator Newlands made this eminently clear at the outset of the debate: "There must always be a commencement for a new legal term in the administration of the law, and certainly in the evaluation of the law we are not always confined to the terms that have existed in the past."[53] In common law, unfair competition consisted of use of the traditional torts, such as libel and assault, by one competitor against another, and the appropriation of a competitor's property (usually trademarks).[54] In an early case that illustrates the common law concept of unfair competition, it was determined that a legal action was sustainable when a clothier used on his products the mark of another clothier, because in doing so he had misappropriated another's valuable property.[55] This area of the law was intended to prevent one competitor from injuring the profits or appropriating the trade values of another; it was not intended to rectify harm done to consumers, and it had no nexus with the common law regarding monopoly.

The earliest use of the term "unfair competition" in the modern sense occurred in 1900 and was reported by the Industrial Commission. This and similar terms were used by witnesses before the Commission to describe severe price cutting, local price discrimination, and selling below cost.[56] The objection to these vigorous competitive methods was that they harmed competitors.

According to scholarly opinion in the period around 1914, the term "unfair competition" implied the need for stringent restriction on competitive activity, and the F.T.C. was, of course, to be the agency to enforce such restrictions. Thus, one scholar, in discussing the new legislation, said that the era of unregulated competition was "at an end." A fair method of competition was any method common to the business concerned.[57] Restrictions on competition, and acting in the manner of a competitor—the antithesis of competition—were thus fair methods of competition. Another student of the proposed trade commission doubted whether competition ought to be restored at all because of its effect on the stability of existing firms; he approved of such a commission as the appropriate instrument to curtail competition.[58] These views represent, in sophisticated form, those of the leading congressional proponents of the F.T.C. Here we can observe the shift of the notion of unfair competition from the common law idea of misappropriation of the fruits of another's labor to the newer notion of activity affecting the stability of existing firms. The most comprehensive contemporary scholarly article on the subject, written by Gilbert H. Montague shortly after passage of the act, summarized the various definitions of unfair competition offered by proponents of Section 5 during the congressional debates. Here is the list (which does not embrace every definition offered):

(a) Every Act of passing off one's business or goods for another's.

(b) All methods of competition tending to restraint of trade or monopoly which have been forbidden by the Sherman Law.

(c) Substantially all violations of the Antitrust laws, including even wrongs arising from interlocking directorates and allied incorporate directorships.

(d) All unfair methods of stifling competition.

(e) All other Acts which the "Commission . . . decides . . . may lead to monopoly or restraint of trade" though not now forbidden by the Sherman Act.

(f) All other Acts affecting a competitor "for which a remedy lies either at law or in equity."

(g) All other Acts which either affect a competitor and are "against public morals" or in any way interfere with economic "efficiency," though heretofore quite lawful and not forbidden by the Sherman Law or by any other law.

(h) All other Acts comprehended within the meaning which "unfair competition" has today in common parlance and in literature.[59]

Summarized in this manner, the views of proponents of Section 5 appear to have little logic or underlying reasoning. Definition a is concerned with a common law tort that restrains one person from appropriating another's labor and has no relation to trusts, restraints of trade, or monopoly. A small business may misappropriate a large firm's labor as readily as a large one may a small one's. Definition c would not justify passage of the Trade Commission bill, since it would substitute for the criminal and injunctive penalties incurred by violation of the Sherman Act a mere slap on the wrist in the form of an unenforceable cease-and-desist order. Definition d merely defines unfair as unfair. Definitions b, f, g, and h, despite their inherent vagueness and the difficulty the act's protagonists encountered in defining the wrong, point to certain forms of proscribed conduct, some of them competitive and others tending to inhibit competition. A sense of the political substance of the concept of unfair competition can be gleaned from the congressional debates.

Senator Newlands argued that the listing of all unfair methods of competition would be a futile gesture; they were too numerous. Further, when one unfair method was prohibited, another was invented to take its place. But, he contended, "we are beginning to realize that there is a standard of morals in trade or that there ought to be." As examples of unfair competition he mentioned local price cutting, bogus independents, fighting brands, tie-in contracts, exclusive dealing, rebates, espionage, and coercion, threats, and intimidation.[60] This is clearly a list of competitive methods that can be employed by large companies or small ones. They are also methods that will not be employed in industries in which competition has been eliminated through collusion or through follow-the-leader signaling. While these methods coud be employed by a monopolist to destroy an extremely small rival, their use has always been far more common in highly competitive industries.

So against what industries and firms was the proscription of unfair methods of competition directed? Senator Borah pointed out that the Sherman Act already prohibited such methods when they were employed by a monopolist or would-be monopolist.[61] The two leading antimonopoly cases made it clear that devices to gain or retain monopoly power would not be tolerated. The Supreme Court, in the American Tobacco decision, described the firm's practice of selling below cost as ruinous competition, and in the Standard Oil decision it referred to "unfair methods of competition, such as local price cutting at the points where necessary to suppress competition."[62] We should note too that Newlands, who originally desired the F.T.C.'s reach to extend only to the 300–500 largest industrial corporations, later changed his mind, stating, "It will not do to classify in such a way as to eliminate the small corporations, for if you do you may eliminate from the operation of the law the most outrageous outlaws."[63] Clearly, then, Newlands intended proscriptions against unfair competition to apply to both large and small firms, and simultaneously to promote competition and to restrict it.

The practice of selling below cost or cutting prices locally may be used by new entrants to an industry or by suddenly invigorated companies seeking to increase their market shares. Section 2 of the Sherman Act cannot be employed against such firms, since there is no danger of their monopolizing trade. With this point in mind, let us re-examine part of Montague's definition *h*, "all other Acts comprehended within the meaning which 'unfair competition' has today in common parlance."

Senator Borah noted that defendants in cartel and monopoly cases had traditionally claimed that they were reacting to brutal or unfair competitors.[64] He cited "common parlance" in the International Harvester case, in which competitors in the agricultural implement business spoke of price cutting as unfair, oppressive, and brutal competition. But, noting the conflict between the Sherman Act and this standard of unfairness, Borah said "that competition oppressive and unfair, as they chose to call it, is proven to have been of unquestionable benefit to the agriculturalists and farmers of the country. They got the benefit of the lower price; when the severe competition ended, the price was ultimately raised."[65] Under the Sherman Act, he observed, "we have given business to understand that we were not concerned with the severity of competition, but only with its preservation, however strong."[66]

The "common parlance" test also implies that businessmen themselves will determine what is unfair, without regard to the public's interest in lower prices. Businessmen are the persons who will use the words. Borah cited a letter he had received from a businessman who favored the Trade Commission bill and complained about the unfair competition of large companies that lowered prices throughout the country. Senator Willard Saulsbury understood unfair competition to include all violations of the ethics of a profession or business or of the customs of merchants, while Senator Cummins, one of the bill's most forceful advocates, argued that the Commission, in deciding whether an act was unfair, "should consult the decisions of the Court, the learning of the time, the *customs of merchants,* the *habits of trade* . . . all of which go to make up our understanding of the words 'unfair competition.' "[67] The context makes clear that "consult" means "adopt," for no way of rejecting the findings of such consultation was advanced. The Supreme Court had not provided any definition of unfairness in an antimonopoly context, and economists do not operate in such ethical terms as "unfair." Therefore, aside from certain practices that shock the conscience of the community, such as selling adulterated foods, businessmen would largely decide what was unfair. And what is unfair to most businessmen is conduct that endangers their stability, their profit targets, or their prevalent way of doing business, conduct that seriously threatens to change the structure of an industry, or, conversely, conduct that might stand in the way of growth. Before 1914, it will be recalled, businessmen were seeking ways to escape the rigors of market competition; now the F.T.C. would do the job handily. And the firms that establish or maintain the customs of an industry are usually the older and larger companies, which are invariably the industry leaders. The greatest threats to them are price cutters, innovators, and others who compete vigorously.

Another theme running through the definitions of unfair competition offered by proponents of the Trade Commission bill is, as we saw in the last chapter, the need to catch monopolistic conduct in its incipiency, before it becomes full-blown. Thus Montague's definition *b* mentions "all methods of competition *tending* to restraint of trade or monopoly," and definition *e* includes "all other Acts which the Commission . . . decides . . . *may* lead to a monopoly or restraint of trade." When Senator Borah asked what was excluded from the scope of unfair competition, Senator Cummins told him what was *not* excluded: conduct "which must ultimately result in the extinction of rivals and the establishment of monopoly."[68] One of Newlands' definitions might even be termed incipient incipiency: "Every new condition and every new practice that might be invented *with a view* to *gradually* bringing about monopoly through unfair competition."[69] Senator Hollis, a strong supporter of the Trade Commission bill, showed why the Sherman Act standards were inadequate to accomplish the bill's purposes: "There may be some doubt as to whether the mere use of an unfair method without more, *by a corporation of no conspicuous size,* would be held to be within the scope of the Sherman Act."[70] The incipiency doctrine would thus allow the F.T.C. to bring an action against any firm engaging in interstate commerce, no matter how small. Vigorous competitors as well as firms that could destroy competition and achieve a monopoly position by employing such methods could be reached under the incipiency doctrine.

The contradiction between stability and competition is also seen in a variation of the incipiency doctrine that added to it the requirement of specific intent. Senator Cummins defined unfair competition as "that competition which is resorted to for the purpose of destroying competition, and of introducing monopoly."[71] Senator Newlands, on the other hand, referred to unfair competition "with a view to destroying a competitor."[72] While Cummins' definition seeks to protect the integrity of the competitive process, Newlands' points to the protection of individual competitors, and hence of stability. Yet one of the bill's opponents, Senator Harry Lane, asked, "Isn't the essence of competition, avarice, selfishness, and the desire to gain and gain at the expense of rivals?"[73]

As we shall later observe in detail, the F.T.C. has devoted considerable attention to protecting competitors rather than competition, and this trend stems in part from the incipiency doctrine as well as from Montague's definition f ("All other Acts affecting a competitor 'for which a remedy lies either at law or in equity' "). The inability to distinguish competitors from competition follows from the incipiency doctrine because "what evidence can [the Commission] look to in its effort to discern an incipient lessening of competition? The obvious resort is to evidence that a competitor has been injured. . . . There seems no way to tell that a competitor has been 'injured,' however, except that he has lost business."[74] Thus the attention the Commission has devoted to what are inherently private controversies with limited impact had its germ in this doctrine of its founders.

Montague's definition g ("All other Acts which either affect a competitor and are 'against public morals' or in any way interfere with economic 'efficiency,' though heretofore quite lawful and not forbidden by the Sherman Law or by any other law") ultimately derives from one of the principal intellectual mentors of the doctrine of unfair competition, economist William H. S. Stevens, whose work was cited with approval in the course of the debates by the bill's proponents.[75] In a book published after the enactment of the F.T.C. and Clayton acts, which contained Stevens' fullest exposition of his theoretical ideas on unfair competition, he stated that "the essence of fair competition is the preservation of the efficient and the destruction of the inefficient."[76] His list of unfair methods includes local price cutting, operation of bogus independents, fighting instruments, tie-in contracts, exclusive arrangements, boycotts, rebates, the monopolization of machinery or goods used in the manufacturing process, espionage, coercion, intimidation, interference, and manipulation.

Some of these practices were already reachable under tort or criminal law, either of which provides a far more effective remedy than a cease-and-desist order. And all of them were already proscribed under the Sherman Act if they were engaged in by a monopolist or monopolizer. In addition, the connection between these methods of competition and efficiency is never shown. Such methods can be employed by highly efficient firms rationally calculating that they can resist retaliation by competitors. Moreover, employment of some of the methods involving price systems may affect distribution efficiencies. The residue of new conduct we are left with, therefore, is the use of certain competitive methods that are not covered by the Sherman Act. And the new law was expected to cover such competitive conduct as well as monopolistic conduct, anticompetitive conduct, tortious business conduct, and criminal business conduct.

The F.T.C. Act's major substantive provision proscribing unfair methods of competition embodied, then, a declaration favoring the promotion of both competition and stability. Its message therefore satisfied a wide range of interested persons, from Louis Brandeis to spokesmen for big business. What was new was that regulatory procedures designed to promote stability, which up to then could be employed only against specific industries, such as railroads and utilities, were now extended to business as a whole. The supporters of an unambiguous policy of competition were dismayed. Senator Borah, one of the most vigorous spokesmen for this group, pessimistically declared that the Trade Commission bill "marks the beginning of the time when the question of competition will be eliminated entirely and we will simply undertake to regulate and control the combinations, however large they may be."[77] Perhaps Borah exaggerated, but the F.T.C. Act did constitute a further inroad upon the ideal of unrestrained competition, just as it added to the protection of the competitive process. In so doing, it was complemented by the companion Clayton Act.

The Clayton Act

The Clayton Act, like the Federal Trade Commission Act, was debated and enacted in 1914, and in general those legislators who supported one act supported the other. During the debates the two acts were considered to be parts of one framework, and they are indeed informed by the same considerations. The reasons advanced

for enactment of the F.T.C. Act were generally also those urged in
support of the Clayton Act.

The Clayton Act, intended as a complement to the F.T.C. Act,
stemmed in large part from the fact that Congress considered some
methods of competition so reprehensible as to require specific proscription, notwithstanding the general proscription of the F.T.C. Act.
These methods were outlawed by those sections of the Clayton Act
that came under the jurisdiction of the Federal Trade Commission.
Section 2 outlaws price discrimination, Section 3 exclusive dealing,
Section 7 stock acquisitions (but not asset acquisitions), and Section
8 interlocking directorates among competitors. Sections 2, 3, and 7,
like the F.T.C. Act, operate on the incipiency principle. Violations
of Sections 2 and 3 are to be found when conduct may "substantially
lessen competition or tend to create a monopoly," while under Section 7 proof is required that stock acquisition may "substantially
lessen competition between the corporation whose stock is so acquired
and the corporation making the acquisition, or to restrain such commerce in any section or community, or tend to create a monopoly of
any line of commerce." Section 8, which absolutely prohibits interlocking directorates among competitors, has been little used; to control
two competitors and place different men on the boards of directors
is a simple matter.

Three principal factors led Congress to pass the Clayton Act in
spite of the relatively clear intention of the framers of the F.T.C.
Act and the Conference Committee that the phrase "unfair competition" was to embrace the specific practices included in Sections 2, 3,
7, and 8 of the Clayton Act.[78] First, the legislative travels of the two
bills were dissimilar. While the Federal Trade Commission bills
originated in the commerce committees of the Senate and House, the
Clayton Act originated in the judiciary committees; and when the
Clayton bill was still in committee, the F.T.C. bill was being debated
on the floor. Second, the Clayton bill originally, and for a long period
in its legislative travels, was a criminal bill, while the Trade Commission bill was at all times a civil-administrative piece of legislation.
Third, and most important, Congress felt particularly strongly about
certain unfair methods of competition.[79] Senator Moses Clapp, one of
the Clayton bill's most forceful advocates, said succinctly that the
four modes of competition proscribed by the Clayton Act were
specific examples of unfair competition.[80]

Price discrimination (Section 2) and exclusive dealing (Section 3) had been singled out as effective methods by which certain trusts had destroyed or sought to destroy smaller competitors. The Clarks and virtually every other contemporary commentator listed these methods among the most notorious employed by the trusts. Again, large firms were accused of debilitating smaller ones, ultimately compelling them to sell their stock to their oppressors. According to the Clarks, price discrimination, even when begun by a small firm, leads to cutthroat competition and sustained selling below the cost of production. Then the smaller firm would, as a last resort, seek to be acquired by the larger one. The restriction on stock acquisitions was purportedly designed to deter this process. Senator Newlands explained the need for the prohibition of interlocking directorates in the following terms: "If an interlocking directorate were used for the purpose of creating a community of interest between two or three or four corporations, that would make them more powerful in their competition with an individual competitor. [Such a device] involved oppression to the independent concern, and thus involved unfair competition."[81]

Like the F.T.C. bill, the Clayton bill was subjected to intense and pointed criticism. Congressman Martin Madden, in particular, excoriated all of the bill's substantive sections because they could be applied without distinction to a vigorous competitor, a monopolist, and a monopolizer. He observed that every sale made injures or is intended to injure a competitor, because "the mere fact of a sale by 'A' deprives 'B' and other dealers of an opportunity to make a sale."[82] Opponents pointed out also that the Clayton bill's proponents focused all their attention on disputes between competitors and ignored the consumer.[83]

Not only was the bill as a whole subjected to criticism; each of the major substantive sections was attacked individually. The substantive provisions of the original criminal version of the Clayton bill were transformed on the way to the ultimate civil-administrative version. Nevertheless, the following comments apply equally to the different versions. Early in the legislative debates, as well as in the later stages, the Clayton bill's major supporters argued that their major purpose was to prohibit individual acts that could ultimately lead to a restraint of trade under the Sherman Act[84]—the same incipiency doctrine that was discussed in connection with the F.T.C. Act.

Section 2, which proscribed price discrimination when the effect *"may be* to substantially lessen competition or *tend to* create a monopoly," was condemned by Congressman Simeon D. Fess because it would deter entrants into new markets. He observed that a firm seeking to enter a market for the first time must make price concessions in order to attract trade from the established sellers. Congressman Samuel Taggart, a supporter of the bill, responded that no exceptions to its proscriptions would be made for newcomers. Congressman Fess then concluded that the price discrimination section favored large established firms since they already had markets in every section of the country and did not have to make concessions to enter.[85]

The same charge—that smaller firms would be deterred from seeking to expand their markets—was employed in connection with Section 3, which outlawed agreements or leases between seller and buyer (or lessor and lessee) whereby the buyer agreed not to handle the wares of another seller (or lessor) when the effect "may be to substantially lessen competition or tend to create a monopoly." Congressman James Graham observed that when a seller sought a foothold in a new community, he usually persuaded a firm to become a distributor by offering to sell only to that prospective distributor, on condition that the distributor would sell only that seller's wares; in this way a seller assured himself of adequate representation against more established, better known competitors. Congressman Frank Willis, concurring, said he had received many protests from small businessmen, especially manufacturers, who claimed that the only way they could sell their products in new or distant markets was through such exclusive dealing arrangements. Great concerns, he pointed out, could maintain their own distribution networks, but small firms had to engage in such arrangements to get their products to consumers in diverse markets.[86] Congressman Madden argued that exclusive dealing was a highly competitive device since each seller offered a prospective distributor a different inducement to handle his product exclusively.[87]

Section 7 prohibited the acquisition of the stock of one corporation by another corporation when the effect "may be to substantially lessen competition between the two corporations or restrain commerce" or may "tend to create a monopoly." This section, it should be noted, proscribed the acquisitions by one corporation of another's stock but not of its assets,[88] probably because the focus of the congressional debates was on holding companies.

Representative Graham opposed the inclusion of this section, claiming it could be aimed only at preventing consolidation of smaller firms, since the consolidation of larger concerns was already a restraint of trade or monopoly under the Sherman Act. Section 7, he concluded, would prevent small firms from combining in order to compete more effectively against established giants.[89] And indeed, Senator Thomas J. Walsh observed, a decision under the Sherman Act had already banned the combination of two railroads, although the market share of the combination was quite small, because the total amount of commerce that would thereby be restrained was substantial in dollar volume.[90] Thus the kind of consolidation that could not yet be reached by the law was one involving small or medium-sized firms, and it was these that were the Clayton Act's targets.

A review of the arguments surrounding the Clayton Act compels much the same conclusion as was reached with regard to the F.T.C. Act. The thrust of the statute is both to restrict competition and to enhance it. Clearly, both proponents and opponents had a point. But the novel element in the Clayton Act is the spread of a bias in favor of stability to previously uncharted territory. The act was not limited to the trusts and could reach corporations far smaller than the top 300–500; on the other hand, it could also reach the destructive practices of the largest firms. As we shall see in later chapters, the agency's enforcement practices reflected this ambiguous heritage.

CHAPTER 3

Organization and Performance

Since March 16, 1915, when the F.T.C. came into existence, one conclusion has consistently been drawn from examinations of the agency: that it has performed badly. The area of the F.T.C.'s substantive jurisdiction has increased greatly since 1915; the internal organization of the agency has been altered frequently; and the focus of its interests has been widened to include consumer protection as well as competition. But the criticism has persisted, from the first major study, published in 1924, to a House Committee on Interstate and Foreign Commerce staff report issued in December 1974. Gerard Henderson, in 1924, pointed to the enormous delay between the commission of an unfair act and the entry of an effective order to stop it, and the criticism is as valid today as it was then. In a recent important case involving vertical integration in the petroleum industry, for example, F.T.C. staff estimated that the case could take eight to ten years to complete—and possibly considerably longer.[1] Indeed, as Lewis Engman, recently chairman of the agency, observed, ten years or more are typically required for important cases, and "specific changes in the Commission's rules of procedure would not drastically reduce the time required to bring this type of a case to a conclusion."[2]

If the F.T.C. and Clayton acts were supposed to stop improper practices in their incipient stages, clearly long delays between the discovery of an unfair practice and its restraint by order prevent the realization of this goal. The problem occurs in minor as well as major cases, particularly when they involve false and misleading advertising—an issue that I shall take up in detail in later chapters. According to Engman, an advertisement typically runs for thirteen weeks or less, but the agency usually takes much longer—sometimes years—to enter an effective order against culpable firms. By the time the agency proceeds against one set of advertising claims, the firm has changed its advertising many times over.[3]

Delay is only the first, and in the eyes of some observers the least important, criticism to be made of the Commission's performance. Delay may be forgivable, but misallocation of resources is not; and critics have charged the F.T.C. with squandering resources on minor matters and failing to take action on matters of substantial importance to consumers and the process of competition. The cases brought by the F.T.C. have involved, according to these critics, petty matters and minor infractions, mostly linked with small firms in highly competitive industries. In the field of consumer deception—to be discussed in detail in later chapters—the agency is charged with devoting inordinate attention to trivia and little to the deceits practiced by large firms advertising in mass media. The American Bar Association Commission summarized this line of argument when it stated:

While simultaneously asserting the lack of manpower and funds to initiate programs to combat ghetto frauds, monitor advertising, and secure effective compliance with orders, the F.T.C. has issued complaints attacking the failure to disclose on labels that "navy shoes" were not made by the Navy, that flies were imported, that Indian trinkets were not manufactured by American Indians and that "Havana" cigars were not made entirely of Cuban tobacco.[4]

A House staff report issued at the end of 1974 concluded that the F.T.C.'s performance not only was inadequate but was getting worse.[5]

Several theories have been advanced to explain the conduct of administrative agencies in general and the F.T.C.'s deficiencies in particular. The most popular may be termed the "bad guy" theory. The Nader group and the American Bar Association, among many others, adhere essentially to this view, which can fairly be summarized as follows: The explanation for the inconsistency between the agency's bad performance and its noble statutory goals is simply bad personnel. Brushing aside other possible reasons for the F. T. C.'s conduct, the Nader group observed that "the real problem of the F.T.C.—and indeed of any faltering agency—can usually be traced to people."[6]

This theory strains credulity. Can it really be true that the F.T.C. has been badly staffed for most of its sixty-odd years? Why have the innumerable criticisms that have been leveled against the agency failed to produce any substantial administrative reform? What is the explanation for the F.T.C.'s alleged concentration on small firms, cases of minor impact, and competitive or small industries? Proponents of the bad-guy theory do not answer these questions but focus on a single deficiency as a universal explanation. They have usually asserted incompetence rather than demonstrated it, using the occasional anecdote to support sweeping statements about the quality of agency personnel. On the basis of a single employee found asleep at his desk during office hours, for example, the Nader group concluded that virtually the entire F.T.C. senior staff was derelict. Such an anecdotal mode of reasoning fails as a proof of the proposition that the F.T.C.'s shortcomings are explained by bad personnel.[7]

A more sophisticated explanation of the F.T.C.'s performance is based on the broad discretion that the F.T.C. Act confers upon the agency.[8] Such vague terms as "unfair" abound in some of the F.T.C.'s statutes. And the agency's jurisdiction extends over almost all manufacturing, trade, and service industries and establishments in the nation. Because of the breadth of its jurisdiction, so the argument goes, the agency has failed to arrive at clear, definite, and predictable standards. So it drifts, changes policies, and is unable to act decisively—a pattern that is interpreted as incompetence. The proponents of this theory claim that precise standards would heighten the impact of the agency's policies; under like circumstances, like treatment would follow; both staff and public would know exactly what the agency's policies were; and the agency's independence in the face of pressure to make individual exceptions would be enhanced.

Precise standards do improve an agency's performance. But the theory fails to explain specific features of the F.T.C.'s conduct. Why, for example, should imprecise standards have compelled the agency to concentrate, if indeed it has done so, on small firms? The particular direction of actions cannot be deduced just from the fact that the agency has wide discretion. Further, the F.T.C. has administered its specific statutes and those that contain vague language in the same manner. The Nader group and the American Bar Association's investigative body criticize the F.T.C.'s handling of the Wool Products Labeling Act and the Fur Products Labeling Act, both of which are

extremely narrow, explicit statutes, as strongly as they do its administration of the more broadly discretionary statutes. Discretion is
exercised when one makes a "choice among possible courses of
action or inaction."[9] The question is, why is discretion exercised in
one way rather than another? A theory of administrative conduct
based on lack of standards does not provide an answer.

Turning away from the sort of sweeping assertion such theories
offer, let us examine in detail some aspects of the agency's behavior
to develop a feel for its operation and performance. First we should
focus more closely on what bad performance means in the context
of F.T.C. activity. Second, we shall want to examine whether the
charge of bad performance is justified or not. Third, we should investigate the agency's organization, enforcement techniques, and
operating style. If we set out to discover instances of statutory transgression, where does an analysis of the F.T.C.'s statutory mandate
and enforcement tools lead us? Finally, we should be able to account,
at least in a general way, for the different courses the agency has
followed at various times.

Output and Outcome

Perhaps the most egregious error committed by critics of the
F.T.C. is failure to distinguish between agency outputs and the out-
comes of agency actions.[10] "Outputs" are the specific decisions
rendered by the agency. An order stating that the XYZ Corporation
shall cease and desist from discriminating in its pricing policies is
output. Beyond output lies the question of impact, or "outcome."
What are the secondary and tertiary effects of specific decisions or of
decisions in the aggregate? What impact do they have on the economic and social environment? Much of the criticism of F.T.C. performance has been directed less at specific decisions than at the fact
that agency decisions have not had a particular impact on the social
and economic environment.

Such critics as the Naderites, after finding what they perceive to
be gross deficiencies in the outcome, or impact, of agency decisions,
draw the unwarranted inference that the agency's output is the cause
of the alleged lack of impact. Moreover, the link between output and
outcome is made not by comprehensive examination of agency decisions during a particular test period, but by citation of selected illus-
trative cases that at first blush appear downright silly. This technique

begs the question of whether regulatory policies—or at least the kinds
of regulatory policy employed by the F.T.C.—are appropriate instruments with which to effect changes in business conduct or structure. Take antitrust policies, for example; a major study has concluded
that they have not had a major impact on economic concentration:

Clearly the needs and requirements of changing technologies and markets
rather than antitrust policies have played the major roles in determining
changes in concentration in American industries. Antitrust had nothing
to do with keeping the clothing industry diffuse and transportation
vehicles concentrated. It was research and development, not antitrust
that led to the lessening of concentration in the electrical machinery,
chemical, and rubber industries after World War II.[11]

The chapters that follow take up such questions as whether regulatory policy is an appropriate instrument for attaining the desired
outcome in particular instances; what the impact of agency decisions
has been, insofar as measurement is possible, in areas to which the
F.T.C. has devoted resources and time; and what the agency's output
has been in specific policy areas, and why. To clear the way for these
questions, we must get an overview of F.T.C. operation and
performance.

Agency Performance

Has the agency's performance been as bad as critics allege? Have
all the firms against which orders have been entered been small?
Examination of the antimonopoly orders entered between November
1917 and January 1965 under Section 5 of the F.T.C. Act shows
that numerous large firms have been involved, as well as many
smaller ones. Between 1917 and 1922 the F.T.C. issued complaints
against the American Tobacco Company (1 F.T.C. 539), the Ward
Baking Company (1 F.T.C. 388), Armour and Company (1 F.T.C.
430), the Beech-Nut Packing Company (1 F.T.C. 516), Sears,
Roebuck (1 F.T.C. 163 and 2 F.T.C. 536), the American Dental
Trade Association (4 F.T.C. 484), and the Goodyear Tire and Rubber Company (5 F.T.C. 484). During the same period it also brought
a great number of complaints against smaller—in many cases very
small—firms.

The pattern of bringing complaints against large, medium, and
small firms has persisted. In 1935–1936, for example, orders under
Section 5 of the act were entered against such giants as the Rubber

Manufacturers Association and its members (21 F.T.C. 176), major steel manufacturers (22 F.T.C. 711), and the leading electrical equipment manufacturers (24 F.T.C. 306), as well as against many small firms. Whatever period we select, the picture is the same.[12] The charge that the F.T.C. has devoted itself almost exclusively to small firms is thus unfounded. The pattern of agency enforcement is far more complex than such a simple generalization allows; if we are to make sense of the agency's actions, we must acknowledge that it has gone after many sharks as well as mackerels and minnows.

Another charge is that the F.T.C. has been almost exclusively concerned with trivial cases aimed at rectifying matters over which competitors have complained rather than at protecting the process of competition. As we shall see in later chapters, the criticism has much truth in it. But, again, this generalization does not give the full picture. Among all the trade practices that regulation is designed to prevent, none is closer to the concept of original sin in theology than conspiracy to fix prices. Economists may debate the pros and cons of mergers, price discrimination, and other practices, but few of them will have a kind word to say about price fixing. Anti–price-fixing actions might therefore be taken as an index of the resources the F.T.C. has devoted to "good" objectives. If so, the critics' argument is suspect. Between November 1917 and January 1925 the F.T.C. issued approximately one hundred complaints (some of which were dismissed) involving vertical or horizontal price fixing and related practices; and many of these complaints involved large firms and important sectors of the economy. From January 1935 through December 1938, another period selected at random, it brought fifty such cases. Little purpose is served by selecting other periods for illustration, for the pattern is consistent. If we take the generally accepted view that orders against price fixing are significant outputs, then we must conclude that the agency has devoted substantial resources to important activities as well as to unimportant ones. The critics have greatly exaggerated the agency's commitment to the trivial; as we shall see in detail in later chapters, it would be accurate to say that it has used its resources both to foster the competitive process and to repress it, in keeping with its contradictory mandate.

The final charge to be examined is that the agency has not been innovative or courageous—at least, not until very recently. This charge is closely related to the "life cycle" theory, which can be summarized as follows: Regulatory legislation is enacted because of popular pressure; after an initial period of widespread public support for the agency created to enforce the new legislation, support begins to dwindle as interest in the agency wanes; the agency then seeks support from the interests it was created to regulate and enforces its policies in a timid and passive manner.[13] Yet analysis of the timing of innovative and courageous actions taken by the F.T.C. shows that they have been irregular but frequent.[14] To see the agency's recent work as uniquely innovative after a long period of sleep is as wrong as to conceive of the agency as running down like the bell of an alarm clock after an initial burst of activity.

The F.T.C. was, indeed, very active in its early years. In this period it attacked the notorious "Pittsburgh-plus" system of pricing steel products, despite the vigorous opposition of the United States Steel Corporation. This method of pricing, by which freight charges were computed as if the steel had been shipped from Pittsburgh, even if its point of origin was closer to the destination, is alleged to have been a major cause of retarded regional development in the South.[15] In its early years, too, the agency sought to prevent, under Section 5 of the F.T.C. Act, acquisition of corporate assets, since the Clayton Act dealt only with acquisition of stock. The courts rejected the Commission's action as an unwarranted extension of its jurisdiction.[16] As a final example from this period, consider the Beech-Nut case; the Supreme Court upheld the F.T.C.'s decision that, even though no explicit agreement to fix prices was involved, the system of merchandising by which the Beech-Nut Packing Company compelled dealers to sell its products at stipulated prices was an unfair method of competition.[17]

The period from the mid-1920s to the mid-1930s has been viewed by some commentators as one in which the agency retreated from its early activism. Yet it can as legitimately be regarded as one of innovation. Instead of relying on the case-by-case approach of the earlier period, most commissioners began to place their faith in a new informal mechanism—the trade-practice conference. In promulgating trade-practice rules to establish areas of cooperation and areas of competition in particular industries, the agency was following the line of argument adopted by Herbert Hoover when he suggested that voluntary cooperation among business enterprises was the most effective form of regulation. These rules adopted in trade-practice conferences were usually developed by the members of an industry them-selves, through the agency of the industry trade association. They both identified competitive practices that would be deemed unfair in the context of the individual industry and forbade practices (such as price fixing) that would violate the Sherman Act. In other words, they both restricted competition and sought to advance it.[18]

So enthusiastic were most commissioners about the trade-practice-rule procedure that in 1927 the agency publicly stated: "A new constructive agency known as the trade practice conference division is proving of substantial assistance to the commissioners and to industry and business in the fundamental work of the Commission—the elimination of unfair practices in commercial competition. This procedure permits an industry to make its own rules of business conduct; to establish its own law merchant, in cooperation with the Commission."[19]

This reliance on trade-practice conferences has been viewed in some quarters as a retreat from hard-line enforcement; in fact it reflected an early recognition by the F.T.C. of a persistent problem (one that the 1975 Magnuson-Moss Act purports to solve). The case-by-case approach is both ineffective as a means of solving industry problems and unfair to the few who are the subjects of orders and therefore are barred from indulging in a particular practice while others remain free to follow it. In 1973 an F.T.C. representative explained that "the Commission, recognizing the inefficiency and some-times inequity of relying solely on formal proceedings, has attempted to achieve its goals through advisory opinions, guides, trade regulation rules and other more generalized measures."[20]

The voluntary approach, which originated in the 1920s, continued to be followed in the early 1930s as part of the administration of the National Recovery Act in the early days of the New Deal—although not without discomfort to some F.T.C. personnel.[21] In the meantime, another major innovative change was taking place in the agency—development of the economic report. The agency had been compiling economic reports since its founding, but it was only in the 1930s that it began to publish controversial, pointed reports on crucial economic issues. The most important of these reports was the one published after a massive investigation of public utility holding companies.[22] Its detailed findings of abuses by holding companies was a major factor in the enactment of the Public Utilities Holding Company Act, which required operating utility systems to be removed from the financial control of holding companies.

While little purpose would be served by a description of all the major F.T.C. reports issued since (or before) the one on public utility corporations, some of the most important should at least be mentioned. Among them were the investigation of chain stores, which was partly responsible for the enactment of the Robinson-Patman Act; several reports on international cartels, including a controversial one attacking the international petroleum cartel; periodic reports on economic concentration, both in the economy as a whole and in specific industries; reports on specific antitrust topics, such as mergers and interlocking directorates; and, finally, the 1968 report on automobile warranties that contributed to passage of the Magnuson-Moss Act. Some of these reports will be discussed again in later chapters. My purpose in citing them here is to illustrate another link in the chain of innovative F.T.C. actions. These economic reports were intended to be used by Congress and the F.T.C. to remedy what were seen as major economic or consumer problems. Their impact may often have been minimal and their findings subject to debate, but the agency's goal is clear: to produce results through innovative policies.

The 1930s saw the Commission take another innovative step when it made a full-scale attack on pricing systems, especially the basing-point system. The story began in 1931, when Frank Fetter, a distinguished economist and former president of the American Economic Association, published an evaluation of the antitrust laws.[23] Fetter charged that uniform pricing systems were the principal device by which industries fixed prices, and he cited as the most notorious of such systems the basing-point system used in many basic industries, such as steel and cement. Under this system, the price quoted to customers was the delivered price, computed by taking the published price for the product at the "basing point" nearest the customer and adding to it a shipping cost computed from the published freight rate from that point. The procedure was followed regardless of the point from which the good was actually shipped—which did not necessarily have to be close to the basing point. The result was that sellers could increase their returns by selling to customers in their own vicinity. For, if the point of actual shipment was closer to the customer than the basing point was, the actual freight cost would be less than the freight cost from the basing point—which was the amount charged to the customer. Under these circumstances the customer paid what is called "phantom freight." Conversely, if the seller was more distant from the customer than the basing point was, and therefore faced actual freight costs that were higher than those arrived at under the basing-point system, he would have to absorb the difference himself.[24]

In 1932, a year after publication of Fetter's book, an F.T.C. economic report on pricing in the cement industry concluded that the multiple-basing-point system of pricing developed by the cement industry tended to lessen price competition and to produce fixed prices. Moreover, the system caused unnecessary and costly cross-hauling of cement.[25] The belief that pricing systems were the root problem of antitrust activity was reinforced when the F.T.C. examined the Steel Code promulgated under the National Recovery Administration (N.R.A.). In contradiction to Sherman Act standards, the Steel Code approved the multiple-basing-point system. The F.T.C. succinctly concluded that "the diagnosis which the Commission makes is that the basing point system not only permits and encourages price fixing, but that it is price fixing."[26]

The terms of the conflict between the restriction of competition enshrined in codes adopted by the N.R.A. and the commitment to competition embodied in the Commission's attack on pricing systems shifted in favor of the latter when the Supreme Court, in the famous "sick chicken" case of 1935, declared unconstitutional an important provision of the National Industrial Recovery Act.[27] From July 1936 through June 1955 the Commission maintained a vigorous attack on pricing systems, entering orders "against price fixing in 46 chosen cases in which it found a delivered pricing method important enough to be specified in the findings or in the order. Twenty-two of these cases were concerned with zone pricing, 9 with basing point systems, 5 with systems of freight equalization, 5 with uniform delivered pricing and 5 with more than one kind of delivered price formula."[28]

In the most important of these cases—that involving the cement producers' trade association and firms in the cement industry—the Supreme Court decided, in 1948, against the defendants.[29] Reaction in the cement and steel industries was so strong that immediately after the Supreme Court upheld the F.T.C.'s decision outlawing the multiple-basing-point system, spokesmen for these industries sought congressional support for a move to overrule the Court. The campaign was successful and a law to this effect was passed by Congress; only a presidential veto saved the work of the Commission.[30] The outcome of the F.T.C.'s activity in the field of pricing was not, as many had hoped, an end to uniform pricing; but this does not alter the fact that the agency had undertaken an innovative and courageous program to attack what was considered the most important antitrust problem.

By the end of World War II, then, the Commission had developed an arsenal of enforcement tools, including case-by-case action, informal and voluntary procedures, economic reports, and broad-scale programs designed to attack such specific problems as pricing systems. These techniques could be and were used together, though the emphasis given to each could and did vary with the predispositions of the majority on the Commission and of key staff members. The postwar period saw the development of innovative legal theories and such major new programs as the attack on corporate mergers that followed enactment of the Celler-Kefauver Antimerger Act of 1950 and a concerted attempt to compel compliance with the Robinson-Patman Act's provisions on advertising allowances in the garment industry.

Vigorous postwar enforcement of the Robinson-Patman Act of 1936 led to an increase in the number of antimonopoly orders issued by the Commission. The contrast with the prewar situation is illustrated by Table 7, contrasting figures for 1955–1960 with those for

Table 7. Number of antimonopoly orders* issued by F.T.C. under various statutes, 1935–1940 and 1955–1960

Statute	1935–1940	1955–1960
F.T.C. Act, Section 5	84	66
Clayton Act		
Section 3	6	12
Section 7	6	8
Section 8	0	2
Robinson-Patman Act, Section 2(a), and Clayton Act, Section 2	26	74
Robinson-Patman Act		
Section 2(c)	3	60
Section 2(d)	3	62
Section 2(e)	0	14
Section 2(f)	3	5

* In some instances an order involved two or more charges.
Data are from Helen W. Soleau and Donnamarie Carr, *Digest of the Federal Trade Commission's Antimonopoly Cases* (Washington, D.C.: Federal Trade Commission, n.d.).

1935–1940. While the total number of actions taken under statutes other than the Robinson-Patman Act decreased very slightly, the increase in the number of orders issued under the Robinson-Patman Act itself indicates clearly the agency's emphasis on enforcement of the price discrimination law in the postwar period. But the new emphasis was not really at the expense of the other statutes; rather, the Robinson-Patman Act was used largely as a supplement to the other statutes. Heavy emphasis on enforcement of the Robinson-Patman Act's provisions continued through the 1960s. In fiscal 1964, for example, 231 Robinson-Patman Act orders were directed at members of the wearing apparel industry alone. And in the mid-1960s the agency also began to move against corporate mergers, with the results shown in Table 8. The antimerger program was supplemented

Table 8. Number of corporate divestitures required under F.T.C. orders, 1965–1972

Year	Number
1965	10
1966	4
1967	10
1968	6
1969	2
1970	4
1971	4
1972	5
Total	45

Source: U.S. House of Representatives, Committee on Appropriations, 92d Cong., 2d sess., 1973, *Agriculture, Environmental and Consumer Protection Appropriations for 1973, Hearings,* pt. 4, p. 515.

by a requirement that the agency be notified in advance of certain types of mergers and, after 1965, by F.T.C. policy statements on particular industries, the purpose of which was to establish guidelines on the types of merger that would be questioned and the types that would not. Another innovation occurred in 1962, when the F.T.C. instituted an advisory program for the business community designed to provide legal opinion as to whether prospective courses of conduct were likely to violate a law administered by the Commission.[31]

In the 1950s and 1960s, then, techniques and procedures developed earlier were still used, but new programs were instituted too. Many of the new programs centered on enforcement of the Robinson-

Patman Act, which, as we shall see in a later chapter, has been sub-jected to considerable criticism. Yet, if the Robinson-Patman Act is a "bad" piece of legislation, the fault lies not with the Commission but with Congress. So long as the statute is operative, the function of the Commission, a creature of Congress, is to enforce it vigorously. And this it has done.

This brief review of F.T.C. performance during the long period from the agency's inception until the storm that burst in 1969 with publication of the Nader and American Bar Association reports indicates that the agency has been continuously innovative and courageous. Its conduct has not followed a life-cycle pattern, with a burst of activity in the early period followed by relapse into a cozy support relationship with business interests in the middle and later years. The explanation for the agency's decisions, for the outcome of those decisions, and for the absence of impact on the environment that is the subject of F.T.C. concern does not lie in personnel de-ficiencies. To understand the agency's performance we need to ex-amine the interplay between the agency's organization and regulatory style and the contradiction between competition and stability which is inherent in its operating statutes.

Organization and Operating Style

The formal organization of the F.T.C. has changed many times since its inception; indeed, formal changes have taken place almost with each presidential administration. Despite the restructuring and renaming of bureaus and the shifting of personnel, however, the agency's manner of transacting business has remained largely un-changed. The best way to understand the Commission's operating style and organization is to examine the course followed from the moment a matter is brought to the attention of agency personnel to the time it is finally disposed of.

Most of the matters the agency deals with are brought to its at-tention by what is ambiguously termed "the public." To pinpoint the exact percentage of matters drawn to its notice by the mailbag route is difficult; one estimate puts the figure as high as 90 percent, and almost everyone who is or has been associated with the agency, I among them, agrees that the proportion is large, probably between 80 and 90 percent.[32] Of this number, a high proportion seems, in my experience and that of other observers, to come directly or indirectly from competitors or other businessmen affected by the practice complained of. The proportion of these complaints which ultimately results in formal action is even higher. The pattern holds equally in the areas of fraud and what the agency terms antimonopoly practices.[33]

This system, under which the F.T.C. acts primarily upon complaints by affected businessmen, originated early in the agency's history. Rule 1 of the Rules of Practice in force in 1915 stated that any person might apply to the Commission to institute a proceeding in respect to any alleged violation of a law over which the F.T.C. had jurisdiction. The rule continued, "The Commission shall investigate the matters complained of . . . and if upon investigation the Commission shall have reason to believe that there is a violation of law the Commission shall issue . . . a complaint."[34] The agency's annual report for 1916 announced that "usually . . . the facts concerning such violations are brought to its attention by persons who have suffered injury from the Act complained of"[35]—that is, by competitors who know what is "unfair."

In 1936, in the course of a congressional hearing, the General Counsel of the F.T.C. stated that an action usually commenced when an applicant reported to the Commission that a competitor was using an unfair method of competition. He outlined industry's view of the weight that it carried with the Commission by virtue of its experience: "The industry feels that, with respect to some practices, which may not be per se unlawful, yet if the great majority of the industry feel that they are unfair, *are uneconomic,* that their judgment about the unfairness of the practice will carry great weight with the commission."[36]

The Commission's annual report for 1956 noted that applications of complaint were the principal source of Commission investigations.[37] In 1957 the agency announced that 80 percent of its cease-and-desist orders stemmed from letters of complaint from the public (without breaking this category down), the remainder from information received from Congress, other government agencies, and Better Business Bureaus, and from investigations initiated by the Commission.[38] Here it should be noted that most of the complaints that reach the Commission through Congress, Better Business Bureaus, and other government agencies also come originally from competitors.

The 1969 American Bar Association report on the F.T.C., based on a wide-ranging investigation of the agency's operations and unlimited access to internal and confidential documents, says that "the involvement of the F.T.C. in matters having a minor impact on consumers may be explained by the fact that the agency often acts at the behest of one group of industry members against another group. Sometimes these complaints of competitors deal with matters of concern to consumers, but often they do not."[39] At another point the report observes that "often the agency has seemed more concerned with protecting competitors of an enterprise practicing deception rather than consumers."[40]

The evidence that most F.T.C. cases—or at least a very large proportion of them—originate with competitors' complaints raises two questions: Why has the agency acted in so many instances at the behest of businessmen? And what are the implications for agency output?

In addressing the first question, let us put ourselves in the agency's shoes for a moment and consider the issues raised by just one among its many obligations—its mandate to stop deceptive advertising. What is the volume of advertising that could potentially deceive? A leading textbook on advertising discloses that

every day 4.2 billion advertising messages pour forth from 1,754 daily newspapers, millions of others from 8,151 weeklies, and 1.36 billion more each day from 4,147 magazines and periodicals. There are 3,895 AM and 1,136 FM radio stations broadcasting an average of 730,000 commercials a day; and 770 television stations broadcasting 100,000 commercials a day. Every day, millions of people are confronted with 330,000 outdoor billboards, with 2.5 million car cards and posters in buses, subways and commuter trains, with 51.3 million direct mail pieces and leaflets, and with billions of display and promotion items.[41]

How can the F.T.C. deal most rationally with the number and variety of potentially violative acts in this area?

It cannot arbitrarily select, among the universe of firms, industries, and advertising messages, a number to investigate; it might guess wrong in too many instances and thus squander valuable resources without result. Such gambling is contrary to the principles of rational administration and would surely draw down upon the F.T.C. the wrath of executive and legislative overseers concerned with the instrumentally rational aim of preventing waste (or the appearance of it) in government expenditures.[42] An approach of this sort would also lead to hostility and pressure from persons who felt that their problems were being ignored or slighted.

Perhaps the F.T.C. might try to develop criteria for selection of cases for investigation based on an industry's sales, the number of complaints about a product, the hazards of a product, advertising expenditures, the number of people reached by an advertisement, the social characteristics of the people reached, and the out-of-pocket losses that could result from a fraud. Clearly if investigations were conducted on the basis of such guidelines, the number of advertisements the agency would have to examine would not necessarily be significantly smaller than it would be if cases were selected capriciously; nor would they be qualitatively different. Such a system would at best be only marginally superior to arbitrary selection; it does not meet the need for a reliable method of gathering information about potential statutory transgressions.

What group of people will be the best source of information about deceptive practices? Consumers are often unaware of a deception that has been perpetrated upon them; if they are aware of it, the chances are high that either they do not know where to complain about it or their information about the nature of the deception is so vague and imprecise as to be useless. Sophisticated academics may know the law and may know where to complain, but they are usually not aware of what is going on in specific lines of commerce. From time to time a group may form that takes it upon itself to represent "consumer interest" or the "public interest"; such groups tend to lose interest or heart after a while, however, and then to disappear—and in any event they lack the resources and legal power to find out very much. They are not, therefore, consistently reliable sources of information for the F.T.C.

The one remaining possible source of information, the business community, might therefore be expected to be the major instigator of complaints (and consequently orders), as indeed it has been. Businessmen are informed about specific events in specific industries, since for the protection of their firms they must be aware of situations that could be disadvantageous to them. They are the only group whose information and interests coalesce; they must always be aware of the moves of competitors, suppliers, and customers. When they feel that a competitor, supplier, or customer has gained an unfair advantage, they complain to the F.T.C. This accounts for the American Bar Association's observation that the agency often acts at the behest of one group of industry members against another group. In this aspect of its operations, the F.T.C. is compelled by its operative statute to act as a conduit for businessmen seeking to solve their competitive problems.

When we consider that the F.T.C. not only must examine advertising but also has jurisdiction over a large number of other unfair methods of competition in its enforcement of the Robinson-Patman Act, the Clayton Act, and various other statutes, the reliance it must place on the business community as its source of information is further accentuated. For, unlike the advertising case, the myriad transactions involved in other areas of this extensive jurisdiction are not made public (except in the case of large mergers, which are covered in the press). Under these circumstances, rational allocation of the funds available for the discovery of wrongdoing requires the F.T.C. to rely primarily on businessmen, the group most knowledgeable about the marketplace.

The result has been that the F.T.C. has devoted a large proportion of its time and effort to small firms and competitive industries. Because adversely affected firms have complained of unfair competition or deception, industries characterized by intense rivalry and by low prices and profit margins—industries whose performance would have gladdened the heart of Adam Smith—have been the subjects of F.T.C. investigation in disproportionate numbers.

It is not surprising, therefore, that

the F.T.C.'s Robinson-Patman enforcement has hit the pygmies notably harder than the titans of trade. Of the 1,040 formal complaints issued during the F.T.C.'s first twenty years of Robinson-Patman enforcement, only 28 percent smote corporations noticed by a listing in *Moody's Industrials* for 1960, and only 13 percent charged concerns ranked among *Fortune's* 1961 directory of the 500 largest industrial or the 50 largest merchandising corporations in the United States.[43]

The reason is, of course, that in industries populated by big concerns, firms know how to signal to each other about price leadership and other problems. In such industries there is generally an informal system whereby a particular firm leads and its competitors follow.[44] The procedure may involve nothing more complicated than competitors' reading about a price leader's moves in a newspaper or trade journal; or it may be based on circulation of new price sheets through salesmen.[45]

Industries with many small competitors cannot regulate themselves as effectively as those with few firms. A small competitor is the most likely to trigger a price war or initiate some other program of vigorous competition, ending the system of self-regulation. Many industries are incapable of self-regulation because of the large number of viable competitors they contain; these industries are unable to cope with or restrain "price cutters" or "aggressive merchandisers" or firms that introduce new marketing or distribution techniques.[46] And the F.T.C. devotes considerable effort to restricting competition in these intensely competitive industries. In 1959, for example, antimonopoly cases absorbed 60 percent of the F.T.C.'s manpower and money[47]—and in many of these cases the F.T.C. was using its authority to produce conditions that simulated industry self-regulation and prevented intense competition.

This pattern holds for many matters to which the F.T.C. devotes its attention. Nevertheless, there remains a sizable number of instances in which F.T.C. action promotes competition or in which sources other than affected businessmen play an important role. In the first case, firms adversely affected by uniform price increases or new terms and conditions of trade instituted by suppliers complain to the F.T.C. of price fixing. To the extent that the F.T.C. acts on these matters, complaints from businessmen lead the Commission both to restrict the competitive process and to enhance it. In the second case, information comes from unhappy consumers, other government agencies, or so-called public interest organizations, or from the F.T.C.'s economic investigations or advertising monitoring activities.

The total number of applications for complaint is very large. How does the agency select from this total the relatively few cases that are investigated? The first criterion is probability of violation. Many of the complaints it receives, especially from disgruntled consumers, clearly do not relate to acts that violate the law; they are therefore dismissed. Complaints from congressmen, on the other hand—many of which come indirectly from businessmen—are given high priority. A more important criterion is the F.T.C.'s ranking at any one time of areas of concern. If a complaint relates to a matter that current F.T.C. thinking places high on the list of priorities, then it is likely to be investigated. (Investigation is ordinarily conducted by one of the many agency field offices, under the supervision of a headquarters attorney.) Until recently, for example, enforcement of the Robinson-Patman Act was a high-priority item; in recent years it has not been.[48]

As we observed earlier, the Commission has always been aware of the limitations of the case-by-case method of investigation imposed on it by the statutory requirement that it serve complaints and enter orders against each "person, partnership or corporation . . . using any unfair method of competition or unfair or deceptive act or practice in commerce."[49] This requirement, which has been amended by the Magnuson-Moss Act (discussed in Chapter 10) was until recently thought to mean that the F.T.C. had to act very much like a court, following a procedure of complaint, answer, and trial, with relatively formal presentation of evidence and full procedural safeguards for respondents, before an order could be entered. The necessity for this course of action was the principal cause of the delay between the commission of an unlawful act and the entry of a final order prohibiting it.

The Commission has used a number of techniques to circumvent the case-by-case method. When an unlawful practice has appeared to be widespread, it has investigated and sought to bring complaints against all of the transgressing members of an industry. Actions were brought, for example, against many record manufacturers and distributors from 1959 through 1961 for the granting of illegal payola to disc jockeys. Between 1959 and 1962 the F.T.C. entered many orders against firms in the citrus fruit industry for violations of the brokerage provision of the Robinson-Patman Act. But while the legal question was settled with the first decision, the facts showing violation had to be proved in each case—and proving violation usually consumes far more resources and time than arguing legal theory. So even if routinization effected some saving, cases of this sort still involved delay and substantial expenditure.

In the late 1960s the Commission developed a new procedure to avoid the case-by-case method, the trade-regulation rule (TRR)—not to be confused with the trade-practice rule, which does not have the force of law. Under the TRR procedure, the agency, having conducted a preliminary investigation, files notice in the *Federal Register* of a proposed TRR and invites interested parties to submit to it written data, views, and arguments and to appear before it to express their views and suggest amendments, revisions, and additions to the proposed rule. Only then does the Commission promulgate the rule. The first test of this procedure involved a rule declaring failure "to disclose . . . the minimum octane number or numbers of the motor gasoline being dispensed" to be an unfair method of competition for refiners and others who sell gasoline to the public.[50] In a suit brought by two petroleum trade associations and thirty-four refiners, the Court of Appeals upheld the power of the agency to issue TRRs, pointing out that "a vast amount of data had to be compiled and analyzed, and the Commission armed with these data had to weigh the conflicting policies of increasingly knowledgeable consumer decision-making against alleged costs to gasoline dealers which might be passed on to consumers."[51] The court then went on to state that the Commission was obligated in such a proceeding to weigh all arguments and facts pro and con.

Whatever doubts might have existed about the appeals court's decision were laid to rest by the Magnuson-Moss Act, which explicitly authorizes the F.T.C. to use TRRs. But does the new procedure make a difference? It is time-consuming: the Octane Rule, for example, was first formally proposed in July 1969, after investigation that began somewhat earlier; yet even before court proceedings delayed it further, it was not to be effective until March 1972. More important, until the enactment of the Magnuson-Moss Act, a TRR amounted to nothing more than a declaration that a certain practice would be considered unfair or deceptive. The Commission still had to prove in each case that the respondent had violated the rule. In other words, until the Magnuson-Moss Act was passed, there was little difference between the method by which the first case in a series indicated what the agency would consider unfair or deceptive and the TRR procedure. It should be remembered, too, that the TRR procedure does not answer in those frequent situations in which a method of competition or a claim is unique. It is useful only when a practice is common in an industry. And its effect is to foreclose a method of competition.

To summarize, the F.T.C.'s jurisdiction is vast in terms both of subject matter (all unfair methods of competition, unfair or deceptive acts or practices, and several specific statutes) and of population (virtually every firm engaged in interstate commerce except those, such as railroads, that are explicitly regulated by other administrative agencies). In contrast to the Food and Drug Administration, which receives all new drugs and must approve them before they can be marketed, the F.T.C. has been provided with no effective tools for discovering violations among the millions and millions of business transactions that take place. Finally, the F.T.C.'s technical competence—its command of skills that would allow it to evaluate quickly many business transactions and claims—is very limited. Because of the breadth of its jurisdiction, the paucity of its tools, and the limitations of the case-by-case method and its feeble variations, the Commission has usually had to depend on the business community for information.

Of course, nothing compels individual human beings to act in a specific manner, and there have therefore been variations in the agency's emphases. In the face of criticism of the so-called mailbag approach, the agency has tended to move away from it. The F.T.C. may also decide from time to time not to enforce certain statutes; such a decision was reached concerning the Robinson-Patman Act in the early 1970s. But a serious cost is then involved: the number of cases brought by the agency declines without any significant commensurate increase in quality. A report of an audit of the F.T.C. by the General Accounting Office in 1975 stated that 97 percent of cases never get beyond the stage of initial investigation, and in more than 60 percent of those formally investigated, no charges are brought. And still "the vast majority of cases are against small businesses, involve relatively unimportant minor details or technical violations of the law."[52] The decrease in the number of cases brought, caused in large part by a decision not to enforce the Robinson-Patman Act, has not, according to a staff report of the House Interstate and Foreign Commerce Committee, led to "an increase in the quality of the consumer protection cases to compensate for this decline."[53] There was a fall in the number of preliminary investigations completed from more than 14,000 in fiscal 1971 to under 4,000 in fiscal 1974.[54]

The agency may—and indeed has—sought to escape the destiny imposed on it by its statutes. Its output may vary in volume and emphasis from one period to another. It has always promoted competition and restricted it. But the outcome of its actions will be subject to criticism as long as the major sanction with which it is provided by statute is the cease-and-desist order. Under this system a transgressor is entitled to a free bite of the apple before the courts can impose any meaningful monetary penalties; so deterrence is minimal. If a sinner is caught and told not to do it again, he can usually adjust his business operations to avoid that sin and turn to another instead. The cease-and-desist order is the legacy of the compromise of 1914 and the continuing contradiction between competition and stability.

PART TWO

REGULATION OF MONOPOLY
AND STABILITY

CHAPTER 4

Exclusionary Practices
and Collusive Practices

As we saw earlier, each era of the agency's existence has seen a different emphasis in output and some innovation. These changes may be due to a variety of factors: a presidential program; the interests and demands of key legislators who take a close interest in the F.T.C.'s work; criticism of agency performance, from either inside or outside government; requirements or obstacles imposed by court decisions; and the predilections of the majority among the five commissioners or even of top agency personnel. I suggest, however, that despite even sharp changes in emphasis or method, the F.T.C. remains essentially the same in its central aspects: its decisions continue to reflect the contradiction between competition and stability; its performance, insofar as it can be measured, continues to fall short of what both critics and agency personnel would like.

Traditionally, the two most important operating bureaus within the F.T.C. have been those dealing with practices that affect competition and those that involve deception. Their names have changed with each reorganization of the agency but their jurisdictions have remained the same. Thus what was known throughout most of the 1960s as the Bureau of Restraint of Trade became the Bureau of Competition in the 1970s, but in all its guises it has been in charge of cases arising under the Clayton Act and the Robinson-Patman Act and most cases brought under Section 5 of the F.T.C. Act's injunction against unfair methods of competition. This bureau is responsible for the development of cases from the initial investigatory phase (usually assigned to a field office), for the trial before a hearing examiner (lately called administrative law judge), and for the appeal, held before the full Commission. Many matters are settled by consent order, by which the Commission and the respondent agree to the entry of an order and upon its terms. Under this procedure, conducted by both field offices and central bureaus, formal proceedings are terminated with the entry of an agreed-upon order, subject to the approval of the Commission.

This chapter will examine the contradictory content of the F.T.C. Act's proscription against unfair competition, showing the manner in which, consistent with the statute, the agency has both promoted competition and restricted it. Cases from 1956–1964 and 1973–1975 will be used to illustrate these contradictory trends. The record of 1956–1964 was seen by the critics of 1969 as typical of the F.T.C.'s bad performance. During that period, party control of the agency shifted from Republican to Democratic. The years 1973–1975, on the other hand, have been popularly portrayed as ones in which the F.T.C. reformed itself and sought to promote the public interest.[1] Section 3 of the Clayton Act will be considered along with the F.T.C. Act, for generally the same divison within the Bureau of Restraint of Trade (or Bureau of Competition) which is responsible for enforcement of Section 5 of the F.T.C. Act is also responsible for enforcement of Section 3 of the Clayton Act. We shall examine first exclusionary practices and then collusive practices.

Exclusionary Practices

Exclusionary practices include exclusive dealing, tie-in selling of two separate commodities, reciprocity, price discrimination, and vertical mergers. All of them are intended to exclude competitors from certain outlets or custom. Such practices may be either signs of vigorous competition—the exclusion of competitors from your customers is what competition is all about—or monopolistic tactics. Robert H. Bork and Ward S. Bowman argue that exclusionary practices appear to be

either competitive tactics equally available to all firms or means of maximizing the returns from a market position already held. . . . Analysis indicates that, absent special factors that had not been shown to exist, so-called exclusionary practices are not means of injuring the competitive process. The example of requirements contracts illustrates the point. The theory of exclusionary tactics underlying the law appears to be that firm X, which already has ten percent of the market, can sign up more than ten percent of the retailers, perhaps twenty percent, and, by thus "foreclosing" rivals from retail outlets, obtain a larger share of the market. But one must then ask why so many retailers are willing to limit themselves to selling X's product. Why do not ninety percent of them turn to X's rivals? Because X has greater market acceptance? But then X's share of the market would grow for that reason and the requirements contracts have nothing to do with it. Because X offers them some extra inducement? But that sounds like competition. It is equivalent to a price cut, and surely X's competitors can be relied upon to meet competition.[2]

Exclusionary tactics may, of course, extend a monopoly position; this would be the effect of a tie-in of a patented (and therefore exclusive) article and an unpatented one. But in most reported instances, exclusionary tactics are competitive devices available both to established firms and to newer firms seeking to enhance their market positions. In preventing the use of such methods of competition, the Commission acts in favor of the status quo in an industry and thwarts competition.

Exclusionary arrangements often play an important role in a firm's plans. In the case of a product assembled from parts made by many suppliers, such as an automobile, exclusivity aids coordination and assures supplies. Exclusivity may be a necessary inducement for someone to undertake the distribution or retailing of a product; in this case the arrangement ensures that products are marketed and made available to consumers on competitive terms. These points were made, it will be recalled, by opponents of the Clayton Act during the course of the legislative debates.

If exclusionary tactics are used as monopolizing devices rather than as competitive devices, the proper remedy is to proceed against the monopolizer under the Sherman Act. None of the cases brought by the F.T.C., however, has involved monopoly; in all of its cases involving exclusionary devices as a competitive tactic, the firms against which it moved were in no position to monopolize their industries. Examination of the relatively few orders in this category during 1956–1964 will make this fact clear.

Exclusive dealing that may "substantially lessen competition" is proscribed by Section 3 of the Clayton Act. During the period 1956–1964 the F.T.C. entered ten orders under Section 3, one of which was set aside by the Court of Appeals and subsequently dismissed because exclusive dealing had not been proved.[3]

Two of these orders were against manufacturers of hearing aids.[4] In the Beltone case the respondent entered into contracts with 167 of its distributors under which the distributors agreed not to sell the products of Beltone's competitors. The respondent, a firm not included in the *Fortune* list of the 500 largest corporations, was hardly in a position to monopolize or dominate its industry. In 1960 there were between 35 and 40 manufacturers of hearing aids, of which 11 were classed as major firms with sales of $1 million or more (one of them being the giant Zenith). Beltone accounted for about 16 percent of total industry sales during the period for which evidence was submitted. In the Otarion case, the respondent's share of total sales by major firms was less than 5 percent. There was just as little danger of monopolization at the retailer level as at the seller level. Entry into retailing is unquestionably easy; there were between 5,000 and 6,000 retail outlets in 1960.[5]

These manufacturers were therefore using exclusive dealing not to monopolize or dominate the hearing-aid industry, but rather to enhance competition. An outlet with allegiance to a single manufacturer will devote his best efforts to selling that manufacturer's products. A nonexclusive distributor may promote some products less vigorously than others. The F.T.C.'s attack on exclusive dealerships fallaciously assumed that a manufacturer has no further competitive interest in his product once he sells it to the distributor; in fact, he has a continuing interest, since repeat sales and reputation depend on the conditions of the retail sale.

The Outboard Marine case illustrates another anticompetitive aspect of the F.T.C.'s actions against exclusive dealing.[6] Because Outboard Marine required its dealers not to handle its competitors' products, the competitors had to create and develop potential outlets and train people to sell their products. The Commission interpreted the respondent's action as a restraint on the marketing of competitors' products, objecting to the fact that the competitors had to develop their own distribution systems. At the retail level, the exclusive distribution system clearly led to a greater number of retailers than there would have been if other manufacturers had shared Outboard Marine's outlets. The evidence showed that most of Outboard Marine's dealers had had no relevant experience before they obtained the dealerships, and further that these dealers were largely engaged in other trades— retailing of sporting goods, undertaking, optometry, barbering, and so on. Evidence was submitted that if eighteen of the most common of these other occupations were selected, their followers would provide in excess of 960,000 potential outboard motor dealers. Even if we allow for the fact that dealers of outboard motors can be located profitably only near water, and exclude those not so situated, the remaining number of potential outlets is still large. Again no harm was shown to have occurred to competitors because Outboard Marine had been monopolizing; the F.T.C. simply restrained a competitive device.

The Mytinger & Casselberry case illustrates another business reason for exclusive dealing arrangements.[7] The respondent, a manufacturer of vitamin and mineral food supplements, sold its products through 80,700 door-to-door salesmen (called distributors). Of all the door-to-door sales of vitamins and minerals, this firm accounted for 61.5 percent; but these sales made up only 8.6 percent of the total value of retail sales of such products. In order to compel distributors to devote their best efforts to selling Mytinger & Casselberry's products and to prevent consumers from associating this firm's products with those of its rivals, the firm required its 80,700 distributors to deal exclusively with it in their handling of vitamin and mineral food supplements. Once more the effect of a restraining order would be fewer distributors than there would have been if competitors had to hire their own distributors. The possibility of monopoly was again remote on all levels.

Exclusive dealing, then, is a competitive device employed by manufacturers for a number of business reasons, and may have nothing at all to do with monopolizing an industry. The reasons are generally related to a manufacturer's desire to differentiate his product from others. A firm that has painstakingly built up its marketing system may want to avoid sharing with competitors the fruits of its labor.[8] Dominant firms can establish product differentiation through intensive advertising; smaller firms must use such techniques as exclusivity to persuade retailers to employ their best selling efforts in order to combat the effects of larger companies' advertising.

The same principle of vigorous competition applies to tie-in sales. In the Photostat Corporation case[9], evidence was brought to show that owners of photostat machines had to purchase paper and chemicals from the respondent if they wished to avoid a labor charge for machine servicing. Photostat did not permit repair parts and accessories to be sold to competitors, "thereby causing costly delays in repairing and servicing machines of owners purchasing competitors' supplies."[10] Photostat's terms could have been met or improved upon by competitors selling copying machines and supplies. And Photostat might have legitimately believed that its competitors' chemicals or paper would produce bad copies on Photostat machines, thereby affecting the product's reputation and subsequent sales. The decision in the case is, however, silent on this point.

Another order against tie-in arrangements illustrates the relationship between price discrimination and other exclusionary practices.[11] Three distributors of proprietary drugs, toiletries, and housewares in Jacksonville, Florida, consented to an order prohibiting them from offering discounts to customers who bought several of their products. Discounts were not offered if the products were purchased individually. The effect of the order was to prohibit a method of competition designed to induce customers to increase their purchases. Monopoly or the possibility of dominance by the respondent was not a serious consideration, since the company was a small regional firm.

The F.T.C.'s propensity to bring cases that would have the effect of stabilizing an industry structure and foreclosing some areas of competition is further revealed in two tobacco-warehouse cases.[12] The cases involved the manner in which local tobacco boards of trade allotted selling times for tobacco in local warehouses during the short selling season and the means by which selling time was allocated to new warehouses. This industry was already characterized by lack of competition among warehouses both because selling time was allocated among warehouses by what amounted to nothing more than local trade associations and because growers were subsidized by the Department of Agriculture. The F.T.C.'s orders did nothing to promote competition among warehouses by enabling them to sell tobacco at any time they desired. The effect was merely to alter the trade association rules for restricting competition. Why the public interest should have dictated use of public funds to stabilize an industry devoted to selling a harmful product is hard to see. It could not be seriously contended that monopoly or its consequences could follow from the operations of the local tobacco boards of trade.

Perhaps the most famous of the exclusionary practice cases in the 1956–1964 period was that involving gasoline refiners and rubber companies and their sales commission plans for tires, batteries, and accessories (TBA).[13] Under these plans, the refiner agreed to promote the sale of the rubber company's TBA products to service stations selling the refiner's products. The rubber company paid the refiner a commission on such sales. The respondents were ordered to cease entering into such plans and to permit dealers to select their own TBA suppliers. No claim was made that there was a danger of monopoly in either the tire or the gasoline refining industry. Rather, it was argued that restraint existed in the sale of TBA products because the dealer's freedom of choice was impaired. But every contract impairs freedom of choice, and the real question in the bargaining relationship between seller and buyer is whether the buyer has a competitive choice before binding himself to a single seller. In these cases, the answer is clear: Almost every locality has many refiners who are ready to sell their products to the multitude of service stations that exist. Moreover, there was no danger that these practices would lead to monopolization of the market for TBA products or impairment of price competition at any level.

Gasoline stations are not the only outlet for TBA products. If some rubber companies were expending resources on the sales commission fees involved in the TBA plans, their competitors would have been better able to compete for sales to other kinds of outlets (and for sales to the multitude of gasoline stations not involved in the sales commission plans). Gasoline refiners as well as the dealers themselves would want their TBA prices to be competitive with prices at other outlets (especially Sears), so prices to the consumer do not become a consideration.

Four other orders issued in 1956–1964 further illustrate the thrust of the F.T.C.'s actions on exclusionary practices. In the Brown Shoe case,[14] the nation's second largest shoe manufacturer, which sells through both company-owned and independent retailers, granted certain benefits to independent stores that promised to concentrate their purchases on Brown's shoes. Approximately 760 stores agreed to Brown's arrangement; these stores constituted about 1 percent of total retail shoe purchases. Because under these agreements Brown's competitors were effectively prevented from selling to a "significant number" of shoe stores, the F.T.C. entered an order against Brown Shoe. It would be hard to find a clearer example of F.T.C. action against a vigorous competitive tactic that was not remotely likely to cause the development of a monopoly. The benefits of the Brown arrangement to retailers—including free signs, business forms, and accounting assistance, participation in low-cost group fire, public liability, robbery, and life insurance policies, and special low prices on certain footwear lines—were of great value to them and might have caused retailers handling competitive lines to exert pressure on the competing suppliers to provide similar benefits. Such bargaining and horizontal competition is effectively prevented, however, by the order in this case, which must have had the effect of impairing competition. Actions that shut out competitors from some sales—which is supposed to be the object of rivalrous behavior—is viewed by the F.T.C. as anticompetitive, just as early opponents of the Clayton and Federal Trade Commission acts warned.

In the Procter & Gamble case[15] another competitive device was struck down. The respondent entered into exclusive contracts with every manufacturer of automatic washers and dishwashers under which the latter packed samples of Procter & Gamble products in new machines. Further, distributors and dealers were paid to recommend only Procter & Gamble products. The respondent entered into a consent order that prohibited these practices. The "injured" competitors, some of them major soap manufacturers, could have retaliated by improving on Procter & Gamble's offer, by using other methods of competition for subsequent sales, or by reducing prices. Instead, the F.T.C.'s order foreclosed a vigorous method of competition that had no monopolistic impact—and which provided consumers with free merchandise.

In the case of Sandura,[16] a small manufacturer of hard-surface floor coverings, the respondent had instituted a system under which distributors sold Sandura products to selected dealers at or above recommended prices; dealers were required to sell at minimum prices and were not permitted to sell the products to any disapproved dealer. The manufacturer was not only small—in a field dominated by such giants as Goodyear, Goodrich, Johns Manville, and Armstrong Cork—but was bordering on insolvency. The Commission admitted that "distributors, dealers, and the consuming public distrusted Sandura as a result of its recent deficiencies, and respondent lacked the wherewithal to finance an advertising campaign to overcome this sales resistance."[17] Therefore it had to use the promise of exclusive territories to induce distributors and dealers to carry its products. Insofar as the distribution system fixed resale prices, it constituted a price-fixing arrangement; but insofar as it was a device to get distributors to carry Sandura products, in an industry in which three other firms made between 77 and 84 percent of sales and Sandura ranked about twentieth in sales and was in dire straits, it carried no danger of monopoly but was merely a method of competition.

The final case to be examined for the 1956–1964 period is that of Luria, a scrap broker in the iron and steel business.[18] The complaint in this case was issued in January 1954, the Commission's order was entered in February 1963, and the Court of Appeals upheld the order in 1968—by which time the condition of the iron and steel scrap industry had changed from one of short supply to one of excess supply. During the Korean War the respondent was able to achieve a dominant position as a scrap broker because many of the largest steel mills purchased all or most of their requirements from Luria. The steel mills were, however, free to purchase scrap from anyone else and to terminate at will any supply arrangements with Luria. The mills claimed that they selected Luria as an exclusive source to ensure reliable and continuous supplies during the shortage caused by the Korean War. Despite these arrangements, Luria's share of the scrap market (exclusive of railroads, shipyards, and fabricators) never exceeded 33 percent. After the Korean War, scrap prices began to decline significantly—hardly a sign that Luria was exercising monopoly power. The F.T.C.'s action restricted a firm's ability to compete vigorously.

This review of the exclusionary practice cases in which orders were entered by the F.T.C. in the 1956–1964 period illustrates the way in which such cases have been used to restrict bargaining processes and foreclose valuable methods of competition. In any contract, a buyer agrees to a restrictive arrangement because he sees advantage in doing so. If other sellers cannot offer equivalent or superior advantages, the one offering the restrictive arrangement should be successful in concluding the contract. This is what competition is supposed to be about.[19] Moreover, restrictive agreements serve the competitive process by allowing a firm (1) to obtain market access, (2) to increase product exposure, (3) to increase distributors' sales efforts, and (4) to determine the quality and character of a distributor's services.[20]

Although in recent years the F.T.C. has backed away from enforcing other parts of its mandate, most notably the Robinson-Patman Act, it has continued to enter orders in restrictive practice cases at approximately the same rate as before. The kinds of restrictive practice that it has attacked have changed to some extent, however. For example, orders have been entered against shopping-center developers who enter into leases with tenants that restrict the merchandise a tenant can sell in the center.[21]

In other cases the F.T.C. has proceeded against arrangements in which contracting parties agree to reciprocal dealing ("I'll buy X from you if you buy Y from me").[22] The firms involved have included both some in the *Fortune* 500 list and many smaller ones. In no case has the question of monopoly or monopolization arisen; in all instances considerable competition has existed. But in each instance the F.T.C. "nails down its finding that competition is injured with the testimony of competitors of the defendant that his activities and aggressiveness may cost or have cost them sales. The conduct that threatens such 'injury' is then prohibited. That this result is profoundly anticompetitive seems never to occur to the Commission or most courts."[23]

Collusive Practices

While F.T.C. action against exclusionary practices tends to eliminate competition, its actions against collusive practices usually reflect concern with maintenance of competition. Collusive practices are those under which firms agree to eliminate competition among themselves. The most common example is price fixing; other collusive practices are agreements among competitors to divide territories and to boycott certain customers. These practices are unlawful per se; to prove a violation, only unlawful agreement need be shown.[24] Collusive practices (or cartel practices), unlike exclusionary practices, are usually designed to eliminate competition; and in some instances competition is eliminated so completely that the conspiracy simulates a monopoly.

Collusive practices have traditionally been treated under the Sherman Act by the Department of Justice as criminal acts. A fine and the threat of imprisonment are certainly greater deterrents than a cease-and-desist order, which is the limit of the F.T.C.'s power in a case of price fixing. There seems no reason, therefore, for the F.T.C. to exercise jurisdiction in a collusion case. An F.T.C. proceeding in such a case can even do harm if the Department of Justice wishes to prosecute subsequently, for under Section 9 of the F.T.C. Act, no natural person may be prosecuted on account of any transaction concerning which he testified or produced documentary evidence in an F.T.C. proceeding. Nevertheless, under liaison procedures in effect between the two agencies, the Department of Justice has given the F.T.C. the green light to proceed in many price-fixing cases.

Procedural difficulties are not a major stumbling block. The most important obstacle to enforcement of the law in the area of price fixing arises from what is known as conscious parallelism, the process by which firms in oligopolistic industries follow identical courses without overt agreement. The result of this process is that firms in such industries may achieve legally by conscious parallelism what they are forbidden to attain collusively. Antitrust prosecution for price fixing thus becomes little more than a game, in which only firms in industries with grossly imperfect informal mechanisms for coordination are caught. Whatever the other merits of antitrust law, then, it fails as a mechanism to assure low competitive prices.

Why should coordinated prices be expected in such industries? In the case of industries that produce identical commodities and have few enough members to permit rapid dissemination of market information, horizontal price fixing is unusual and unnecessary. Yet uniformity in list price is almost inevitable. Any general reduction in price by one competitor to increase his custom will be matched by his rivals; the initiator will thus gain nothing. Similarly, except during periods of unusual shortage, one seller cannot raise his prices unless he can be sure he will be followed shortly and in equal amount by his competitors. The result is that a system of signaling develops in the industry whereby the price leader raises list prices and is either followed, not followed, or followed in lesser amounts by other members of the industry. Uniform list prices can thus be achieved without price fixing. The process of surreptitious price discrimination and experimentation in selected markets or with selected customers (condemned by the F.T.C.) erodes the price structure. As Almarin Phillips states, "Because of the smallness of the group of firms in simple, oligopolistic markets, the conclusion is certain (if an obvious price war is not in existence) that the firms have—in a behavioral sense—communicated and, to a degree, agreed on certain aspects of conduct. . . . Their agreement . . . may be as complete as that reached through the use of explicit and overt communication and a formal organization in markets in which firms are many."[25]

Of course, conscious parallelism does not enable oligopolists to charge any price they desire. Actual prices are affected by such factors as the existence of substitutes, the level of demand, conditions of supply, the bargaining power of buyers, the level of imports and the threat of further imports, the extent of product differentiation, and transportation costs.[26] Moreover, if significant changes in market shares occur as the result of nonprice competition, one firm may reintroduce price competition. These factors have led some economists to conclude that oligopolistic industries respond to market forces in their long-run price fluctuations even if not in the short run.[27] Thus the forces that tend to produce uniform prices, whether through collusion or conscious parallelism, are counteracted by other forces that tend to promote price competition. If competition is assumed to be the more desirable form of market behavior, F.T.C. policy should favor those mechanisms, such as price discrimination, which firms employ in order to compete in price. And this argument is strengthened by the futility of the policy of entering orders that command firms to compete in price.[28]

The outcome of price-fixing orders may not be what it was expected to be; but how are the F.T.C.'s decisions to be explained? Before we attempt to answer that question, let us place ourselves again in the position of the agency as it seeks to attack price-fixing conspiracies. To search for conspiracy in all of the many industries in which member firms charge identical prices would be a waste of resources. So once more the agency must rely largely on a rational source of information—businessmen affected by alleged agreements, whose knowledge and gossip coincide with their self-interest. Such businessmen are either customers adversely affected by a uniform and sudden rise in prices or competitors who for one reason or another refuse to go along with the conspirators and blow the whistle on them. A second source of information about horizontal price-fixing arrangements can be government agencies that either have received identical bids from various suppliers or have recognized a peculiar pattern of bids in which competitors appear to take turns at receiving contracts; but most of these cases have been pre-empted by the Department of Justice for criminal prosecution under the Sherman Act.[29]

Given the probable sources of information about possible instances of price fixing, in what kinds of case is the Commission likely to find sufficient evidence of collusion to issue a complaint? The analysis offered earlier suggests that one likely class would be cases involving unconcentrated industries—those in which producers are numerous and small. In such an industry, firms may lack sophistication in concealing evidence, or may even be ignorant of the law concerning horizontal price fixing. Their numbers also work against successful conspiracy, for the greater the number of firms involved, the greater the chances of a squealer. These factors make a conspiracy in this type of industry, if it occurs, a likely target for the F.T.C. And indeed the Commission has often proceeded in cases of this kind. For example, it has entered orders against fishermen and clam diggers who have banded together in regional associations. In these instances, most of them involving relatively small sums of money, fishermen acted together to raise prices to canners, who of course were displeased.[30] Although price fixing may always be bad in principle, the actual impact of these agreements on the consumer was slight, since there was still substantial competition in the industry; the fishermen faced competition both from those who caught the same kind of fish in other areas and from those who caught other kinds of fish that could be used as substitutes.

A second kind of case in which evidence is readily available arises from public disclosure of collusion by the colluders themselves— usually through a trade association. The many cases brought against price fixing by the F.T.C. after the demise of the N.R.A. illustrate the type. During the N.R.A. period, industries were urged by the federal government to develop "codes of fair competition." The government's concern to prevent prices from falling during the Great Depression led it to sanction, even to encourage, pricing systems that promoted uniformity, such as the basing-point system. When the N.R.A. was declared unconstitutional, many industries continued to follow practices that would have violated the antitrust laws but for the N.R.A.[31] The F.T.C. then proceeded to prosecute various trade associations and their member firms for collusion to fix prices, basing its findings of conspiracy in considerable part on actions taken publicly and with government approval. Orders were entered against trade associations and their members in the cement, steel, lead pigments, rubber tire, and chain manufacturing industries, among others.

Since the 1930s, trade associations have grown considerably more sophisticated in their efforts to avoid any taint of price fixing. Under the guidance of expert counsel, the executives of trade associations and individual member firms have done everything possible "to avoid creating any suspicion that there are [price-fixing] agreements."[32] Moreover, as we have seen, in oligopolies conscious parallelism serves the same purpose as overt collusion and makes collusion unnecessary in most instances. If for some reason large firms do want to engage in collusive price fixing, they can usually do so without leaving incriminating evidence around. For all these reasons, the number of price-fixing cases brought by the F.T.C. against large firms and important trade associations has declined substantially since the 1930s, and today, such cases are exceedingly infrequent.

A rare exception was the American Cyanamid case. The respondent pharmaceutical manufacturers were accused of having violated the F.T.C. Act by securing patents through misrepresentation and the withholding of vital information from the Patent Office and then utilizing the patents to fix the prices of certain antibiotics.[33] The complaint was brought in July 1958; the Commission's first decision was made in December 1963; and the F.T.C.'s order was affirmed by the Court of Appeals in September 1968. Since the improperly obtained patent had been secured in January 1955, more than thirteen years had elapsed between the original wrong and the entry of an order correcting it. The F.T.C. obtained its data for the pursuit of this matter from the public record (proceedings of the Patent Office), from an economic analysis of the antibiotics industry by its own staff, and from a detailed investigation of the pharmaceutical industry by the Senate Antitrust Subcommittee.

The antibiotics conspiracy case marked the end of the road for the F.T.C. so far as cases of horizontal price fixing are concerned. A very few cases of this sort have been brought subsequently,[34] but none of them has been of such importance. The F.T.C. has labored mightily in this area to promote competition, bringing many cases over the years; but the outcome of this effort has been minor, at best. Price levels do not appear to have been greatly affected by orders entered in horizontal price-fixing cases. In the area of vertical price fixing, the story has been different.

Vertical Price Fixing

If a manufacturer or distributor enters into an agreement with a retailer whereby the retailer is to sell products at a fixed price, the manufacturer or distributor is said to be guilty of vertical price fixing. The Supreme Court in 1911 declared this practice to be an unlawful restraint of competition;[35] but since then the decision has been largely nullified by legislation permitting the states to enact fair-trade laws— legislation that was passed by Congress at the behest of the proponents of lawful resale price maintenance, including such strong advocates of the original Federal Trade Commission Act as Louis Brandeis and George Rublee.[36] Almost all states have passed such laws, although the inflation of the 1970s has led several to rescind them.

The Miller-Tydings Act of 1937, which established the ground for fair-trade laws, was enacted to a considerable extent because of pressure from drug retailers and was designed to curb the discounting practices of department stores and cut-rate drugstores.[37] In most states, manufacturers of branded goods may use the fair-trade principle to set resale prices, except that if the manufacturer is also a distributor or retailer, he may not establish resale prices for customers who are also competitors, since this would constitute horizontal price fixing. In addition to fair-trade laws, many states have also enacted statutes that forbid selling below cost, require a minimum markup, or use some other device to set a floor under prices.[38]

The F.T.C. began to devote attention to resale price maintenance, or vertical price fixing, as early as 1918 and has attacked the practice ever since,[39] entering a large number of orders in cases where fair-trade laws have not applied and where something more has been involved than a simple refusal to deal with price cutters. As early as 1922 the Supreme Court upheld the Commission's right to declare vertical price fixing an unfair method of competition.[40] In these cases, therefore, the F.T.C. has sought to promote competition in the face of intense pressure to legalize resale price maintenance.

It would be a mistake, however, to think that this holding action has been the F.T.C.'s only activity in relation to vertical price fixing. It has also acted in support of businesses seeking to curtail the competitive opportunities of other businesses. And in this respect enforcement of the law on vertical price fixing has had rather the same effect as enforcement of the Robinson-Patman Act. In 1955–1956, for example, five orders were entered against publishing houses that required their retailer customers, but not their book club customers, to sell books at fixed minimum prices.[41] While the vertical price fixing was indefensible in terms of its effect on prices, the major problem here was the differential treatment accorded the different channels for distribution of the respondents' books. Book clubs, the newer mode of distribution, had bargained with publishers to gain an advantage over traditional booksellers. But as a result, consumers benefited, for they could get books at lower prices through the book clubs. In its results, therefore, the arrangement differed substantially from the fair-trade form of vertical price fixing, which has the effect of establishing uniform (higher) prices for all customers. Booksellers who sought relief through F.T.C. action did so because they wanted artificially maintained prices, not because they wanted to share with the public the benefits that would accrue from an order prohibiting vertical price fixing. In the Doubleday case[42] the hearing examiner found that "bookseller witnesses were unanimous in their desire for price maintenance, and the secretary of the American Booksellers Association said his membership was practically unanimous against any change therein." In short, the dealers' complaint, and the reason these cases were brought, had to do with discrimination against booksellers, not with an attack on fair trade.

In similar vein, two cases were brought against manufacturers of electric razors who opened new channels of distribution by themselves in competition with their customers, with whom they had entered into fair-trade agreements providing for resale price maintenance.[43] Again, dealers objected to the disturbance created by the new competition stemming from the manufacturers' forward vertical integration rather than to the resale price fixing itself.[44]

Several cases involving price wars in the marketing of gasoline illustrate the way in which orders against vertical price fixing have been used as an adjunct to orders against price discrimination intended to quell price wars.[45] Each of these cases has arisen from the circumstances of a price war and has involved two counts, one of price discrimination, the other of vertical price fixing. As the earlier discussion of price discrimination in the sale of gasoline demonstrates, the effect of F.T.C. decisions in this area has been to prevent price wars and to maintain prices, since the major oil companies are effectively prevented from aiding dealers in price wars and dealers do not themselves have the resources to engage in a lengthy price war. Orders against vertical price fixing have the same effect. During the price wars from which these cases arose, petroleum producers entered into consignment agreements with station operators under which the latter became mere agents of the producers in the sale of gasoline (though not in the sale of other products). Under these agreements, producers set the prices of gasoline during the price wars. Thus, just as in the matter of price discrimination, the producers became, through consignment plans, full participants in the price wars, and were more or less obligated to give assistance to affected dealers. The Commission struck down the consignment arrangements, however, as being a surreptitious form of price fixing, thus effectively excusing producers from participating in price wars. And because station operators generally have only meager resources at their command, the effect has been to deter price wars—an intense form of price competition.

Clearly the F.T.C. has brought some cases against vertical price fixing to promote competition. This conclusion follows fairly obviously from the nature of the offense. Equally, however, if less obviously, some cases have had the effect of promoting stability. Orders relating to resale price fixing have been used as a weapon to prevent the destabilizing effects of price wars in gasoline marketing and to try to limit the inroads being made upon traditional booksellers' markets by book clubs. But since the enactment of legislation permitting states to pass fair-trade laws, the agency's actions have amounted to little more than guerrilla strikes against a few of the transgressors who have stepped beyond the bounds of fair-trade protection. They certainly cannot be interpreted as a comprehensive national policy to prevent price fixing at the retail level. The F.T.C.'s policy in bringing such cases in the face of the widespread use of fair-trade agreements is, in fact, another instance of the fundamental contradiction between competition and stability.

Conclusion

The cases discussed in the course of our examination of the F.T.C.'s actions against exclusionary and collusive practices under Section 5 of the F.T.C. Act and Section 3 of the Clayton Act are typical of the greater part of its Commission's conduct in these areas. But they do not exhaust the range of cases. A few cases have been brought, for example, in matters involving collusive territorial or customer allocation or boycott.[46] Usually, but not always, the respondents in these actions have been relatively small firms.

If we look at the body of cases as a whole, the most striking point about them is the way in which they reflect the fundamental contradiction between competition and stability inherent in the statute. The second feature to stand out is that most of them (though not all, certainly) reflect the F.T.C.'s dependence for information about possible violations on the business community—those customers, suppliers, and competitors who are seeking adjustment of relationships among themselves. The relationships adjusted in cases of exclusionary practice are horizontal and restrict competition; in collusive practice cases, as we have seen, the relationship to be adjusted is frequently vertical or complicated in some other manner. The vertical adjustment that has followed some of the collusion cases has often promoted horizontal competition; in some of the cases involving vertical price fixing, however, changes brought about by new modes of distribution have been checked.

As we have seen in the American Cyanamid case and in the cases brought against firms employing the collusive basing-point pricing system, when the Commission has available to it sources of information other than the business community, it proceeds vigorously. But wrongdoers do not ordinarily flaunt their misconduct, and collusion is often not necessary to obtain uniformity in prices. So despite its good intentions, the F.T.C. is reduced to the patchwork practice of instituting cases on an ad hoc basis. It has gone on some fishing expeditions, and occasionally it has come up with a big catch. But such a hit-and-miss method of case selection used on a regular basis would be irrational in light of the Commission's sweeping jurisdiction both in subject matter and over persons. Accordingly, the impact upon the national economy of F.T.C. action in these areas has been minimal. The agency's decisions on collusive practices have had no discernible effect on inflation. Nor do its decisions on exclusionary practices appear to have had much effect on the well-being of business units in the aggregate, which respond primarily to changes in such factors as the availability of money, the rate of cost increases, and demand.[47] Because of the nature of its regulatory process, the F.T.C. has largely failed both the proponents of competition and the proponents of stability.

CHAPTER 5

The Robinson-Patman Act

The most important amendment to the Clayton Act is the Robinson-Patman Act of 1936. Indeed, most F.T.C. antimonopoly complaints since 1936 have been brought under the Robinson-Patman Act. Yet few laws have occasioned so much criticism from economists and legal draftsmen, and the act is widely regarded as the product of an organized political effort to preserve the traditional marketing system of independent merchants against the encroachments of mass distributors and chains, whose low prices made them popular with consumers during the business crisis of the 1930s.[1] The conventional manufacturer-wholesaler-retailer system of distribution that existed at the beginning of the twentieth century began to change in the 1920s as large retailers bought directly from manufacturers, bypassing the wholesaler. Chain stores of all kinds increased their share of retail sales, from 9 percent in 1926 to 25 percent in 1933.[2] After World War II the development of discount houses, rack jobbers, and other novel forms of distribution continued the trend.

Chain buyers secured wholesaler discounts from suppliers; this advantage, combined with the operational efficiencies permitted by their large size, vertical integration, and centralized management, gave them lower costs than the traditional retailer could achieve, and the savings could be passed on to the consumer in the form of lower prices. The reaction of the bypassed wholesalers was to seek protective legislation of various kinds, including taxation of chain stores, fair-trade laws that would permit resale price maintenance, and a new law on price discrimination.[3]

During the depression of the 1930s, chain stores filled the need that many people felt for a scapegoat to blame for their woes. The demise of small retailers was attributed to "evil" chain-store practices, and this conclusion was bolstered by a misreading of the evidence collected by the F.T.C. in the course of an investigation of chain-store retailing. The investigation actually found that the chains' ability to sell at lower prices than small independents was primarily the result of the lower costs that chains could achieve because of their high volume, limited service, and uniform principles of management; it did not flow from their alleged buying advantages.[4] Nevertheless, the sentiments of those who supported the Robinson-Patman Bill were well expressed by Huey Long, who declared: "I would rather have thieves and gangsters than chain stores in Louisiana."[5]

Although the Robinson-Patman Bill was promoted as legislation to protect retailers, it was initiated by the U.S. Wholesale Grocers Association, with the active support of the National Food Brokers Association and the National Association of Retail Druggists. In fact, the bill was drafted by the attorney for the U.S. Wholesale Grocers Association.[6] The chains adopted the defensive strategy of trying to weaken the bill through amendments. In the clash between the various kinds of business involved, the consumer's interest was nowhere represented.[7]

Congressman Wright Patman stated that the purpose of the bill was "to give all of the independent merchants of this country the same rights, privileges, benefits, and opportunities as the larger chains or concerns receive, and no more."[8] The only mention of the consumer in any of the reports that accompanied the bill was a blanket assertion that "it is not believed that the restoration of equality of opportunity in business will increase prices to consumers." This consoling observation was followed by the statement that price discrimination would lead to monopoly at some uncertain time in the future, and hence to higher prices to the consumer.[9]

Opposition to the bill was led by Congressman Emanuel Celler, long considered a proponent of vigorous enforcement of the Sherman Act. He stated, in a minority report on the bill:

The advocates of this bill include many independents unable to meet competition which is easily met by their efficient fellow dealers, and as well wholesale grocers catering to such small dealers handling the basic necessity, food, and asking for unnatural restraints upon their most efficient competition. . . . Unfortunately, housewives and the consumer generally are not organized, their voice is not articulate. But retail grocers and the retail druggists, and the wholesalers catering to them, have banded together and have raised a lot of commotion and issued forth reams and reams of propaganda in support of this bill, but no thought have they given to the consumer.[10]

Section 2 of the Clayton Act was amended by Section 2 of the Robinson-Patman Act in several significant respects. To the effects clause of old Section 2 proscribing price discrimination that might "substantially lessen competition or tend to create a monopoly in any line of commerce" the Robinson-Patman Act added an injunction against discrimination that might "injure, destroy, or prevent competition." The intention was to reduce the amount of proof needed to show anticompetitive effects.

New subsections 2(c), 2(d), and 2(e) do not concern pricing directly, but relate rather to the methods chains allegedly used to gain advantage over smaller rivals, including the granting or receiving of false brokerage or discounts in lieu of brokerage (section 2[c]), the granting of discriminatory advertising allowances to competing customers (section 2[d]), and the rendering of disproportionate services to competing customers (section 2[e]). These subsections make the named activities offenses per se; thus it is not necessary to show that those discriminated against have actually suffered loss in sales or profits. These subsections have been used principally against small businesses in highly competitive industries.[11]

Section 2(f) imposes liability under certain conditions upon buyers who solicit or receive price concessions under Section 2(a). Proof is more difficult under 2(f) than under 2(a), however, and it has therefore been involved in few cases.[12]

The food wholesalers, food brokers, and retail druggists who promoted the Robinson-Patman Act also supported fair-trade legislation, which similarly precludes price competition among retailers.[13] And as they pushed for new price-discrimination and fair-trade legislation at the national level, they urged other legislation at the state level, including laws forbidding sales below cost at the retail level and laws requiring a certain markup over cost.[14] From the Sherman Act, a statute designed to prevent price rises, we move with this act—and in the name of antitrust—to laws intended to prevent price reductions. As one of the Robinson-Patman Act's numerous critics succinctly puts it, the new statute is a complete perversion of the Sherman Act which it is supposed to further amend. The intent of the Sherman Act was to preserve a competitive framework so that the whole of society, as consumers, could benefit through the operation of free markets. If the competitive framework is to operate, then there must be a possibility of injury to competitors. The prevention of injury is most likely to lead to a reduction in competition. If no one is hurt, there is a strong probability that no one is competing. The Congressional approach indicates a desire to preserve the status quo, rather than competition.[15]

Equally important, the new law sought to limit the benefits accruing to firms that attempted to modernize distribution systems or to introduce innovations in marketing. Under the Robinson-Patman Act, a buyer who lowers his costs through innovations in storage, transport, or delivery arrangements may not achieve a competitive advantage by receiving lower prices; so innovations are discouraged.[16]

An Overview of Enforcement

The Robinson-Patman Act, unlike any other statute examined thus far, stands unambiguously on the side of stability and against vigorous competition. The small entrepreneurs who lobbied for passage of the Robinson-Patman Act hoped it would prevent the development of new modes of distribution and retailing. This hope was of course not realized; retailing and distribution have been streamlined, and chains have largely replaced "mom and pop" stores. In the battle over enactment, the small independents, standing on the side of stability and the preservation of older systems of distribution, were opposed by chain stores and mass distributors, standing, at least in this battle, on the side of vigorous competition. The independents won the legal battle but were unable to stem the tide of modernization. They did bequeath to the F.T.C., however, a statutory tool that the Commission could and did employ against several important methods of competition. What the independents did not foresee was that this weapon could be used against them as well as against chains and mass distributors. In providing the F.T.C. with a law that, more than any other, equated injury to individual competitors with injury to competition, they gave it a weapon it could use against firms of any size—large, medium, or small—which employed the proscribed methods.

Until the early 1970s the Commission enforced the law heartily.

Table 9. Number of antimonopoly orders issued by the F.T.C. under various statutes, 1945–1965

Statute	Number
F.T.C. Act, Section 5	201
Robinson-Patman Act	
Section 2(a)	171
Section 2(c)	237
Section 2(d)	248
Section 2(e)	6
Section 2(f)	20
Clayton Act	
Section 3	22
Section 7	35
Section 8	1
Total	941

Data are from Helen W. Soleau and Donnamarie Carr, *Digest of the Federal Trade Commission's Antimonopoly Cases* (Washington, D.C.: Federal Trade Commission, n.d.).

Table 9 shows the number of antimonopoly cease-and-desist orders issued between 1945 and 1965. In a few cases, where the respondent was charged with two offenses, orders are counted twice. But I have counted only those orders issued under Section 2(e) of the Robinson-Patman Act that did not also include a prohibition under Section 2(d); most of the 2(e) cases also included a 2(d) charge. And I have counted under Section 5 of the F.T.C. Act those cases brought under Section 3 of the Clayton Act that charged violation on both counts; again, most Section 3 cases included both charges. Cases that were dismissed by the Commission are excluded; but since we are interested in the F.T.C.'s output, cease-and-desist orders entered by the Commission but ultimately reversed by the courts are included. Of the 941 orders, 682 (72.48 percent) were for violation of the Robinson-Patman Act. To say that the bulk of the F.T.C.'s antimonopoly activity was in the area of Robinson-Patman Act enforcement is therefore no exaggeration. Moreover, most of the cases brought under this act used the sections relating to advertising allowances and brokerage payments, for which proof is relatively easy.

The Robinson-Patman express came to a screeching halt in the 1970s. In 1969 the American Bar Association issued its report on the F.T.C., and this was followed by two semiofficial reports, the White House Task Force Report on Antitrust Policy (Neal Report) and the President's Task Force Report on Productivity and Competition (Stigler Report). Thereafter condemnation of the Robinson-Patman Act and the F.T.C.'s enforcement of it became virtually official doctrine. In June 1975 President Gerald Ford singled out the Robinson-Patman Act as the prime example of a regulatory statute that restricted price competition and artificially enhanced prices. The reason criticism of the Robinson-Patman Act ceased being merely a subject of academic comment and became one of executive concern was, of course, inflation. One must be extremely cautious in inferring causation, but it is a fact that wholesale prices have risen more rapidly in product classes that have been the subjects of intensive F.T.C. action under the Robinson-Patman Act than in product classes that have not.[17]

Whether or not enforcement of the Robinson-Patman Act actually causes prices to rise, many public officials, both in the executive branch and in the F.T.C., now believe that it does. For example, Commissioner Mayo Thompson, in a speech before the Federal Bar Association in 1975, stated that "if there were no price discrimination, there would be precious little price competition in the real world. There is a choice to be made, in other words, between keeping prices 'equal' and high, or letting them be unequal and a great deal lower."[18] In support of his conclusion Thompson quoted an executive in the furniture industry—at one time the subject of a great deal of F.T.C. effort—who argued that furniture prices would have been 10 to 20 percent lower without F.T.C. action.[19]

In light of the new widespread disapproval of the Robinson-Patman Act, the F.T.C., as a matter of deliberate policy, began to de-emphasize the statute, with the result that many fewer cases have been brought under it in the 1970s. In congressional testimony, agency personnel have replied to adverse comparisons of the number of anti-monopoly complaints brought since 1970 with the number brought in the previous decade by pointing out that the 1960s were years of Robinson-Patman enforcement, and that less emphasis is placed now on this statute.[20] In fact, no cases at all were brought under the Robinson-Patman Act in the first three months of 1975. But whether the agency will be able to go on ignoring the act, given the support it continues to receive from large and small businesses and the rise in the rate of business failures in the mid-1970s, is questionable.[21]

Let us now look more closely at the reasons both for the antipathy to the Robinson-Patman Act and for the support it receives by examining the Commission's output in this area. We shall concentrate on the years 1956–1964, which are typical of the period in which the agency enforced the act vigorously. The major provisions of the statute will be examined separately.

Price Discrimination

Price discrimination is not a sophisticated or complex concept; it is defined legally as "merely a price difference."[22] Any price difference will do. The straitjacketing effect of the legal concept of price discrimination as simply a price difference is revealed when one considers all the types of pricing activities that are produced by this sweeping definition.[23] As far as the types of price difference available to sellers are concerned, the list of proscriptions includes:

- Quantity discounts (discounts that rise as the quantity purchased in a single sale increases)
- Volume discounts (discounts that vary with the amount purchased in a given period)
- Trade and functional discounts (based on the purchaser's position in the distribution hierarchy)
- Customer classification without functional classification
- Price differences based on area or locality
- Differentials dependent on delivery methods
- Arbitrary price differences

These discounting procedures can be varied or combined in a multitude of ways, and each can be unlawful under the Robinson-Patman Act (primarily because it is relatively easy, as we shall see, to satisfy the requirement that injury be shown). The effect of this sweeping definition is, of course, to freeze prices and make them unresponsive to competitive considerations. If all forms of price differentiation are blocked, experimentation in lowering prices is deterred, since a medium-sized or large firm is unlikely to experiment by reducing prices to all customers throughout the nation simultaneously. The process of reducing prices is usually begun by granting small-scale price concessions, for

trial and error pricing yields more adequate information than market surveys. Such pricing often is the first step in the progressive undermining of a previous price level and the establishment of a new one. Professor Malcolm P. McNair of Harvard has described the process as

CARL A. RUDISILL LIBRARY
LENOIR RHYNE COLLEGE

follows: "The process of changing a price typically begins when one customer feels himself strong enough to force a price concession, either an outright concession, or something in the nature of a fringe benefit. . . . The grapevine carries the story, and soon other dealers are dickering for concessions. If market conditions are sufficiently weak, they gain the concessions; and then finally when the manufacturer actually announces a new price, he is merely recognizing a condition which in fact already exists."[24]

In restricting this process, "the Robinson-Patman Act tends to be a price fixing statute hiding in the clothes of anti-monopoly and pro-competition symbols."[25]

In short, the price uniformity required by the Robinson-Patman Act tends to stop reduction of prices. A seller reduces prices selectively at his peril. Therefore, in industries with a tendency toward price uniformity, gradual adjustment of prices through selective or experimental reductions is discouraged. In these industries, prices are usually changed by a process of selective adjustment to specific conditions in specific markets; then at some point the industry observes that the general price level has changed.

Compliance with the law also inhibits bargaining, which is an essential element in the competitive process. If everyone pays the same price to the supplier, buyers tend to adopt a live-and-let-live approach and stop trying to wring concessions from suppliers. The effect is to keep prices above the level they would reach if each purchaser knew that his competitors might have bought at a lower price.

In most cases the law requires only minimal showing of the competitive effects of price discrimination, and this fact, too, puts a brake on competition. To prove violation, one must show not only that price discrimination has occurred, but that the discrimination may have an anticompetitive effect. As it has been applied at the level of the seller's customers (secondary line), the "effect" requirement has come to mean nothing more than that "the competitive opportunities of certain merchants were injured when they had to pay (the seller) substantially more for their goods than their competitors had to pay."[26] Thus in secondary-line cases the fact of price differences virtually implies the possibility of injury. In altering prices to comply with the law, the seller tends to raise the lower price (which is almost always the newer or less common price) rather than lower the higher price.

Cases involving harm to sellers' competitors (primary line) have required a more stringent showing of incipient injury than have secondary-line cases. The tendency of compliance with the law to produce price uniformity at higher levels than would obtain under more competitive conditions is, however, still clear. A Supreme Court decision that did not involve the F.T.C. shows the effect clearly. A pie manufacturer, dominant in Utah, sued three national competitors for selling pies more cheaply in Utah than elsewhere. The Court held that this beneficence to Utah's consumers was unlawful since the plaintiff's profits were reduced because it had to match its competitors' lower prices.[27]

The defense of meeting a competitor's price reinforces the tendency for prices to be uniform at a higher level than would obtain if freedom of pricing existed. To discriminate in price to meet a competitor's price is lawful, but prices cannot be reduced below that point. The conflict between the Sherman Act and the Robinson-Patman Act is evident here in two senses. First, prices will be higher than they would be if more vigorous competition (lowering prices beyond competitors' levels) were possible. Second, "an agreement between competitive purchasers as to what they will pay a single seller is illegal under the antitrust laws. The same uniformity in price, however, may be required under the Robinson-Patman Act."[28] Further, if a seller is to meet a competitor's price he must "have the most intimate knowledge of the terms offered by . . . competitors. This promotes price rigidity."[29]

In price discrimination and related areas, the F.T.C. has devoted a great deal of its attention to such highly competitive industries as the food, garment, and automobile parts industries. We turn next, therefore, to an examination of the Robinson-Patman Act's prohibition against price discrimination as it has been applied in the food industry.

Price Discrimination and the Food Industry

Structurally, most food-product industries show little sign of becoming monopolies or oligopolies in which there is danger of tacit price agreement or price leadership of the kind found in automobile or steel manufacturing. Of the more than 140 classes of food products listed in the 1958 five-digit manufacturing census classification, only just over 40 had four large manufacturers accounting for at least 50 percent of the total value of shipments.[30] Moreover, there are a great number of firms in the various food-manufacturing industries, an indication that entry into these industries is relatively easy; for example, in 1958 there were 2,646 meat packing firms, 1,095 natural cheese manufacturers, and 637 pickle and sauce manufacturers. In the food industries in which the absolute value of shipments is greatest, concentration is lowest. For example, there were 5,008 firms in the fluid milk processing industry in 1958; the four largest accounted for 23 percent of the total value of shipments, the eight largest for 29 percent, and the fifty largest for 45 percent.[31] Food industries with lower absolute values of shipments, of course, usually have fewer firms than the large industries (such as fluid milk, bread, and meat packing). But even in those with relatively high concentration (for example, cereal breakfast foods) it has been by no means unusual for an independent firm to have a greater share of the market than multiproduct firms several times its size, a phenomenon that again indicates vigorous competition.

The food industries are characterized by intense interproduct competition. Most shoppers' food budgets provide for food products beyond the basic necessities, and a wide variety is available to choose from. The fact that the products among which they choose may be assembled within the confines of a supermarket puts limits on manufacturers' freedom of pricing. In the few food industries not affected by interproduct competition (such as milk, bread, and meat), low concentration, low barriers to entry, and large numbers effectively preclude monopolization of the industry.

The food industry is also highly competitive at the retailer level, where low rates of profit on sales compel sharp bargaining between retailer and the manufacturer or middleman. If we calculate the weighted average of net profits after taxes as a percentage of sales, we find that for the ten largest chains it was 1.3 percent in each of the years from 1957 to 1964; for the thirty largest retail grocers, average net profit after taxes was 1.3 or 1.2 percent of sales every year from 1957 on. These figures indicate efficiency, intense competition, and high turnover. The share of the grocery store business accounted for by supermarkets has grown dramatically since the end of World War II; in 1963 their business amounted to 52.7 percent of all grocery store sales.[32] This development was not very surprising given the supermarkets' clear superiority over other grocery outlets in the quality and quantity of goods carried, in location, and in general attractiveness. Nationally the grocery industry is not highly concentrated. In 1963 the four largest chains made 20 percent of total grocery store sales, the twenty largest 34 percent (the latter figure showing little change from the 1958 ratio). The chains are strongest in the cities. In 218 standard metropolitan statistical areas the four largest firms in each area averaged 50.1 percent of sales in 1963, the eight largest 62 percent, and the twenty largest 74.3 percent. In many areas, at least one strong local chain exists—Jewel in Chicago, for example. Entry into the retail grocery business must be assumed to be easy since there were 244,838 stores in 1963.[33]

As might be expected, both horizontal competition and vertical bargaining are intense in the food industries, and the dissatisfaction felt by the firms that suffer in the process explains the F.T.C.'s activity in this area. In a case dismissed by the F.T.C., the Commission observed that "in the highly competitive food field differences of a few cents on a case of goods will make or lose a sale."[34] The low profit rate on sales and the price differences that exist attest to the intensity of horizontal competition.

Nineteen price-discrimination orders entered by the F.T.C. between 1956 and 1964 involved the sale of vendor-label food products under arrangements that the F.T.C. found had deleterious effects on some buyers; only four of these orders were entered against companies big enough to be found in the *Fortune* 500 directory. Even when a major company was involved, it does not follow that the transgression was a major one. For example, Foremost Dairies[35] was charged with favoring Barbers, an eight-store independent grocery chain in Albuquerque, New Mexico, over competing retailers; but the total amount of money involved was not great. The Albuquerque market had sustained several milk price wars—to the delight of local consumers—and the order in the case was the F.T.C.'s way of attempting to stabilize the market for the benefit of processor-distributors and to deter price cutting in the future. The Commission conceded that Barbers was in no position to monopolize the sale of milk in the area; it was simply a hard-bargaining small grocery chain.

In general, whether we examine the 1956–1964 period or any other in which the F.T.C. actively enforced the Robinson-Patman Act, we find that a large proportion of the secondary-line cases in the food industry involved either relatively small firms or large firms in minor activities. There is no way of accurately measuring the impact

of this activity on pricing in the food industry, but insofar as enforcement of the act operated as a deterrent, the result was restriction of
competition and promotion of stability in market structure.

F.T.C. action was directed not only at specific industries but also at
certain kinds of practice and behavior, in whatever industry they
might be found. Nowhere is this clearer than with respect to price
wars, of which the Foremost case is but one example.

Price Wars

Consistent with the role it has played in stabilizing competitive
structure and conduct, the F.T.C. has also been involved in stopping
price wars, especially in the petroleum industry. In petroleum marketing, price cutting is not ordinarily initiated by the big firms; once a
price war has begun, however, the large companies are necessarily
involved by virtue of their size. Price wars, a frequent occurrence in
petroleum marketing, "result largely from refusal of smaller firms in
the industry . . . to follow the pricing philosophy of the giants.[36]
But the giants must then respond, and so become involved in the
price cutting.

The cases that arose from local price wars during which Sun Oil
and American Oil lowered gasoline prices to dealers involved in the
wars exemplify the role the F.T.C. has played. The Sun Oil case was
ultimately affirmed by the Supreme Court; the American Oil order
was set aside by the Court of Appeals.[37] The patterns were identical
in both cases. A service station carrying the respondent's brand of
gasoline was forced to reduce its prices because of a price war started
by another station. Accordingly the dealer sought reduced prices
from his supplier in order to compete effectively with other brands.
The supplier granted a temporary allowance to the dealer involved
in the price war, but this action precipitated demands for reduced
prices from other local dealers carrying the same brand but not involved in the war. The supplier's refusal to yield to these demands
prompted the dealers to complain to the F.T.C.

Most gasoline price wars are caused by one of three types of situation: (1) surplus gasoline moves into the market or a seller has an
excess supply; (2) the distributor level is characterized by low laid-
down costs; or (3) cut-price retailers selling unbranded gasoline and
self-service retail operators enter the market, or established independent operators seek to increase their sales at the expense of stations

carrying major brands. Typically the stations carrying major brands have responded to price wars by seeking to restrict competition. Suppliers, faced with the prospect of having to reduce prices to aid their stations involved in a price war, are equally anxious to end the war.[38] The methods employed by the industry to stabilize retail prices have ranged from unlawful price fixing to the use of local-government regulations (passed at the behest of the affected dealers and suppliers) forbidding oversize signs announcing retail price or prohibiting sales below cost.[39]

In the Sun case, the Commission held that the respondent could not use the defense of "good faith meeting of competition" to justify the allowance it gave to the dealer involved in the price war, enabling him to meet other dealers' prices. Under this ruling suppliers are effectively excused from participating in the vigorous competition of a price war; for they will hardly lower prices to all dealers in the area in order to aid the few involved in a price war, and they cannot otherwise assist dealers to meet competitors' prices. The dealers' lack of resources makes only two results possible: either dealers are deterred from engaging in price wars, or, if they are foolish enough to promote a price war, it ends quickly. If a dealer does not survive a price war, the supplier can always replace him in this easily entered retail trade. The F.T.C., then, helps suppliers to avoid the intense competition of a price war. And the Robinson-Patman Act deters price flexibility in two ways: first, as we have seen, the concept attached to price discrimination promotes uniform pricing; in addition, the "meeting of competition" defense reinforces the tendency to uniformity. This aspect we shall now examine in more detail.

Meeting Competition

Under Section 2(b) of the Robinson-Patman Act, a seller may rebut a prima facie case of price discrimination by showing that the lower price was "made in good faith to meet an equally low price of a competitor." In one important case the Commission held that this defense is available only if the seller is seeking to retain old customers; prices cannot be legally lowered to obtain new customers by meeting the prices of their current suppliers. Thus the aggressive competitor who seeks to divert trade from his more complacent competitors is put on notice that the F.T.C. views his conduct as unlawful.[40]

The Tri-Valley case[41] dramatically illustrates the anticompetitive effect of the F.T.C.'s position on this defense. The Tri-Valley Packing Association, small canners of fruits and vegetables, charged grocery chains that maintained buying offices in San Francisco less than customers that did not. The Commission described the market as vigorously competitive; indeed, San Francisco's California Street market, in which buyers and sellers bargained fiercely, virtually fulfilled the Smithian vision. The respondent, whose sales were only $22 million, was dwarfed by many other members of the industry and was hardly threatening to monopolize food canning. Tri-Valley defended its price discrimination by showing that its prices to the favored buyers only met other sellers' prices. But the Commission disallowed the defense, holding that to prove good faith the respondent would also have to show either (a) that the prices Tri-Valley was meeting could be cost justified or otherwise excused, or (b) that the respondent had reason to believe that this was the case. Under this ruling, the defensive requirements for meeting the statutory burden are increased, with the effect of further rigidifying the price structure; and in order to charge a discriminatory price to a customer served by a competitor, a firm must know a good deal about the competitor's costs and general pricing system. In short, to comply with the Robinson-Patman Act a firm meeting a competitor's price must know almost as much about the competitor's business as he does about his own. And this sort of information is usually obtained through the kind of cozy relationship with competitors that the Sherman Act frowns upon. Thus, to comply with the Robinson-Patman Act one is invited to violate the Sherman Act.

Robinson-Patman and Marketing Innovation

The statutory prohibition against price discrimination not only points to price rigidity but also deters marketing innovation. Indeed, as we have noted, attempts to prevent changes in marketing methods provided a major impetus for the statute's enactment. Two cases will illustrate this point. In the first, the General Foods Corporation, one of the largest food processors, favored one group of distributors— the so-called wagon distributors (ICWDs)—over wholesalers in the resale of General Foods products to restaurants, hotels, hospitals, and other quantity buyers.[42] The discrimination began in 1946, when General Foods, dissatisfied with the level of its sales to institutional purchasers, entered into contracts with ICWDs who sold directly from their trucks to the institutions. The ICWDs received favored discounts because they sold aggressively, maintained adequate stocks, arranged displays, and demonstrated products. The Commission's order prohibiting such favoring of ICWDs penalized General Foods for innovation. The effect of the order is to deter the development of new, efficient modes of distribution and to stabilize existing market structures. And many other F.T.C. orders have similarly penalized firms for their marketing innovations.

The second case concerned another important marketing innovation, the use of "private labels" bearing a name chosen either by the retailer or by his distributor (the former is found more commonly in larger chains—for example, A & P's Ann Page label; distributor labels are seen more often in independently owned supermarkets and small chains). Although private-label brands still make up only a small percentage of all grocery items carried in supermarkets, they are generally associated with product lines with a high sales volume. Products sold under private labels are usually priced below merchandise of comparable quality sold under the manufacturers' labels. Aside from the obvious benefit to consumers of the lower prices of private-label items, this system of merchandising brings major gains to food retailers. Many of them could, if they wished, integrate backward to produce the private-label product currently being purchased from a manufacturer. This potential threat acts to restrain the manufacturer in his pricing both of goods bearing his own label and of private-label products; and the threat is considerably greater if the retailer already has an established private-label product than if he had to create consumer acceptance for a new one.[43]

The major proceeding focused on this problem was the bitterly fought Borden evaporated milk case, ultimately won by the F.T.C. before the Supreme Court.[44] The principal legal issue was whether the evaporated milk sold under a private label was of "like grade and quality" to the physically identical product packed under the manufacturer's label. The Borden Company had been selling evaporated milk under its own label since 1892. In 1938 it began packing and selling private-label evaporated milk of the same grade and quality. Private-label prices were consistently lower than Borden-label prices. Borden argued that the discrepancy was justified because its brand name, which had been promoted for many years, added to the value of the product. The Commission rejected the argument, however, and found that smaller competitors, selling primarily private-label products, had suffered injury because they had lost customers to Borden. Injury was also found on the secondary level, since some retailers and wholesalers were too small to have their own private labels. Borden, most of whose sales were of milk bearing the Borden label, was ordered not to sell at discriminatory prices. Compliance with this decision would be likely to entail raising the price of the smaller volume private-label line. It should be noted that after twenty years of selling private-label evaporated milk, Borden's share of the evaporated milk market was only 10.7 percent—hardly a monopoly position. The import of the F.T.C.'s decision was that private-label marketing was to be actively discouraged; but it has not had this effect, as a trip to the supermarket quickly demonstrates.

Most F.T.C. decisions in price discrimination cases point in the direction of stability, but the picture is not entirely unambiguous. For in some of the cases involving territorial price discrimination, monopolizing conduct has been present. Indeed, the alleged territorial price discrimination of Standard Oil and other trusts provided one argument for enactment of the original Section 2 of the Clayton Act.

Territorial Price Discrimination

Prices usually vary from area to area with the intensity of competition, the number of competitors, and general market conditions. But in some instances territorial price discrimination has been used to monopolize. The key indicia employed by the courts and the F.T.C. to distinguish monopolizing conduct from competitive conduct are: "(a) monopoly or overpowering position of the seller in wider markets; (b) aggressive objectives toward smaller and weaker rivals; (c) deep sustained undercutting of rivals' prices . . . (d) persistent sales below the seller's cost; and (e) actual or impending demise of a seller's sole rival in a particular market."[45] The Commission has persistently failed to distinguish between the two types of cases and has treated both as violations of the Robinson-Patman Act—though the courts (particularly the Seventh Circuit Court of Appeals) have restricted the Commission. The few cases involving predatory practices might have been more fruitfully prosecuted by the Department of Justice as criminal attempts to monopolize under Section 2 of the Sherman Act; indeed, the Justice Department has at times brought such cases.

The reasons for the rare occurrence of territorial price discrimination that is truly monopolistic have been carefully analyzed by John S. McGee:

Most would probably agree that predatory price cutting is unappealing, if not ludicrous, when the minimum efficient size of a firm is small relative to the market and the skills necessary to enter are not rare. This, I should think, rules out most if not all trade and agriculture. Predatory price cutting would require large relative size—i.e. monopoly power—which raises the possibility against the monopoly directly. It also rules out firms with minority market shares, I should think. Indeed, even a firm with high regional but low national share is not a very good candidate, since other national firms are a menace to advancing prices . . . afterwards. A firm which has a very high national market share but which faces numbers of rivals in most or all regions is not a prime candidate for predator either. Not only is this situation symptomatic of potential entry everywhere, but it would be more than slightly expensive to kill off present rivals. . . . Holding prices below average variable costs would be frightfully expensive. . . . For those who want to exorcise against "predatory" price cutters, where are they least unlikely to be found? Look for a prosperous and liquid firm with high national share of the sales of a distinct product, with no rivals most places and with very few elsewhere. Rivals should be operating in absolutely small markets. There should be powerful impediments to entry. . . . Rivals should be poor, illiquid, and—for some reason—incapable of borrowing.[46]

While some of the F.T.C. cases have involved nothing more than diversion of trade from one competition by another,[47] several have shown evidence of monopolizing elements. These latter cases have generally involved small industries in which one seller dwarfs the rest. For example, in the Maryland Baking case the respondent was a dominant national manufacturer of rolled sugar cones. Its only competitor was a local firm in the Washington-Baltimore area. The respondent lowered the price of its product in the Washington-Baltimore area with proven intent to destroy its rival, whose share of the Washington-Baltimore market fell from 91 percent to 58 percent. But it should be noted that even in this apparently classic case of predatory price cutting, the respondent did not destroy its small local competitor, which was able to bypass jobbers and sell directly to retailers. This new method of distribution actually increased the victim's total business, since it stimulated the local firm to sell chocolate-coated cones to ice cream manufacturers.[48]

In another case of predatory territorial price discrimination, the respondent, the Forster Manufacturing Company, was the leading manufacturer of wooden skewers, wooden ice cream spoons, and clothespins; its total sales in 1957 amounted to only about $6 million, but it dwarfed its rivals.[49] The developed facts clearly showed that Forster had specifically intended to destroy its rivals and in some instances had priced its products below variable cost to do so.

Cases like Maryland Baking and Forster are, however, few and far between. The overwhelming proportion of the F.T.C.'s effort in matters of price discrimination has been in the direction of promoting stability and limiting competition. Rarely has it stepped in to aid the competitive process. Yet these instances of action on price discrimination to aid the process of competition, few as they are, make a better record than the agency has achieved in enforcing other sections of the Robinson-Patman Act.

Inducing Price Discrimination

Although the principal demons identified by the Robinson-Patman Act's proponents were big buyers, particularly chain stores, the section of the act designed to curb the knowing receipt of discriminatory prices has been employed most frequently against small firms or buying groups of small firms. During the period 1956–1964 the eleven orders entered under Section 2(f) were against groups acting together to buy automotive parts and their jobber members.[50] And this industry, like most that have received the F.T.C.'s attention, is, as we shall see, highly competitive.

The automotive parts industry is essentially an adjunct of the automobile repair industry. Since most repairs must be made quickly, it is essential that parts be available. The problem of availability is complicated by the great number of parts required for each automobile in each model year. Some parts for different models are interchangeable, as are some parts for automobiles of the same make in different model years, but the number is very limited. Further, the number of car dealers, repair shops, gas stations, and automotive wholesalers that must be supplied with parts is enormous; in 1968 there were more than 400,000 service centers for automobiles. Complex distribution channels have been developed to cope with the problem; one channel leads to the automobile dealer and a second to independent repair outlets; but there is considerable interchange between the two. In addition, a parts manufacturer may sell to warehouse distributors (WDs) or to jobbers, or he may sell through a manufacturer's agent or even through other parts manufacturers.[51]

Many of the distributor intermediaries have mixed trade status. Many WDs, for example, sell to both jobbers and repair facilities; the percentages sold to the two classes of customer vary widely. Some WD warehouses contain only a small portion of the inventory carried by other WDs. Secondary jobbers may sell to both repair establishments and ultimate consumers. To complicate the distributive structure further, some manufacturers purchase parts from other manufacturers to round out a line and warehouse them. Thus there is intrachannel as well as interchannel competition.[52]

Manufacturers of automotive parts compete vigorously for good outlets, for two reasons: the number of large, good outlets is limited; and wholesalers prefer to buy from as few sources as possible. Accordingly, there is keen price competition in the industry at all levels from manufacturer to repair shop. The ultimate consumer conceives of repair work primarily as a service and is not particularly conscious of the price of parts. So repair shops do not shave prices of parts; they charge the manufacturer's suggested list price. The repair shops' concern, therefore, is with the margin between the cost of parts to them and the manufacturer's suggested list price. Their attempts to increase this margin, by purchasing parts at lower prices from their suppliers, trigger similar attempts to increase margins right up the line to the manufacturer.[53]

Jobbers can increase their margins by purchasing parts at the lower prices usually offered to another functional category in the distributive chain. This fact, coupled with the mixed (and often unclear) trade status of most of those in the distributive chain, creates a price structure with many different prices at each level. Each buyer's suspicion that his competitor may be paying less than he is leads him to push suppliers harder for lower prices. This pressure is resisted in varying degrees by manufacturers because the value to them of jobbers and WDs varies with advertising expenditures, missionary work, the number of products carried, and market coverage. These differences in the extent to which manufacturers resist demands for lower prices cause still more price variation.[54]

The distributive structure of this industry differs from that of any other in several respects: (1) In relation to total wholesale sales volume, automotive wholesalers are more numerous than wholesalers in any other business. (2) The average automotive wholesaler is small compared to wholesalers in general. (3) The greater part of automotive wholesaler sales is made by small firms. (4) There are very few large automotive wholesalers, but the largest are very large because they have numerous branches. (5) Redistribution from one wholesaler to another before the part reaches the repair establishment is common. (6) The automotive wholesaler's average sale is small in relation to sales by other kinds of wholesalers. (7) Automotive parts wholesaling is a relatively high-cost business.[55]

The F.T.C. brought several cases against manufacturers under section 2(a) of the Robinson-Patman Act, seeking to have them neatly classify customers into functional categories and rigidly abide by prices established for each category. In the Airtex case the respondent was charged with favoring wholesalers who belonged to buying groups over those who did not. In the American Ball Bearings case the respondent classified customers into three groups: jobbers, distributors, and WDs. The Commission found that some customers were not performing the functions of the categories to which they were assigned (particularly jobber groups without warehouses). Accordingly, the respondent was ordered not to discriminate in price to competing customers. In another variation on the theme, a manufacturer was ordered not to favor the distribution chain going from auto manufacturer to franchise dealers over the channel to independent repair outlets.[56]

The orders against buyers under Section 2(f) were directed at associations of jobbers who had banded together to enhance their bargaining power. In these cases the Commission, interestingly (and correctly), characterized the automotive parts business as highly competitive. Net profits of parts jobbers varied between 1 and 4 percent.[57] Typically these cases involved jobbers who received WD discounts from manufacturers although they did not operate a warehouse (or, alternatively, they operated a warehouse but for only some purchases). In other words, the buying group was a front for the jobbers, who received their merchandise directly from the manufacturers, bypassing the warehouse, and were also billed directly. The orders entered by the F.T.C. forbid jobbers to receive preferential prices, either directly or through their buying organizations.

Aside from these cases relating to the automotive parts industry, the effect of which was to freeze and stabilize existing functional classifications, F.T.C. orders under Section 2(f) have been few and far between. In no case has monopoly power been present. In contrast, the number of orders entered under those sections of the Robinson-Patman Act that deal with brokerage and advertising allowances, has been enormous.

Brokerage

As we observed in Chapter 1, some forms of nonprice competition can easily be translated into quantitative terms. For example, an advertising allowance granted by a supplier to his purchaser will be specified in terms of a certain reimbursement by the supplier for each dollar expended by the buyer in advertising the seller's products. The remaining civil sections of the Robinson-Patman Act are aimed at these forms of competitive activity that are readily translated into monetary terms.

Forms of nonprice competition that cannot be readily translated into quantitative terms (such as competition in inventiveness) are, in general, relatively unsusceptible to the kind of cumulative retaliation to which price cutting is subject. "Price is the foremost variable to be regulated by quasi-agreements because there is no special skill . . . involved in undercutting. There are no limits to effective retaliation, even in the very short run."[58] For this reason, a firm's highest regulatory priority is restraint of price competition and those forms of nonprice competition that can readily be translated into quantitative terms.

Among the most common forms of nonprice competition that can be converted into price terms in the food industries are payments to brokers or payments in lieu of brokerage. The function of a broker is to bring together a buyer and a seller who might otherwise experience difficulty in locating each other. Thus markets that are highly fragmented on both the seller's and the buyer's side are most likely to need brokers, and only in such market situations can the F.T.C. find unlawful brokerage or unlawful discounts in lieu of brokerage. Slightly less than half the cases involving brokerage brought between 1956 and 1964 were in the citrus fruit industry, either against packers who granted brokerage payments to purchasers who were buying for themselves rather than as brokers, or against brokers who accepted brokerage on their personal purchases, or against either sellers or

buyers who engaged in sales through a brokerage business owned
or controlled by the buyers in question.[59] In these cases the F.T.C.
was seeking to prevent the hard bargaining that prevailed in the
citrus fruit business, where price concessions were made and received in the form of brokerage allowances. Usually both buyers and
sellers were small and numerous—the very opposite of a monopolistic
situation. The F.T.C. was again restraining competition and bargaining, and was effectively inducing the industry to give up price
competition.

Section 2(c) prohibits sellers from granting a brokerage fee or
"any allowance or discount in lieu thereof" and forbids brokers and
buyers to receive brokerage fees when the broker is under the control
of either the buyer or the seller. The provision is absolute; no showing of injury or incipient injury is required for a violation to be
proven. This absolute prohibition has been of great significance for
the F.T.C. in two respects. First, the absence of any requirement that
competitive impact be shown has enabled the Commission to enter
orders against very small companies; and second, proof of statutory
violation is very easy. As a result, the F.T.C. has used Section 2(c)
as one of its bread-and-butter statutes to create impressive statistics
on the number of orders it has entered—a tactic designed to coax
additional appropriations from Congress. More than 160 orders were
entered against respondents under this section during the period 1956–
1964 alone. With fewer than five exceptions, the orders were all entered against individuals or firms in the food industry, the vast
majority of them against very small firms. The respondents in these
cases were often too small to be incorporated and so bore such names
as "J. Parker Lampert doing business as Mission Fruit and Vegetable
Co." and "John H. Ginsbach doing business as Alamo Fruit Distributors Ltd."[60]

Section 2(c) also prohibits brokers from passing on brokerage
payments to buyers as part of the bargaining process. This rule in
fact obligates the F.T.C. to enforce the guild rules of food brokers.
Thus a sugar broker who granted a portion of his sales commission to
two small buying associations for retail grocers was prohibited from
doing so again.[61]

The brokerage provision of the Robinson-Patman Act originated
from the N.R.A. and its codes of fair competition. These codes prohibited secret rebates, and in some instances all rebates; many in fact

went so far as to ban payment of brokerage commissions to buyers.[62] The brokerage provision of the Robinson-Patman Act was patterned on these codes; according to Congressman Patman, "there was greater unanimity of the industries of America upon a trade practice rule prohibiting absolutely secret rebates, etc., than upon any other rule put into effect under the National Recovery Act."[63]

The act's proponents saw the payment of brokerage as an indirect form of price concession; brokerage constitutes payment for a service that can be translated into price terms. The brokerage provision in effect outlaws a particular form of competition; it forbids something that can be interpreted as a price concession made through what purports to be a brokerage payment.

Advertising Allowances and Furnishing of Services

Another common form of nonprice competition that can be translated into quantitative terms is the furnishing of valuable services to customers or the payment of money to customers for the performance of these services. Sections 2(d) and 2(e) respectively prohibit sellers from making payments for services to buyers and from furnishing services or facilities to buyers unless such payments or services are made available to all competing buyers on proportionally equal terms. The services for which suppliers typically pay include cooperative advertising, distribution of samples, mention of a supplier's name in a radio or television program, special in-store demonstrations of the seller's product, instructions to store clerks to push the seller's product, and "services within a retail store, such as furnishing a window display, giving away premiums, placing the product in a preferred location in the store or furnishing special selling equipment, show cards or the like." Services rendered by the seller for the buyer and cognizable under Section 2(e) include provision of a demonstrator or payment of the salary of the buyer's sales personnel, provision of special containers or labels, furnishing of advertising and demonstration aids, provision of free goods, and extension of "special terms, such as allowing mail or telephone orders at a discount, allowing a cash discount, allowing the purchaser a rebate for the non return of unsaleable merchandise, or permitting the purchaser to buy F.O.B. at a lower price than that charged other customers."[64]

Sections 2(d) and 2(e) act as restraints on the various listed forms of competitive activity in virtually the same way that Section 2(a) acts as a brake on price competition. There are two principal respects in which Sections 2(d) and 2(e) differ from Section 2(a). Sections 2(d) and 2(e) can be violated without any showing of incipient competitive harm. At the same time they can be violated only by discriminatory treatment of competing customers. In contrast, Section 2(a) can be violated by any price differences (such as territorial price differences that involve noncompeting customers) but theoretically requires some showing of anticompetitive effect.

The per se character of Sections 2(d) and 2(e) has allowed the F.T.C. to play the numbers game with these sections too and to enter many orders under them. Most of the respondents have been small members of highly competitive industries. Once again it could not seriously be maintained that monopoly would result from the practices enjoined by the Commission under these provisions or that competitive processes were being impaired. Rather, these sections restrain competition in services and allowances. The practices covered by these sections can be used to retaliate against price cutting and are intimately connected with price competition, which in turn can be used to counter these methods of competition. The restrictions thus affect price competition. Small manufacturers, who must be selective in granting allowances and services, are the principal victims of Sections 2(d) and 2(e). Large manufacturers can afford a cooperative advertising program covering allowances to many or all retailers; small manufacturers with many customers cannot afford to offer advertising allowances to all of their competing customers. Further, a small manufacturer often wants to avoid the possibility of substantial losses by experimenting with a particular form of nonprice competition before adopting it wholesale, to determine whether it will be successful. Under the law such selective experimentation is effectively prohibited; so, since the losses that could result from general employment of the contemplated nonprice form of competition could be large if it were unsuccessful, the small manufacturer is effectively prevented from introducing it. Not surprisingly, therefore, many respondents under these sections have been small manufacturers who have sought to evade the law. Orders against larger companies have often involved single payments to retailers for "anniversary" sales or other such nonrecurring events.

More than 350 orders were entered under Section 2(d) during the period 1956–1964, far more than under any other antimonopoly provision administered by the F.T.C. Of this number, about 200 were entered against manufacturers of wearing apparel, an industry group that had approximately 34,500 members at the time.[65]

The facts of Section 2(d) cases are extremely simple. The respondents, in most instances small firms, are charged with granting cooperative advertising allowances to certain favored customers without making such payments available on equal terms to the favored customers' competitors. The reason some customers receive such payments while others do not is that the former bargain successfully for such allowances and the latter do not. Such bargaining is the very essence of competition; its repression may be justified under Sherman Act standards only if there is a threat of monopoly. No such threat has ever been even remotely in prospect in F.T.C. cases.[66]

Sections 2(d) and 2(e), like the brokerage provision of Section 2(c), had their origins in the N.R.A. codes and were designed to limit competition in the interests of stability. Although the language ultimately adopted in the statutory provisions differs from that of the original Patman proposals, the idea of restricting competition in advertising allowances and services can be traced to the counsel for the U.S. Wholesale Grocers Association. During the debate on the provisions, opponents of the two sections pointed out, prophetically, that the application of these sections would penalize small manufacturers who could not afford to grant proportional advertising allowances or services to all of their customers.[67]

Conclusion

The Robinson-Patman Act, passed largely at the behest of small-business groups during the Great Depression, has been charged by one of its more vehement critics with outlawing "all bargaining as the process is understood in the business world."[68] This reproach may be a bit strong, but there is little question that the act is clearly arrayed on the side of stability and against the competitive process. More than any other statute examined so far, it confuses injury to specific competitors with injury to the competitive process. As we have seen, there have been some instances in which the act has been used to aid the competitive process; but the overwhelming proportion of cases brought by the agency under the Robinson-Patman Act have reflected the principal thrust of the statute in damping down the competitive process.

For many years Robinson-Patman cases were the bread and butter of the Commission's antimonopoly work. But in recent years, as a result of considerable adverse criticism, the F.T.C. has virtually ceased to enforce the act. The past and the present of Robinson-Patman enforcement raise two questions.

As far as the present era of nonenforcement is concerned, the question is one of administrative responsibility: What right does an appointed group of administrators have to disregard an obligation imposed on it by Congress? A high official of the F.T.C. told me that "the Robinson-Patman Act is a thing of the past." Perhaps so, but abrogation of an act is a legislative responsibility and should not be a matter of administrative whim. The serious misgivings that have been felt because of the failure of police officials to enforce certain laws should give pause to those who would excuse such administrative arrogance.[69] Nor should it surprise anyone if vigorous enforcement of the Robinson-Patman Act becomes a thing of the future as it has been a thing of the past.

For the past, the question is: What has been the impact of the considerable effort the F.T.C. has devoted to enforcing this law? There is little support for the view that it has made a significant difference to the American political economy. True, wholesale food prices have risen faster than many other wholesale prices, but there is simply no evidence that the discrepancy has been caused by F.T.C. activity in this area. As with other areas in which F.T.C. orders have proscribed certain forms of conduct, the agency's substantial output has had little impact. Indeed, a senior official of the agency's Bureau of Competition conceded privately in 1975 that the F.T.C. had come to look upon orders proscribing particular practices as being of little value; for this reason, he said, the agency would in future concentrate on cases and orders that would affect the structure of an industry.

CHAPTER 6

The F.T.C. and
Economic Structure

Most of the F.T.C. activities discussed so far have pertained to problems of improper or culpable conduct. But antitrust philosophy since the Sherman Act has also operated on the assumption that the very structures of some industries are inherently wrong and must be altered. The classic cases are the 1911 decrees ordering the breakup of the American Tobacco and Standard Oil trusts. These cases illustrate the underlying relationship between conduct and structure; certain forms of conduct must be prohibited because they lead to monopoly or simulate monopoly. And monopoly, the argument goes, is the opposite of competition, which the Sherman Act was purportedly designed to protect.

Since the Sherman Act, the ability to restructure an industry has been seen as a powerful antitrust tool. Yet this tool was not explicitly granted to the Commission under Section 5 of the F.T.C. Act, which makes available only the restricted power to order a firm to cease and desist from certain practices. Only under Section 11 of the original Clayton Act was the F.T.C. explicitly empowered to effect structural relief. Under this section, it could order divestiture of stock in the case of a stock acquisition "where the effect of such acquisition may be to substantially lessen competition" between the acquiring and acquired corporations or "tend to create a monopoly of any line of commerce."

Early in its career the Commission sought to enlarge its powers of relief under Section 5 of the F.T.C. Act, beginning, predictably enough, in the realm of mergers. In one of its earliest merger cases, that against Swift and Company, the agency attacked stock acquisitions under both Section 5 of the F.T.C. Act and Section 7 of the

Clayton Act, ordering Swift "to cease and desist from further engagements in unfair methods of competition [and] from further holding, owning, controlling, directly or indirectly, the stock or assets of the two [acquired] companies."[1] In the appeal, however, the brief for neither the Commission nor the respondent mentioned the charge under Section 5 of the F.T.C. Act; it was therefore ignored in the court's decision and in the later Supreme Court decision.

The issue of whether the Commission was empowered to order structural relief under Section 5 of the F.T.C. Act was first raised specifically in the Eastman Kodak case,[2] in which the respondent acquired three laboratories that were equipped to manufacture positive movie prints from negatives in order to obtain a commitment from other movie-print manufacturers to buy only American—that is, Eastman—film. If the movie-print companies would not buy American, said Eastman, they would find Eastman competing with them by producing movie prints in the acquired laboratories. The Commission found a violation of Section 5, and in order to prevent the continuation of monopoly and restore competition, it issued an order requiring Eastman Kodak to divest itself of the three laboratories.

The case reached the Supreme Court in 1927, and the reversal handed down by the Court appeared to deny the F.T.C.'s power to effect structural relief under Section 5 of the F.T.C. Act. The Court stated that "the Commission is empowered to prevent the using of 'unfair methods of competition' . . . and . . . to issue an order requiring the offender 'to cease and desist from using such method of competition.' The Commission exercises only the administrative functions delegated to it by the Act, not judicial powers. . . . It has not been delegated the authority of a court of equity."[3] The decision was not without its ambiguities, since it confused the agency's remedial powers under Section 5 with the question of whether the agency had jurisdiction over asset acquisitions. Nevertheless, the Commission construed the decision as imposing an absolute barrier to its "authority under any circumstances to direct a divesture of physical properties."[4] Given the temper of the Supreme Court in the 1920s, no other conclusion would have been reasonable.

In the post–World War II period, however, a Supreme Court that was considerably less hostile to the powers of administrative agencies began to allow the F.T.C. more leeway in fashioning relief. In a case involving misrepresentation of the fiber content of overcoats, the Commission entered an order that, among other provisions, banned the use of the word "Alpacuna" to describe the coats made by the respondent. In upholding the Commission's power to control the use of a valuable trade name, the Supreme Court stated that "the Commission is the expert body to determine what remedy is necessary to eliminate the unfair or deceptive trade practices which have been disclosed. . . . The courts will not interfere except where the remedy selected has no reasonable relation to the unlawful practices found to exist."[5] The Court confirmed the new latitude afforded the F.T.C. in 1952, when it stated that "Congress expected the Commission to exercise a special competence in formulating remedies to deal with problems in the general sphere of competitive practices."[6]

Two further steps were necessary before the Commission could begin an all-out assault on economic structure under Section 5 of the F.T.C. Act: approval by the Supreme Court of a definition of "unfair methods of competition" broad enough to include the existence of certain economic structures, and an explicit recognition that divestiture of property was an appropriate form of relief under Section 5. The first was achieved in 1966 when the Supreme Court declared, in a case involving alleged unfair practices in a shoe franchising program, that the F.T.C. may properly attack not only practices that violate the spirit or the letter of the antitrust laws but also practices that "conflict with the basic policies of the Sherman and Clayton Acts even though such practices may not actually violate these laws."[7] Thus, if monopolizing constitutes violation of the Sherman Act, joint monopolizing by a few firms could plausibly constitute violation of the Federal Trade Commission Act. Power to order divestiture under Section 5 was conceded by an appeals court in 1971. In a case involving alleged monopolization of emblematic jewelry for national college fraternities, the appeals court upheld an order requiring the respondent to divest itself of part of its business. The court stated that the order of divestiture was reasonably related to the unfair practices and was adequately designed to restore competition.[8] The way was thus open for the F.T.C. to attack oligopoly, even in the absence of merger or consolidation, and, as we shall see later in this chapter, its first case, against the breakfast-cereal industry, was brought only a year later. In the meantime it kept busy employing its other major tool against corporate concentration—the revived Section 7 of the Clayton Act.

The 1950 Antimerger Law

The antimerger provision of the original Clayton Act forbade only stock acquisitions and did not reach a merger or consolidation effected by the acquisition of assets. The reason for this omission was that the act's sponsors had had their sights aimed narrowly on holding companies, a form of consolidation effected by stock acquisition. Moreover, the Sherman Act already forbade acquisition by any method if the effect would be to restrain trade or create a monopoly,[9] a fact that the 1914 opponents of Section 7 used to support their claim that the Clayton Act was directed at small and medium-sized firms whose merger activity could not be prohibited under the Sherman Act. In any event, the Commission's enforcement of the original Section 7 was hampered, until 1950, by restrictive court decisions.[10] Of the fifty cases brought by the F.T.C. under Section 7 before 1950, all but one were dismissed, either by the Commission itself or by the courts.

In that year, however, Congress amended Section 7 of the Clayton Act in three major respects. First, the 1950 amendment covered asset acquisitions as well as stock acquisitions. Second, the reach of the provision was extended. The old act proscribed only those stock acquisitions that might result in a substantial lessening of competition between the acquired and the acquiring corporation; as amended, however, it reached vertical and at least certain categories of conglomerate mergers as well. Third, the definition of areas covered by the provision was sharpened. The original version contained some imprecise and inconsistent descriptions of the geographical and product markets in which the possible effects of acquisition were to be measured; the amendment altered the language to make it clear that the possible effects were to be measured as they affected any line of commerce in any section of the country.[11]

The amendment did not, however, alter the thrust of the original Section 7; the incipiency standard of the F.T.C. Act and the Clayton Act as a measure of possible anticompetitive effects remained. Indeed, it could reasonably be argued that the sharpening of the language of Section 7 made proof of possible anticompetitive effect even easier than before. In any event, the amendment's standards follow the approach of the Clayton Act in reaching conduct in its incipiency.[12]

The proponents of the 1950 amendment argued that mergers increased concentration, and therefore an amendment was needed to stop them. They had an important weapon in hand—a 1948 F.T.C. report on mergers that proclaimed that "if nothing is done to check the growth in concentration, either the giant corporations will ultimately take over the country, or the government will be impelled to step in and impose some form of direct regulations in the public interest."[13] At even the most basic level, this argument runs into serious problems: somewhat naively, it ignores the power already wielded by large corporations; it also confuses the absolute size of firms with concentration; most important, it ignores the fact that industry concentration ratios had not increased since 1903.

If there were a real possibility that monopoly might be achieved through merger, a vast increase in concentration through asset acquisitions might have been expected before the 1950 act was passed. In fact, nothing of the sort happened. Economist George Stigler compared the concentration of twenty industries at the turn of the twentieth century with the pattern in the 1930s and found that concentration actually declined in fourteen industries, increased in two, and remained about the same in four.[14] A later investigation concluded that industry concentration levels were approximately the same in 1952 as they had been in 1902.[15] Indeed, between 1939 and 1958 the share of domestic output originating in highly concentrated industries declined and the share originating in highly unconcentrated industries increased.[16]

The statistical evidence that concentration had not increased since the end of the first merger wave in 1902 not only is overwhelming but was known to the advocates of the amendment to the Clayton Act. A 1950 article by two respected academicians, published in a prestigious scholarly journal and reprinted in the Senate hearings, concluded that recent mergers had had very little effect on corporate concentration.[17] The study provided ammunition for Senator Forrest Donnell, one of the principal Senate opponents of the amendment.

There was therefore little reason in 1950 to believe that mergers provided important impetus to high concentration. And if in any industry monopolization should be attempted or achieved through merger or consolidation, the Justice Department could sue the violator under Section 2 of the Sherman Act. What, then, were the arguments for the amendment? The most important reason for congressional action stemmed from a general antipathy to bigness. Congressman Estes Kefauver, a principal advocate of the 1950 amendment, stated in 1947:

It is no accident that we now have a big Government, big labor unions, and big business. The concentration of great economic power in a few corporations necessarily leads to the formation of large Nation-wide unions. The development of the two necessarily leads to big bureaus in the government to deal with them. . . . The control of American business is steadily being transferred from local communities to a few large cities in which central managers decide the policies and the fate of the far flung enterprises they control. . . . Through monopolistic mergers the people are losing the power to direct their economic welfare. When they lose the power to direct their economic welfare they also lose the means to direct their political future.[18]

The value of maintaining small-scale enterprises was thus central for at least one important group among the amendment's proponents. And the benefits that were presumed to flow from small-scale enterprise were as much political as economic. Put another way, the amended Section 7 of the Clayton Act was designed to protect competitors as much as competition. Further, the objection to bigness had equal cogency whether the bigness came through merger or through internal growth. Finally, whether or not there had been a trend concentration, the 1950 amendment was intended to operate as an insurance policy against the possibility that mergers might bring about changes in the economic structure. Policy on mergers thus partly supported stability. But whether an antimerger policy would or could protect the integrity of the competitive process is, as we shall see, a matter of considerable debate.

The Problem of Concentration

Several economic theories relate concentration to prices and profits. To examine them all would be both time-consuming and counterproductive. Brief mention of three will suffice to advance our evaluation of the F.T.C.'s output and impact.[19] The first theory, initially set forth in 1838 by Augustin Cournot, is that prices rise as concentration rises. The second, associated with the name of William Fellner, is that, short of monopoly, the degree of concentration bears no relationship to price. And the third, first advanced by Edward Chamberlin, is that below some critical level of concentration, prices behave competitively while above it they behave monopolistically.[20] The original formulations of these theories have been considerably refined and qualified, but the debate as to their respective merits continues among economists of industrial organization at the empirical level.[21]

Most of the empirical investigations have found a positive, if not strong, correlation between profits and industrial concentration, though the industry sample and years selected have made a significant difference to the degree of correlation. Thus for the manufacturing sector in the 1936–1940 period Joe Bain (writing in 1951) found a 4.4 percent difference between the average profit earned in industries with high concentration (eight firms accounting for at least 70 percent of value added in the industry) and average profit in those with low concentration.[22] Twenty years later Yale Brozen carried forward into the postwar era data on the industries covered by Bain's (and others') work, enlarged the number of industries sampled, and found that the relationship between concentration and profits did not hold. Rather, "rates of return in this group of [concentrated] industries moved toward the average rate in subsequent years as time passed allowing capacity and structure to adapt. The concentrated industries behaved competitively."[23]

Other recent studies have strongly suggested that variations in profit rates are either not associated with concentration at all or are only weakly associated with it. Instead, Stanley Ornstein finds, "most of the explained variation in profit rates comes from economies of scale in production, changes in industry demand, and changes in firm demand."[24] Harold Demsetz concludes that "most if not all of the positive correlations between profit rates and concentration uncovered by some earlier studies can be attributed to variations in the size of firms, not the degree to which markets are concentrated."[25] Thus the higher profit rates found in highly concentrated industries are due to the greater proportion of output accounted for by large firms. In such concentrated industries, large firms produce more efficiently and at lower average cost than their smaller competitors.[26] A 1969 study of firm size and productivity supports this hypothesis by showing that the biggest firms in a large sample of industries tend to have higher rates of productivity than other firms in the same industries and that industries with the highest concentration have the highest productivity while those with lowest concentration have the lowest productivity.[27]

While the methodologies used and the interpretations put on data continue to be subjects of debate, these and similar studies nevertheless point to conclusions important for public policy. An explicit policy of deconcentrating industry through use of Section 5 of the F.T.C. Act is, at the very least, fraught with danger. If the argument that bigness begets efficiency is correct—and the evidence tends to show that it is—then deconcentration would be unwise,

because considerable economies of large-scale production or other advantages of existing large firms would then be lost with no compensation in the form of lower prices. If the sizes of all firms are limited by deconcentration policies to be no larger than moderate-sized firms in their industries, then it will be the costs of the moderate-sized firms that determine prices. . . . Since persistent market concentration seems to be associated with economies of scale or other forms of superior performance by existing large firms in concentrated industries, a move to deconcentrate such industries is very likely to increase, not decrease, cost.[28]

And as we saw in our discussion of conscious parallel pricing, the prices of goods produced by large oligopolistic corporations displayed a generally slower rate of increase over the period 1947–1971 than did market-determined prices.[29] A headstrong deconcentration policy might have the effect of raising costs and prices and retarding economic development by sharply reducing profits that could be employed for expansion, cost reduction, or innovation.

Even those who disagree with the findings of a Demsetz or a Brozen still agree that an atomistic market structure is neither feasible nor desirable. Economies of plant size, in raising of capital, and in procurement all argue for oligopoly, even if at a lower level of concentration than currently exists in many industries. But no conclusive evidence exists to justify the serious disruption that could result from a deconcentration policy. Leonard Weiss has written that the cost of such a policy "in confusion and litigation would be huge, and the problem of large firms pulling their punches to stay below the magic number would be far more widespread than it is today."[30] Ralph Beals has found that prices in concentrated industries rise more slowly than prices in competitive industries during periods of economic expansion; if he is right, then a policy of deconcentration might promote an unnecessarily high rate of inflation.[31] For those who hold different views, even a moderate degree of respect for the opinions of those with whom they disagree would dictate caution. As we shall see when we examine the F.T.C.'s attack on the cereal industry, a deconcentration policy may well be a serious error. But if caution appears the best policy with respect to existing levels of concentration, can the same be said in regard to structural change effected through merger?

Antimerger Policy: The Opponents' Case

Arguments can be advanced both in favor of mergers and against them. On the pro side, first, a "merger represents a way of exiting from an industry—often it is the only practicable way"; in any event it is preferable to bankruptcy. Further,

easy exit from an industry significantly lessens the risk of, and thus encourages, initial entry into the industry. Few would enter a poker game if chips could never be cashed in. Overly stringent merger rules thus will curb the birth rate of new companies; and new companies are a vital source of technological innovation and competitive vigor. Mergers permit companies to grow rapidly when that is necessary in order to achieve cost reductions that are obtainable only with large size. It is true that these efficiencies could eventually be achieved by internal growth; but growth is a slow process, and the interim losses of efficiency—losses not just to the owners but to the entire society—are irrevocable. Mergers permit removal of the facilities of a company from the control of unimaginative or lazy or corrupt management. It is the only competitive threat that the managers of many large corporations face as individuals. The "corporate raider," like the price cutter, is loathed by staid, traditional corporate managers.[32]

Second, mergers that produce large firms or mergers with large firms may provide a number of benefits: (a) technological integration in development and the ability to produce compatible technologies, (b) an integrated research staff, (c) the ability to install costly processes that firms could not afford singly, (d) resources large enough to absorb the enormous marketing costs of introducing new products, (e) increased ability to take risks, with respect both to the amount of time that can be invested and to the product areas in which research will be undertaken.[33]

Third, merger may effect substantial economies of scale and thus improve allocation of resources. While the evidence on this point is, as we saw earlier, hardly definitive, the National Industrial Conference Board study demonstrating that both size and concentration of firms are positively related to productivity is significant.[34] If these relationships do hold, an antimerger policy would penalize economic efficiency and waste economic resources.

Fourth, mergers may play a role in promoting innovation and may also lead to an increase in the number of firms in existence. Fred Weston and Stanley Ornstein argue that "there is strong economic logic to suggest that the opportunity for starting a new firm and then selling out on a capital gains basis to another corporation may represent an important stimulus to entrepreneurial activity, and the formation of new firms with new products." Further, the stimulus to prospective entrepreneurs of capital gains through sale of their firms may result "in a larger business population and less concentration than otherwise would exist."[35]

Another line of reasoning in favor of mergers that do not violate the Sherman Act's proscription against monopolization is inconsistent with the arguments so far outlined. This second line of thought is based less on hypothesizing than on hard data. The two principal arguments are, first, that mergers do not lead to increases in either concentration or efficiency, so public resources should not be wasted in opposing them, and second, that mergers are undertaken not with the explicit intention of substantially lessening competition or monopolizing, but for a variety of other reasons. To aid our evaluation of these arguments, Table 10 provides a breakdown of mergers in the

Table 10. Mergers in the manufacturing and mining sectors involving acquisition of large firms, by type of merger, 1948–1973

Type of Acquisition	1948–1962		1963–1972		1973	
	N	%	N	%	N	%
Horizontal	217	15.1	86	9.4	13	23.6
Vertical	162	11.3	88	9.6	7	12.7
Conglomerate						
Product Extension	670	46.6	468	51.0	10	18.2
Market Extension	58	4.0	27	3.0	6	11.0
Other	330	23.0	248	27.0	19	34.5
Total	1,437	100.0	917	100.0	55	100.0

Source: Federal Trade Commission, *Statistical Report on Mergers and Acquisitions* (Washington, D.C.: Government Printing Office, 1974), pp. 147–148.

manufacturing and mining sectors in cases where the acquired firm had assets of $10 million or more. As this table shows, most mergers of large firms in the manufacturing and mining sectors in the post–World War II period have been conglomerate mergers, either of the product extension type or of the pure conglomerate type. This pattern contrasts sharply with that of the prewar period, in which horizontal mergers predominated. In the period 1926–1930, for example, 75.9 percent of mergers were horizontal, in the period 1940–1947 62.0 percent were horizontal.[36] Any theory of the causes of postwar mergers must therefore, if it is to be plausible, explain the preponderance of the conglomerate type. But that is not all; the theory must also explain why mergers follow the wavelike pattern shown in Figures 1 and 2.

The data illustrated in these two figures have been interpreted to mean that firms merge largely for quick financial gain and that prospective market power is only a minor consideration. Weston, for example, ended his investigation of merger activity by concluding that "the special influences accounting for the heightened postwar merger activity have been shown to be (1) an unprecedentedly high peacetime tax structure, (2) low price-earning ratios of common stock, and (3) a desire to achieve rapid expansion in order to increase sales in a strong sellers' market."[37] And *Fortune's* report on a study it had conducted argued that the post–World War II boom in conglomerate mergers was associated with a "bull market that offered unusual opportunities to issue new activities."[38] With the recession of 1969–1970 and the downturn in the stock market that accompanied it, the opportunity to make profits through conglomeration faded. With this incentive gone, the number of mergers involving acquisition of big firms declined sharply, as Figure 2 illustrates. This theory, which is supported by the statements of a number of persons intimately associated with the post–World War II merger wave, thus tends to show that financial considerations unconnected with any desire to exercise market power have provided the principal motivation in most conglomerate mergers.

But what of the other types of merger? A survey of 412 firms, of which 93 responded, revealed a variety of reasons for horizontal, vertical, product extension, and market extension mergers. The ten most important reasons cited were the desire to (1) complete product lines; (2) increase market share; (3) make full use of existing market-

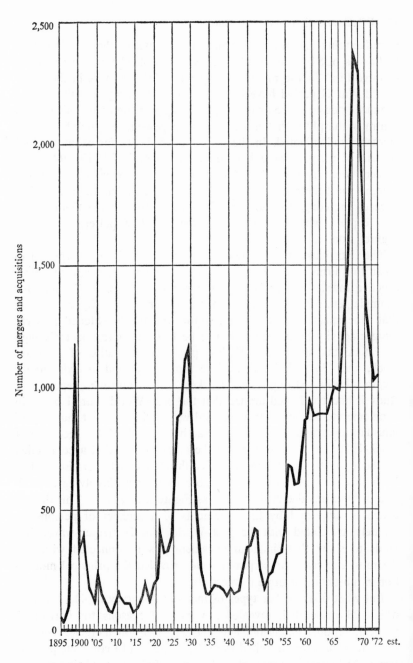

Figure 1. Acquisitions of manufacturing and mining companies, 1895–1972
Source: Tom Cardamone Associates for *Fortune* magazine, April 1973, p. 71.

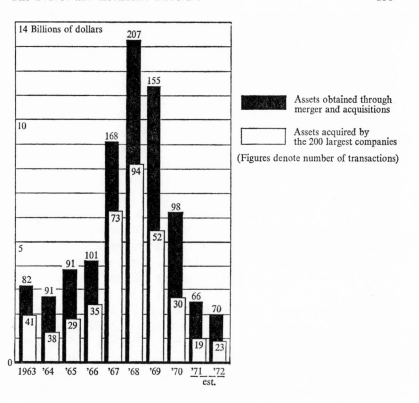

Figure 2. Acquisitions of large firms, 1963–1972
Source: Tom Cardamone Associates for *Fortune* magazine, April 1973, p. 71.

ing capabilities, contacts, or channels; (4) offset unsatisfactory sales growth in present markets; (5) capitalize on distinctive technological expertise; (6) obtain patents, licenses, or technological knowhow; (7) meet the demands of diversified customers; (8) make full use of existing production capacity; (9) increase control of sales outlets; and (10) reduce dependence on suppliers.[39] Each of these reasons is consistent with either competitive behavior or an attempt to exercise monopoly power. The survey does suggest, however, that at least in some mergers, motives other than the desire to make a killing on the stock market played a major role.

No definite conclusion can be reached, then, on firms' motives in undertaking mergers. The advocates of the "financial gain" hypothesis have made a strong if not overwhelming case. At the same time, even if managers' initial reason for seeking consolidation has nothing to do with designs on the market, it does not follow that after the merger they will not take advantage of their new position to exercise market power. How, then, do firms fare after merger, and what have been the effects of mergers? Here the answers are clearer, but still not entirely unambiguous, since the trends that have been discussed have depended very much on choice of base years and standards of measurement. For example, an influential government report showed that "between 1948 and 1967, there was a persistent and substantial upward movement in the share of assets controlled by the 200 largest U.S. manufacturing corporations . . . [and] the sharpest rise occurred in the last two years, when merger activity reached an all-time high."[40] Three factors have influenced this finding: the period selected; the use of assets as a measure; and the fact that the asserted relationship between mergers and increased concentration, although one of concomitance rather than cause and effect, is seen as a causal one.

But different statistical games produce different results. If one examines the 200 largest corporations in 1954, one finds that by 1968 their total assets rose only 0.4 percent; but if the assets of the 200 largest corporations in 1954 are compared with the assets of the 200 largest corporations in 1968, the increase was 11.5 percent.[41] By taking one measure of concentration, one discovers little change; when the other is taken, the change is considerable. An even more important question is whether assets are the best standard of measurement. In recent years many large corporations have included foreign as well as domestic assets in reporting total assets. But more important, since large firms tend to be capital-intensive, their total assets are large relative to sales. If an alternative measure of concentration—value added in manufacture—is used instead of assets, the share held by the 200 largest manufacturing firms is considerably reduced. When assets are the measure, concentration for the 200 largest firms in 1954 and the 200 largest in 1968 rose from 50.8 percent to 62.3 percent; but when the measure is value added, concentration for the 200 largest firms in 1954 and the 200 largest in 1967 (a period shorter by one year) grew 37 percent to 42 percent.[42]

The hypothesis that mergers have been a principal cause of concentration is thus partly undermined in that the supporting proposition—that concentration has greatly increased since the end of World War II—is weakened by the use of value added in manufacture as the measure of concentration, a less biased measure than assets. A question of even greater significance is that of the nexus between mergers and increases in concentration. The important study by Alfred D. Chandler mentioned in Chapter 1 shows, it will be recalled, that since the end of the first merger wave, the principal cause of changes in industry concentration has been changing technologies and markets, not mergers.[43] And other studies have shown that the industries that have experienced greatest increases in concentration have not, in general, been those in which the greatest number of mergers have occurred. Indeed, "mergers have been a minor factor in the rise in the share of value added in manufacturing accounted for by the 50 largest firms. Most of the acquisitions of firms with assets of $10 million and over, carried out by the 200 largest manufacturing firms, are attributable to firms ranked 51 to 150. And these firms show only a minor rise in their share of value added in manufacturing."[44]

As we have seen, the three types of conglomerate merger account for most of the mergers that have taken place in the postwar period, and studies of the behavior of the conglomerates after merger show once again that there has been little, if any, effect on concentration. There is no indication that the larger size of the acquiring firm has significantly increased the market share of the acquired firm. In fact, an F.T.C. study of nine major conglomerates showed that in many instances conglomerates lost part of the market previously held by acquired firms.[45]

If the postwar merger movement has had no clear effect on industrial concentration, the reason may be that merger provides no magic road to lucrative profits for the acquiring firm. Studies conducted through 1970 generally concluded that the investment performance of firms active in acquisition had been neither better nor worse than the average investment performance of other firms in the same industries. The F.T.C. reached the same conclusion in 1972.[46] But more dramatic evidence was provided in a 1973 *Fortune* study of conglomerates: "Heavily burdened by debt incurred in the expectation of prolonged prosperity, a number of them have proved to be financially weak in an era of economic uncertainty. Several conglomerates have even been conducting 'remnant sales' to raise cash."[47]

The arguments of the opponents of an antimerger policy might be summarized as follows: Merger is almost invariably a competitive device and can serve such useful functions as facilitating entry into or exit from an industry. Monopolistic intent and the strong possibility that this aim may be realized may occur in a few instances, but these exceptions may readily be reached under Section 2 of the Sherman Act. But most mergers are not undertaken for such purposes, and there is little likelihood that monopolistic conduct will result from them. Even during the great merger wave of the post–World War II period, concentration—correctly measured in terms of value added in manufacture—has increased only marginally, and the available evidence indicates that mergers had nothing to do with even this slight increase. Therefore, the antimerger policy embraced in the 1950 amendment to the Clayton Act operates in most instances not to promote competition but to protect structural stability. It protects competitors, not competition.[48]

Antimerger Policy: The Proponents' Case

Some of the economic reasons that the Clayton Act's proponents advanced in its favor have already been discussed. I do not propose to rehearse them again in detail here, but will merely examine some of them briefly from a different perspective. So far as the political reasons advanced by Senator Kefauver are concerned, these are not usually debated seriously by economists, and consideration of them will be deferred until the concluding chapter.

The first of the reasons advanced in justification of merger policy under the Clayton Act—and one that applies only to horizontal mergers—is that a linear relationship exists between industry concentration and the degree to which firms in an industry act like a monopoly. Put another way, this theory holds that "the greater the degree of oligopoly, the greater the ease of oligopolistic coordination, and thus the closer market performance results will be to the monopoly solution."[49] This view is, as we have seen, vigorously disputed by other economists, who claim that many additional factors are of importance in determining profits, such as the rate of growth of demand, the nature and speed of technological change, product differentiation, the goals of individual firms, and the degree to which sellers operate in other markets. Empirical studies have come to different conclusions on the question.

A similar and related argument is that prices tend to approach closer to monopoly levels as concentration increases. As we have seen, however, the evidence does not appear to support this supposed correlation. Even Gardiner Means, the architect of the theory of administered prices, once disowned the notion.[50] This is not to suggest that no relationship at all exists between pricing behavior and concentration, but rather that it is complex and nonlinear. Once a certain degree of concentration is passed, as it is in most American industries, no relationship appears to exist between prices and concentration. As one observer has noted, with "relatively small numbers sellers' actions may have an appreciable effect on each other. If one seller drops his price, for example, rival firms may be seriously affected. This must be considered by the foresighted price maker when setting his prices, with the result that prices tend to be sticky."[51] Once this point has been achieved, the relationship between prices and concentration is very tenuous until the monopoly level is reached.

Price rigidity in oligopolistic industries has been explained by a host of factors that have little or nothing to do with concentration: demand inelasticity, cost rigidity, marketing techniques, and so on.[52] Richard Ruggles has concluded, on the basis of a detailed survey of various industry sectors in 1929–1932, that "at no stage in the discussion has it been necessary to consider the effect of industrial concentration to explain the relation between the fall in direct costs and the fall in price."[53] A review of the studies that have been made of these relationships observes that "it has not been established that there is a unique correlation between the degree of concentration and either the degree of discretion available to the firm, the types of business practices pursued, or the character of the economic effects."[54] The F.T.C. has never seriously argued in the merger cases it has brought that a linear relationship between industrial concentration and economic performance exists; rather, it has simply assumed that it does.

Perhaps the most compelling argument advanced by the proponents of a vigorous antimerger policy is that, given the uncertainty surrounding the effects of mergers, it is less costly and difficult to prevent mergers than to dismantle an unwieldy corporate apparatus many years later, after the costs of a merger have been discovered, when the operations of the acquiring and the acquired firms have become integrated. The Clayton Act is thus an insurance policy against the possibility of great economic loss; at relatively little expense the possibility of great benefit is achieved by requiring divestiture shortly after merger. The first answer to this argument is that mergers are not likely to inflict damage and that a hands-off policy can save both public expenditure and the economic cost that results from disruption of a firm's activities. Besides, decisions in merger cases that have gone the government's way have been Pyrrhic victories. A 1969 study of merger decrees concluded that approximately three-quarters are ineffective by the standards developed. Instead of ordering divestiture, the F.T.C. entered orders forbidding certain marketing practices. To formulate an effective decree, especially after an acquired firm has become closely integrated into the joint corporation, is often extraordinarily difficult.[55] Further, achievement of the required divestiture may involve problems if the properties to be separated are large; such properties can usually be bought only by big firms, which may breach the statutory standards in making the acquisition.

Any discussion of antimerger policy must be inconclusive. Points are scored on both sides. Let us look at the act's administration for further clues.

Mergers and the F.T.C.

As with so many other aspects of the F.T.C.'s administration of the laws under its jurisdiction, the agency's performance on mergers has been the subject of much critical comment. The Nader group's study of antitrust enforcement found in its examination of merger activity that between March 1961 and January 1970 only fifty-six complaints had been issued and forty-six orders entered by the Commission. Further, the mean time that had elapsed between a complaint and the issuance of an order (that is, before any court appeal) was 32.6 months. The paucity of complaints—6.2 per year—and the length of time taken in responding to them were viewed by the Nader group as evidence of bad performance.[56] The Department of Justice's Antitrust Division brings roughly the same number of complaints per year in the manufacturing and mining sectors as the F.T.C. The grand total of twelve or thirteen complaints per year hardly keeps up with the merger rate; for between 1953 and 1972 the average number of large acquisitions (those involving firms with assets of $10 million or more) in manufacturing and mining was seventy per year.[57] Moreover, many of the F.T.C.'s complaints have been brought not in the manufacturing and mining sectors but in retailing; and others have not concerned large acquisitions. Clearly, the agency's output in merger activity has not remotely kept pace with acquisitions.

In fact, however, the explanation both for the long delay between acquisition and Commission order and for the enforcement agencies' inability to keep up with important acquisitions during periods of high merger activity lies not in any dereliction of duty but in the nature of an antimerger proceeding. Although the F.T.C. and the courts have greatly simplified the criteria for a finding of unlawfulness, the burden of evidence imposed on each side in litigation is still immense. The government must first establish in detail the facts of acquisition. Next it must learn what the product market properly is and justify the definition it arrives at on the basis of the intricacies of the particular industry, including close substitute products, ease of entry into the industry, and the viability of competitors. Then it must develop data on market shares and seek to determine the reasons for the division of the market and for changes over time. It must also justify its selection of a particular geographical market to test the effects of merger by examining such factors as sales and transportation patterns. Finally it must try to show, through the testimony of economic experts, affected businessmen, and others, that a range of anticompetitive effects have occurred or will occur as a result of the acquisition. Even if it can be demonstrated that some such ultimate results are probable, the burden of producing evidence is great indeed. Merger proceedings are further complicated by the fact that respondents do not idly sit by and watch the government present its case; they develop evidence with which to rebut the government's case and erect affirmative defenses. In turn the government must investigate and rebut the respondent's evidence. In addition, as in virtually all litigation, and especially in big cases, there are ample opportunities for procedural side issues and delay. Under these circumstances, most contested merger cases must involve great effort and time, despite the attempts of courts and the Commission to simplify the rules governing illegality.

When all this is considered, the explanation for the F.T.C.'s alleged failure to have much impact on postwar mergers would appear to lie not in the Commission's personnel or policy but in the unsuitability of litigation as a means of controlling supposedly undesirable behavior. No evidence exists that would tend to show that the agency has not used its resources effectively to produce a reasonable output in its antimerger work. It has won most of the cases it has brought, and it has shown no hesitation in attacking very large firms. Between 1965 and 1972, for example, it entered orders against Imperial Chemical Industries, Gates Rubber, Textron, Allied Chemical, Occidental Petroleum, Procter & Gamble, and Texas Industries. Moreover, recognizing that its activity in this area would be most effective if it were concentrated on a few industries rather than scattered through the economy, the F.T.C. has focused attention on the food, cement, and department store industries.

Horizontal Mergers

During the 1960s and early 1970s the law on horizontal mergers was considered to be clear. In the Philadelphia National Bank case of 1963[58] the court held that a merger that gave a firm control of an "undue" market share and which resulted in a "significant" increase in concentration was unlawful unless the respondent clearly showed that the merger was not likely to have any anticompetitive effect. In a 1966 case the Supreme Court ruled that a combined market share of 7.5 percent was an "undue" share.[59]

In 1974, however, the Court backtracked slightly in a case involving merger of two coal producers that raised their market shares from 7.6 to 12.4 percent in one market and from 15.1 to 23.2 percent in another. Since electric utilities are the major consumers of the nation's coal, and since they usually enter into long-term contracts, a coal producer must have substantial coal reserves to compete effectively. The reserves of the acquired firm in the case were low, and the Court concluded that its competitive viability was considerably less than mere production statistics would indicate. The Court therefore held that the merger was not likely to lessen competition substantially.[60] This case thus marked the first inroad upon the doctrine that statistics are virtually conclusive in horizontal merger cases.

In general, however, the Commission has followed the statistical guidelines established by the Supreme Court, and the market shares at issue in the cases it has brought have often been relatively small. A typical horizontal merger case involved the fourth largest salt producer (4.7 percent of the market); this firm was charged with violating the law by acquiring the sixth largest salt producer (4.2 percent of the market). In another case the second largest manufacturer of sporting goods acquired the fourth largest; after the merger the combined firm accounted for only 18.5 percent of total sales of sporting goods, yet the acquisition was challenged.[61]

Thus in the case of horizontal mergers the tendency of the F.T.C., abetted by the Supreme Court's decisions, has been to follow a per se rule and to give no consideration to any defense except that of the pending failure of the acquired firm. Words like "concentration" are used in F.T.C. proceedings for their talismanic properties in order to strike down virtually all horizontal mergers without regard to any of the considerations that have been advanced here. The results have been much as might be expected: the amendment (as enforced under this approach) has had some deterrent effect on mergers. While 31 percent of large acquisitions in the manufacturing and mining sectors in the period 1948–1953 were horizontal, the proportion dropped to 12 percent in the period 1960–1964.[62]

In the horizontal merger cases brought by the F.T.C., the likelihood of monopolization has clearly been extremely remote, and such a consideration could not have formed part of the rational motivation of either the acquirers or the acquired. Rather, as we observed earlier in the chapter, the likelihood is that mergers were effected in order to gain competitive advantage through economies of scale in research or distribution or through complementarity in managerial or technical talents. While such gains might arguably come about gradually through internal expansion, the merger route provides a quick way of achieving them by opening up at least the possibility of rapid gains in efficiency. The thrust of the F.T.C.'s approach to horizontal mergers that involve only small increases in market concentration is, however, not to enhance competition but to maintain the status quo.

Vertical Mergers

Vertical integration through merger involves the acquisition of a supplier of raw materials (backward integration) or of a purchaser of the firm's products (forward integration). Firms traditionally acquire suppliers or, more commonly, customers not to monopolize an industry or destroy competitors but to ensure supplies or outlets. A study of vertical integration in manufacturing between 1899 and 1948 concluded that "most of the vertical integration which took place in the period was apparently motivated by a desire to *rationalize* flows by assuring efficient facilities for sales and distribution or assuring needed raw materials rather than from any widespread tendency to add the profits of suppliers or distributors to the profits of manufacturing."[63]

The F.T.C. and the Justice Department attack vertical mergers because they believe that the acquiring firm purchases a captive market and thereby excludes its competitors from that portion of the market. In essence, this is the only theory employed by the F.T.C. and the courts in declaring vertical mergers unlawful.[64] But critics see a fallacy in the theory that

by buying a firm one thereby acquires its customers. Instead little more is bought than a hunting license. The costs and difficulties of getting customers and the risks of losing them that the acquired firm experienced are still present. The ultimate consumer will buy from someone else if he is not competitively served by the acquired firm. The merger in no way affects the alternatives of these customers; if they were poor before the merger, they are not worse after it.[65]

Furthermore, any competitive move by the newly integrated firm can be matched or beaten by other firms at the level of either the acquiring firm or the acquired firm. If firms are unable to compete effectively against the vertically integrated firm by lowering prices or offering some other concession, they have only demonstrated their inefficiency and regressiveness.[66] Thus when monopoly or monopolizing conditions are not present, vertical integration by merger may be viewed as a competitive device.

Much of the F.T.C.'s activity in the field of vertical mergers has been in the cement industry. Since 1959 it has filed more than fifteen complaints that have involved acquisition by cement producers of ready-mix concrete producers. The industry therefore provides a good field for examination of the effects of vertical mergers: do they foreclose competition, or, in the absence of economies of integration, do they simply transfer profits? According to the F.T.C., in 1964 about fifty-two cement companies in the United States operated 181 plants; but because cement is very heavy, transportation costs are high and effective geographical markets small, and therefore the number of producers operating in any one geographical market is considerably fewer than fifty-two.[67]

The 1960s saw a rash of acquisitions by cement companies of ready-mix concrete firms, averaging more than ten per year during

1960–1966 and four per year during 1967–1969.[68] The reason for this pattern is suggested by a study of the cement industry which discloses that around 1958 the industry entered a period of overcapacity, which led at times to severe price cutting. In an attempt to preserve their market shares, many firms acquired ready-mix firms and used them as captive markets. This explanation may seem to confirm the foreclosure hypothesis; but other evidence points in the contrary direction, for many cement firms lost a considerable amount of money on their ready-mix operations and were more than happy later to divest themselves of their acquisitions. Moreover, many firms were opposed to vertical integration by merger but engaged in it as a defensive move when their competitors integrated. Thus, in the instance of forward vertical mergers in the cement industry, "foreclosure . . . has been too costly to be worthwhile," and sales of acquired ready-mix divisions could have been anticipated even without F.T.C. intervention.[69]

Vertical integration by merger is thus a competitive device used by a firm either to gain a competitive advantage or to defend its share of the market when others engage in such mergers. At the same time, however, it is a device to thwart another part of the competitive process by putting an end to bargaining and substituting a captive relationship. Yet like other strategies it can be a fool's errand if economies are not effected. The discovery that one part of a vertically integrated business is operating at a loss inevitably leads to the sale of the losing division in order to cut costs, even without government intervention.[70] If, on the other hand, vertical integration effects economies, the trend is desirable and will continue, through merger or otherwise.

Conglomerate Mergers

Conglomerate mergers are customarily classified in three subcategories: (1) product extension (acquisition of a firm in a closely related business); (2) market extension (acquisition of a firm in the same business that does not compete with the acquiring firm because it operates in a different geographical market); and (3) pure conglomerate. As we noted earlier, product extension mergers have predominated in manufacturing and mining. The F.T.C. has entered a number of orders involving market extension and product extension mergers but none against pure conglomerates. (The Department of Justice has attacked pure conglomerates as well as other types.)

The Commission has used four major guidelines in cases of conglomerate merger: (1) a merger that produces efficiencies that go beyond those of either the acquired or the acquiring company's competitors should not be permitted; (2) if a merger gives the acquiring company greater resources than competitors ("a deeper pocket"), the merger should not be allowed; (3) if an acquiring company could possibly engage in predatory or exclusionary practices, there is a strong presumption that the merger is improper; and (4) if merger substantially increases the size of the firm, barriers to entry into the acquired company's industry may be raised, and this likelihood weighs strongly against approval of the merger.

The leading case of the product extension type concerned Procter and Gamble's acquisition of Clorox, a manufacturer of liquid bleach, an easily made product. Objection to the merger did not stem from any charge that Procter & Gamble, a diversified manufacturer of soap products, contemplated using exclusionary practices, but rather from the efficiencies that resulted from the acquisition.[71] The Commission based its finding that Procter & Gamble's acquisition had violated the law on such indicia as the substantial cost savings, particularly in television advertising, achieved by the merged firm, and the efficiencies that resulted where a sales force added one more product to an already substantial line of soap and detergent products. In other words, the order to divest was based largely on Procter & Gamble's alleged achievement of efficiencies and hence lower costs; as a result of these efficiencies, especially in network advertising, it was further alleged, barriers to the liquid bleach industry had been raised.

Analyses of the supposed economies in advertising have suggested that they did not in fact exist. The F.T.C. simply accepted published advertising rates rather than inquiring into prices actually paid. When the prices that were actually paid are examined, it is clear that little or no advantage accrued to large buyers.[72] Even if economies could be effected, as the Commission charged, is this a sufficient reason to condemn a merger? As we have seen, the industrial battleground is strewn with casualties who thought they could attain benefits from merger but failed. The F.T.C. has adopted a particular attitude not because it disapproves of efficiency per se, but because of the potentially destabilizing effects of mergers.

The attempt to maintain the status quo, regardless of the efficiencies or benefits that merger might bring, is further illustrated by the Reynolds Metals case.[73] In that case the largest producer of aluminum foil acquired the largest converter and seller of decorative florist foil, whose sales of $497,000 per year amounted to about one-third of total sales of this product. Here the F.T.C.'s position was based not specifically on efficiencies but on the fact that Reynolds was substantially larger than any other firm in the florist foil industry, a discrepancy that "opened the possibility and power to sell at prices approximating cost or below and thus to undercut and ravage the less affluent competition." This is the so-called deep-pocket theory.

Such predatory conduct has, of course, occurred and can be reached under the Sherman Act if it reaches the proportions of monopolization or attempted monopolization. But such cases are not common, and in most cases predation appears improbable. In an industry with relatively small sales, low profits, and a pattern of slow growth (such as florist foil), the costs of driving out competitors are apt to be too high relative to the potential gain. If, on the other hand, the industry is a lucrative one, driving out smaller competitors is futile, since any effort to achieve excessive profits attracts re-entry into the industry; so why should a firm incur the losses needed to drive out competitors? Finally, unless a single firm is much larger than its competitors, the costs of predatory conduct on a scale sufficient to drive out competitors are apt to be overwhelming. The very small number of F.T.C. cases that involve true predatory pricing shows that indeed firms rarely find such conduct worthwhile.

The Reynolds case also illustrates the third guideline under which the F.T.C. declares conglomerate mergers unlawful without looking closely at the facts—the possibility that exclusionary practices might occur if the merger were approved. The line of conjecture here is even more tenuous than the speculation involved in estimating effects when exclusionary practices actually occur. This crystal-ball gazing, this conjecture about the effects of exclusionary practices that might occur, cannot even be contradicted by facts showing that the contemplated results have not occurred.[74] Since there is no end to the exclusionary practices that may be envisioned, the effect of this guideline may be to discourage acquisition of firms in small, inefficient industries.

The entrance of a firm into another industry—whether through horizontal, vertical, or conglomerate merger—almost necessarily brings some economic benefit. Even exponents of the traditional antitrust viewpoint concede that because diversified firms are better able than single-product firms to shift resources, they can, for example, devote greater effort to product improvement.[75] The older firms in an industry, faced with the entrance by acquisition of a firm that threatens competition based upon efficiencies derived from diversification, "will be under heavy pressures to improve, rather than worsen, their competitive performance. They will be forced to cut costs, to improve their product, to lower their price in order to survive.[76]

Not every entrance into a new industry by merger results in efficiencies, but the F.T.C. has explicitly condemned acquisitions that do lead to such efficiencies. And this condemnation follows from the agency's statutory directive, since an acquisition may "lessen competition" to the extent that older firms' survival is threatened by their inability to compete effectively with the newcomers.

The fourth F.T.C. guideline on conglomerate mergers, that involving ease of entry, is illustrated by the Foremost Dairies case, an example of market extension.[77] Foremost, a processor and distributor of fluid milk, ice cream, and related products, made fifty-two acquisitions, some of which were of the market extension type. The F.T.C. found that these acquisitions were unlawful because potential new entrants, seeing Foremost's great national strength, would be deterred from entering the markets in which Foremost had made acquisitions. The problem with this argument is that it stops at the first step in one of those chains of reasoning with which strategists love to play games. To take the strategic argument but one step further, the fact that there are potential entrants will discourage entry. In this case Foremost's entry adds nothing to any barriers. To take the argument another step further, the knowledge that entry is very much discouraged will in fact encourage someone to enter since the likelihood of further entry is low. The ease-of-entry argument thus leads to an unending series of propositions. And it is further complicated by such questions as whether one or many potential entrants exist and how easily industry members can increase supply in response to changed market conditions; the answers to these questions (and others) will affect a firm's decision on entry,[78] but the F.T.C. does not take them into account.

Conglomerate mergers, then, have been attacked by the F.T.C. on the basis of a number of questionable theories. These mergers, like horizontal and vertical mergers, are undertaken to achieve market and financial objectives. But whether or not a firm succeeds in attaining these objectives depends more on production, technological, and marketing effectiveness than upon the fact of merger. People's worst fears about mergers have proved to be largely unfounded. Even many of those who deplore bigness in business have come to discount anti-merger policies as effective means of reducing economic concentration. John Kenneth Galbraith, for example, has complained:

If a firm is already large, it has as a practical matter nothing to fear under antimerger provisions of the Clayton Act. It will not be demerged. It can continue to grow from its own earnings; if discreet, it can even, from time to time, pick up a small and impecunious competitor, for it can reasonably claim that this does little to alter the pattern of competition in the industry. But if two medium-sized firms unite in order to deal more effectively with this giant, the law will be on them like a tiger. Again, if large, you are exempt. If you seek to become as large, or even if you seek to become somewhat larger, although still much smaller, you are in trouble.[79]

The F.T.C., aware of the problem and aware that the problem was concentration, not mergers, prepared for its frontal attack on oligopoly. As we saw at the beginning of this chapter, only in recent years have the legal tools for an assault on what the agency has termed "shared monopoly" been approved by the courts.

Shared Monopoly

On April 26, 1972, the F.T.C. dropped a bombshell by signing a complaint against the four major producers of ready-to-eat breakfast cereals, charging in effect that their oligopolistic domination of the industry constituted an unfair method of competition.[80] As *Business Week* put it, "For years, federal antitrust theorists, economists and lawyers have considered ways to push through the courts a successful attack on oligopoly. . . . Lots of talk and law journal articles have come out of their deliberations, but never a law suit. . . . Now the Federal Trade Commission says it will file a complaint against the four big producers of ready to eat breakfast cereals, claiming they are a 'shared monopoly.' "[81] Obviously, if oligopoly could be attacked in one industry, it could be attacked in another, and it was not long before another complaint was filed, this time against eight of the major oil companies, on July 18, 1973.[82] It is no exaggeration to say that these cases constitute the most important antitrust development since the 1911 monopoly cases against Standard Oil and American Tobacco.

In view of the extraordinary complexity and uniqueness of the petroleum industry, we shall focus on the less complex breakfast cereal industry in an attempt to understand the agency's theory of complaint.

In essence, the complaint charges that for thirty years the respondents had engaged in acts that had the effect of maintaining a highly concentrated, noncompetitive market structure in the production and sale of ready-to-eat (RTE) cereals. The first of the allegedly unfair methods was the promotion of approximately 150 new brands of cereal between 1950 and 1970 and the artificial differentiation of basically similar products through intensive advertising, which had the effect of creating high barriers to entry into the RTE industry. Second, through persistent deceptive advertising the respondents misled consumers into the "mistaken belief" that the respondents' products were superior to and different from other RTE cereals; this strategy allowed the respondents to obtain monopoly prices and exclude competitors. Third, by controlling shelf arrangements in retail markets Kellogg interfered with and restricted the exposure of the products of smaller firms; and the other respondents acquiesced in this practice. Finally, the "shared monopoly" structure of the RTE cereal industry was enhanced by a series of acquisitions.

The results of these practices, the F.T.C. alleged, were artificially inflated prices, excessive profits, lack of product innovation, blocked entry into the industry, and lack of meaningful price competition. The proposed relief included the establishment of new competitors and provision to such new competitors of know-how, trade names, and other benefits on a royalty-free basis for a specified period.

Let us look at the RTE cereal industry in the light of the complaint, examining first relative market shares in 1967 and 1969 and total sales of the RTE manufacturers in 1974, as shown in Table 11. The first striking point about the data shown in this table is that the industry leader is considerably smaller overall than its major competitors. Kellogg derives 80 percent of its revenues from RTE cereals, while its competitors depend far more on other sources— 92 percent of Quaker Oats' revenues, for example, come from other sources and only 8 percent from sales of RTE cereals.[83] Even so, Kellogg's larger competitors have been unable to shift Kellogg from

Table 11. Market shares, total sales, and corporate size of firms in the break-fast cereal industry, 1967, 1969, and 1974

Firm	1967 Market Share (percent)	1969 Market Share (percent)	1974 Sales	1974 *Fortune* Rank
Kellogg	43	45	$1,009,818	200
General Mills	22	21	2,000,103	94
General Foods	18	16	2,986,692	58
Quaker Oats	7	9	1,227,345	163
Nabisco	5	4	1,793,049	153
Ralston-Purina	3	4	3,073,210	55
Others	2	1	—	—

Sources: Complaint, *Kellogg Company et al.,* F.T.C. Dkt. 8883 (1972); *Fortune,* December 1967 and May 1975.

its leading position in this lucrative market. So much for deep pockets.

Table 11 also reveals that even in the short period between 1967 and 1969 market shares varied. Indeed, intensive advertising and the introduction of new brands attest to vigorous nonprice competition in the industry. (In 1967 approximately fifteen cents of every revenue dollar was being spent on advertising, and during that year, brands that had been introduced within the previous ten years accounted for 25 percent of sales.) Nor does the introduction of new brands guarantee success. General Foods, for example, blundered badly both in introducing fruit cereals and in reducing the size of its boxes; and the magnitude of such a mistake can be appreciated when one realizes that there is ordinarily a three-year lag between development and introduction of a new cereal. Because of the risks involved and because the RTE cereal industry is surprisingly capital-intensive, even Procter & Gamble, the twenty-eighth largest corporation in the United States in 1975, decided not to enter the industry, despite its high profits.[84]

Competition in the breakfast cereal industry is manifested in several other ways. First, there is considerable competition between RTE cereals and other products eaten for breakfast, including such newcomers as instant breakfasts and egg substitutes. There is no reason to doubt that there is considerable cross-elasticity of demand between RTE cereals and a dozen other breakfast products. Second, the RTE cereal makers compete not only in introducing new brands but also in introducing new kinds of RTE cereals, such as sugar cereals, vitamin-fortified cereals, and, most recently, "natural" cereals.

Such innovations may cause dramatic shifts in market shares, and indeed in 1967 Kellogg's market share declined in these newer kinds of cereal.[85]

The F.T.C.'s objection is to allegedly inflated profits and prices. While cereal makers' profits could certainly be described as high, they are not extraordinarily so. Kellogg, for example, ranked one hundredth among the *Fortune* 500 in returns on sales in and forty-sixth in returns on stockholders' equity. But high profits should be expected from an efficient firm in a growing industry. Price competition may indeed be restricted, but as we saw in Chapter 4, such is often the nature of oligopoly. Why reduce prices if your competitors can readily do the same? If demand is sufficient to sustain a given price level, why not maintain it? If demand declines, retailers—the cereal maker's customers—will cut the amount of valuable shelf space assigned to the product, creating pressure for price reductions. Finally, as the discussion of concentration at the beginning of this chapter indicates, it is far from clear that creation of new firms will either reduce prices or alter the areas in which the industry now competes and those in which it does not.

In grossly underestimating the extent to which competition exists in the breakfast cereal industry, the F.T.C.'s innovative attack on oligopoly manifests once again the Commission's blindness to the internal contradiction between competition and stability which characterizes American industry and public policy's response to it. But the great merit of the shared-monopoly approach, aside from its administrative originality, is that it directly confronts the relationship between economic structure and consumer welfare, which is, after all, what trade regulation policy is ultimately supposed to be about. In general, the F.T.C.'s antimonopoly policy appears to have had little or no effect on consumer welfare, at least in the realm of prices, if we take into account the rampant inflation of the 1970s and the fact that during 1967–1972 prices rose considerably faster in less concentrated industries than in highly concentrated ones.[86] As I have sought to show, the fault lies not in the F.T.C.'s output but in the premises and nature of public policy on monopoly regulation. But has the F.T.C. been more successful when it has focused its attention on the consumer directly? We turn now to this question.

PART THREE

THE F.T.C. AND
THE CONSUMER

CHAPTER 7

Advertising, Deception, and the Wheeler-Lea Act

Whatever the F.T.C. may have done since the Wheeler-Lea Amendment was passed, before that its position on deceptive practices emphasized principally, if not exclusively, their effects on competitors and other businessmen. The effects on consumers were of minor concern—nor could they be otherwise given the statutory thrust of Section 5 of the Federal Trade Commission Act, which declared unlawful "unfair methods of competition," not acts unfair to consumers. While, as we have already observed, the two concepts need not conflict, they can create different priorities.

In contrast to the extensive discussion of antimonopoly practices, little attention was paid to deceptive practices in the 1914 legislative debates, and that little did not treat the subject as separate from the antimonopoly thrust. Rather, deceptive practices were subsumed within the general category of acts by which one competitor unfairly abused others. Thus in the course of the hearings on the Clayton Act the charge was made that associations of retail lumber dealers made deceptive statements about mail-order lumber houses in order to deprive the latter of custom.[1]

In the congressional debates the notion of deception was conceived within the common law framework of misappropriation of the fruits of another's labor. Frequently the fruits appropriated were a firm's trade values, usually a trade name or trademark. In cases of misappropriation, the value protected is the financially valuable goodwill that the plaintiff has developed in the trademark or trade name, not the consumer's interest in the truth.[2] In the course of the debate on the F.T.C. Act, Senator Cummins cited as an instance of unfair com-

petition a new firm that called its product Crystal White Laundry
Soap in order to capitalize on the excellent reputation of an older
firm's White Laundry Soap.[3] And Senator Newlands agreed that a tire
manufacturer who falsely claimed his tires to be the equal in quality of
the more expensive tires of established competitors was guilty of unfair competition. Interestingly, Newlands assumed that the competitors
would bring the matter to the Commission's attention.[4]

In short, one searches the record in vain for any indication that the
sponsors of the F.T.C. Act intended the consumer to be the beneficiary of prospective F.T.C. action in the area of deceptive practices
(although it should be pointed out that consumers may benefit from
F.T.C. action). The intended beneficiaries were competitors harmed
by deception.

Further confirmation of this intention is found in reports issued by
the Commission and the Bureau of Corporations in 1916, two years
after passage of the Federal Trade Commission Act; they linked with
deceptive practices such things as enticement of competitors' employees, industrial espionage, and secret concessions to suppliers or
customers.[5] These practices, although morally reprehensible and of
legitimate concern to competitors, have little to do with consumers.
But from the beginning the F.T.C. grouped these practices and mis-
appropriations together as "deceptive practices," in contrast to practices that allegedly restrain trade. Although the agency sought to stop
both kinds of practice principally to aid competition rather than consumers,[6] the great volume of deceptive practice cases compelled
separate treatment.[7]

How, then, was the notion of unfair competition, as applied to such
acts as deception and industrial espionage, understood by the early
advocates of the F.T.C. and the agency's personnel during this
period? Essentially, the concept was based upon developments in
the Anglo-American law of torts. The law of torts is designed to
provide for social stability by declaring conduct that may lead to
breach of the peace to be an actionable wrong. Included in such
conduct are assault, deceit, negligence, and malicious prosecution,
and these acts constitute torts whether or not they take place in a
commercial context. Independent legal considerations began to develop
concerning some of these practices, however, when they occurred in
a commercial context. For example, the common law notion of unfair competition—the appropriation of the fruits of another's labor—

stems from the older idea of conversion—appropriating someone else's property without legal right—an act that clearly invites social disruption.[8]

The great breakthrough in commercial tort law occurred in 1853 in the classic English case *Lumley* v. *Gye*.[9] Since the use of physical violence or intimidation, in commercial relations or otherwise, clearly constitutes tortious conduct, the use of force to cause breach of contract would clearly be actionable. But in *Lumley* v. *Gye,* inducing a breach of contract was for the first time held to be tortious regardless of the means employed, on the grounds that since breach of contract is an actionable wrong, a person who "maliciously procures" such wrongdoing ought to be made responsible. The new doctrine was readily transplanted to America.[10]

Without going into more detail on Anglo-American legal history, we can see how commercially tortious conduct came to have the two meanings of conduct involving such traditionally tortious acts as violence, intimidation, and appropriation of another's property, and acts that are "malicious" in relation to competitors and involve tainted means.[11] Such conduct and the various business methods allegedly employed by trusts were lumped together by the proponents of the F.T.C. Act and early Commission administrators as unfair methods of competition. Thus the way in which early deceptive advertising cases were grouped with cases involving such practices as commercial espionage and treated as unfair methods of competition begins to make more sense: false advertising involved a tainted means of maliciously injuring competitors.

Other characteristics of the early deceptive practice cases have also been carried over into more recent times. Paramount among them is the triviality of many cases. A large number of them involve small firms, minor products, and small sums, and are of relatively little importance to anyone's health or safety. Gerard Henderson relates, for example, that "one case in which a complaint was issued, testimony heard, briefs filed, and a formal decision rendered, involved a family quarrel over the right to use the name 'Phillips Old Time Sausage' in the District of Columbia."[12] Such cases have been of major consequence to the respondents' competitors, however. Henderson notes that many have concerned attempts to divert customers either from specific and identified competitors or from a rival line of goods.[13]

A good number of the deceptive practices against which the F.T.C.

moved in this early period involved activities about which trade associations were deeply concerned, fearing debasement of whole product lines. The F.T.C. condemned, for example, the practice of selling products made of artificial compounds as ivory or jade—a matter that was of major concern to the vendors of ivory and jade. Trade associations had adopted stringent codes governing deceptions of this type, but they could not compel adherence; so the F.T.C. was called upon to enforce them.[14] So it went until 1931; the F.T.C. devoted its energies in the area of deceptive practices largely to cases of minor importance to consumers but of great moment to affected industries or competitors. In 1931, however, the Supreme Court rendered a decision that affected both deceptive practices as covered by the original F.T.C. Act and the changes wrought by the Wheeler-Lea Amendment.

The Raladam Case

About 1910 the Raladam Company, a manufacturer of patent medicines, developed from the thyroid glands of animals a preparation that purportedly was effective in weight reduction.[15] The Commission challenged claims in the respondent's advertising that the preparation was a scientific remedy for obesity. In the course of the trial, five reputable physicians supported the F.T.C.'s claim that the preparation was not scientifically prepared, and six agreed with the respondent that it was. The Court of Appeals, reversing the F.T.C., held that such words as "scientific" are inherently ambiguous and express opinion rather than fact, thus accounting for the split in the doctors' testimony. The court also held, however, that the F.T.C. had not shown injury to competitors, and the implications of this ruling aroused much controversy.

The Raladam case was one of several brought by the F.T.C. at the urging of the American Medical Association (A.M.A.), which was engaged in a campaign against remedies used without the interposition of a medical doctor. In the trial the Commission did not produce evidence of actual or possible harm to competing manufacturers, resting content with a showing that certain doctors found the respondent's claims deceptive. The Court of Appeals held, and the Supreme Court later affirmed, that this evidence was insufficient. The Commission could proceed only if present or potential manufacturers of the same or rival products were affected. The Supreme

Court reasoned that since the word "competition" implied the existence of present or potential competitors, the modifying word "unfair" implied that for the Commission to assert jurisdiction, present or potential rivals must be injured or threatened in their trade. Moreover, the Court said, merely to show that Raladam's advertisements would probably increase its business was insufficient, since there is no necessary connection between increased sales and injury to competitors. Finally, the Court made explicit the requirement that rivals who claim to be injured by a practice must show that they are in competition with the respondent in the sale of the same or similar products, and that business has been diverted or is likely to be diverted from them to the respondent as a result of the practice.

After the F.T.C.'s cease-and-desist order was set aside, the Commission brought another case against Raladam, in 1935. This time the agency meticulously showed that Raladam had many rivals selling in the same markets. Moreover, the F.T.C. found that Raladam had made many misleading and deceptive statements about competing products, and from this fact it inferred that trade had been diverted from the competitors to Raladam. This time the Supreme Court had no difficulty in affirming the Commission's order.[16] The ease with which the Commission won the second case raises the question of whether the first decision so hampered the Commission's ability to protect consumers as to make new legislation necessary, as was argued in the debates on the Wheeler-Lea Amendment of 1938.

One point of view was, and is, that indeed new legislation was badly needed. The House report that accompanied the new legislation states:

By the proposed amendment to Section 5, the Commission can prevent such acts or practices which imperiously affect the general public as well as those which are unfair to competitors. . . .

This amendment will also enable the Commission to act more expeditiously and save time and money now required to show actual competition and the injurious effect thereon of the unfair methods in question.

At the present time, both in the investigation of unfair methods of competition and in actual proceedings after the issuance of a formal complaint, the Commission must develop the jurisdictional prerequisite, even though the methods or practices involve representations that are flagrantly false or deceptive and dangerously injurious to the purchasing or consuming public.[17]

But other knowledgeable commentators have argued that the first Raladam decision impeded the F.T.C. not one whit. As early as 1924 Gerard Henderson observed that "it is rare that a deceptive practice . . . is not a method of competition. Two men are commercial competitors . . . [and] any practice, device, or course of conduct adopted by either to improve his relative position as compared with the other, or to prevent the other from gaining on him, is a method of competition."[18] But perhaps the most important evidence that the F.T.C. was not hampered by the requirement that deception be shown to be an unfair method of competition is that contained in a statement made by the Commission's chairman, Ewin Davis, after the Raladam case: "It is the rarest case in the world, if it ever exists, where the consuming public is adversely affected by false and misleading advertisements that a competitor is not also affected, and consequently we would have the requisite showing of competition."[19] At another point in his statement Davis said, even more affirmatively, that "the competitor is always affected if the consuming public is adversely affected"—because consumers would be induced to divert their trade to the unfair competitor.[20]

Contemporary commentaries in the law reviews also supported the opinion that the Raladam case constituted no obstacle to the F.T.C. in bringing a case. Nor were additional burdensome evidentiary requirements imposed on the agency because of it; the evidence necessary to prove a violation was about the same before and after the Wheeler-Lea Amendment. Finally, a 1938 examination of deceptive practice cases brought by the F.T.C. after the amendment was enacted indicated that they could easily have been brought under the F.T.C. Act before the amendment.[21]

In summary, then, the traditional legal reasons given for amending the term "unfair methods of competition" to include "unfair or deceptive acts or practices" are not entirely convincing. Nevertheless, the F.T.C. had sound reasons for urging new legislation. First, the *possibility* certainly existed that cases of deception could arise which did no injury or prospective injury to competitors. Second, the new language would at least marginally reduce the burden of proof by eliminating the requirement that competitors be produced as witnesses. Third, and most important, the Commission could make consumer protection an important new area of concern for public policy. Instead of dealing with the competitive process alone, it could add another vast field to its area of concern. In the area of consumer affairs, however, the F.T.C. had a major rival in the Food and Drug Administration (F.D.A.); the relationship between the two agencies was to play an important role in the shaping of both the amendment to the F.T.C. Act and new food and drug legislation.

The New Food and Drug Proposals

An examination of the genesis of the new food and drug and related legislation of the 1930s compels the conclusion that the food and drug industries supported enactment of the Wheeler-Lea Amendment in order to undercut more stringent proposals that would have subjected them to criminal penalties. Those who favored the imposition of such criminal penalties sought to place jurisdiction over food and drug advertising in the F.D.A., while those who opposed the institution of a strong deterrent wanted the F.T.C. to have jurisdiction over such advertising. The terms of the Wheeler-Lea Amendment, which vested jurisdiction in the F.T.C., reflect the battle that took place between the two sides.

On June 12, 1933, in response to urgent requests from officials of the F.D.A., Senator Royal S. Copeland of New York introduced a bill to improve regulation of food and drug advertising.[22] The bill failed to pass Congress that year and for several consecutive years, largely because of the effective opposition mounted by drug interests, whose tactics throughout the battle were first to fight against enactment of a stringent law and then, as a second resort, to try to have the F.T.C. granted as much jurisdiction as possible over food and drug advertising, at the expense of the F.D.A.

The Copeland Bill sought to amend existing food and drug legislation in several crucial respects. First, it proposed that F.D.A. jurisdiction be enlarged to include mechanical devices and cosmetics. Second, it sought to forbid the advertising of drugs for tuberculosis, cancer, and other diseases for which self-medication could be dangerous. Third, it wanted to forbid representation of a drug as a cure when it had only a palliative effect. Fourth, and for our purposes most important, it sought to invest jurisdiction over false advertising of drugs in the F.D.A. The significance of this provision lay in the substantially greater powers of enforcement enjoyed by the F.D.A. relative to the F.T.C. Under the Copeland Bill, the F.D.A. would have powers of factory inspection under some circumstances, could seek injunctions to deny a company the right to make interstate shipments, and could levy heavy penalties and even impose prison terms.[23] The F.T.C., in contrast, could only enter a cease-and-desist order.

In every session of Congress from 1933 through 1937 Senator Copeland introduced his bill, which regularly failed to be passed, in part because of the F.T.C.'s vehement opposition to any surrender, or even sharing, of its power to regulate advertising. The Copeland bill that was finally enacted in 1938 was a much weaker law, and succeeded only because a calamity that caused several deaths roused public opinion and created demand for a new law that would guard the public from unsafe drugs.[24]

In 1935 one of the principal legislative tactics of the United Medicine Manufacturers of America, a leading pharmaceutical trade association, was to support F.T.C. retention of jurisdiction over drug advertising; drug manufacturers much preferred the Commission's slow-moving cease-and-desist procedure to the criminal prosecution authority of the F.D.A. Similarly in 1936 "the move to strip FDA of proposed advertising authority, leaving all advertising regulation with the Federal Trade Commission, was spearheaded by the Proprietary Association and the Institute of Medicine Manufacturers," which supported F.T.C. jurisdiction so that, if a bill were passed, "it would be as ineffective as possible."[25]

In 1937 the food canners joined the drug trade associations in opposing the Copeland proposals because of their seizure provisions. Once again the drug associations sought to have the F.T.C. retain exclusive jurisdiction over drug advertising because, as *Business Week* put it, "it is candidly admitted by food, drug and cosmetic advertisers that regulation by the Trade Commission would be less onerous than regulation by the Food and Drug Administration." The new drug proposals were not enacted. Congressman Clarence Lea, cosponsor of the Wheeler-Lea Amendment and chairman of the House Interstate and Foreign Commerce Committee, was instrumental in pigeonholing the Copeland Bill so that the Wheeler-Lea Amendment would reach the House floor first.[26]

By June 1937 it was clear that the function of the Wheeler-Lea Amendment was to block strong legislation on drugs by vesting exclusive jurisdiction over food and drug advertising in the F.T.C. *Business Week* observed that Congressman Lea was "sworn" to exclusive F.T.C. jurisdiction. And he incorporated modified provisions and definitions from Copeland's bill into his own so that it would appear that F.D.A. jurisdiction over food and drug advertising was unnecessary. In response to Lea's tactics, consumer groups planned to seek criminal jurisdiction by the Department of Justice if efforts to establish F.D.A. jurisdiction failed; they regarded F.T.C. jurisdiction over food and drug advertising as virtually worthless.[27]

Neither the Copeland nor the Wheeler-Lea bill reached the floor in 1937, but early in 1938, under the expert management of its sponsors, the Wheeler-Lea Bill reached the floor first.

The Wheeler-Lea Act

The F.T.C. recommended new legislation to outlaw "unfair or deceptive acts or practices" in its annual report for 1935. Such a bill was first introduced in 1936 by Burton K. Wheeler in the Senate and Lea in the House.[28] Its use as a device to block a vigorous drug bill was recognized almost immediately.

The sponsors of the Wheeler-Lea Bill portrayed it as a moderate, responsible bill consistent with the original Federal Trade Commission Act's purpose of guiding business through advice, information, and nonpunitive orders. The bill was asserted to provide for an expansion of the agency's area of concern to embrace consumer protection as well as the suppression of unfair competition; as Congressman Lea put it, "the principle of the Act is carried further to protect the consumer as well as the competitor."[29] Lea further observed that his bill had widespread business support, claiming—perhaps with some exaggeration—that 95 percent of business firms supported it.[30] Certainly such important trade associations as the American Pharmaceutical Manufacturers Association, the American Grocery Manufacturers Association, the Cooperative Food Distributors Association of America, and the National Association of Retail Grocers enthusiastically endorsed it. In contrast, as we have noted, consumer groups opposed the bill because they felt it provided an inadequate deterrent to false and misleading advertising of drugs.[31]

Aside from the negative aim of heading off passage of strong legislation on drugs, what did concerned business groups hope to see accomplished through the Wheeler-Lea Bill? In the course of the congressional hearings, the F.T.C.'s chief counsel gave some answers, based upon his discussions with businessmen. He pointed out that there are deceptive practices that an industry wishes to see stopped because they reflect adversely upon the industry as a whole and therefore can affect sales. But adoption of such a practice by one member of an industry compels other members to follow suit in self-defense. To prevent this sequence of events, "they [industry members] want permission to come before the Federal Trade Commission, put down on paper the practices they consider unfair, uneconomic and agree among themselves."[32]

As this statement indicates, business sought administrative protection against conduct that was bad for an industry as a whole or which was uneconomic. What kind of deceptive conduct fits this description? Obviously, deception that is likely to be quickly discovered by the consuming public and to lead to reduced demand for the generic product, thus harming not only the company engaging in the deceptive practice but other firms as well. This interpretation is supported by Charles Jackson's study of New Deal food and drug legislation, in which trade sources are cited as suggesting "that many prescription manufacturers felt that their business might be increased if more restrictive practices were placed on the marketing of proprietary balms."[33] In the same vein a leading trade journal, *Advertising and Selling,* pointed out that the drug distribution trade as a whole is harmed when deceptive claims are made for quack medicines.[34] And as the *Wall Street Journal* observed editorially on April 22, 1936, the F.T.C. is the proper agency to stop such claims because most of those against whom the agency proceeds in its atempt to block practices that are "unfair to competitors" are small fry, some of whom ordinarily market quack medicines.[35]

Thus business sought a statute that would discriminate finely—one that would deter false claims, whose discovery might adversely affect sales of a product class but would not penalize firms that made exaggerated claims only in response to the pressure to increase sales. Business sought a law that would preclude only certain kinds of claims, not one intended to deter all wrongdoers from making false advertising claims inimical to consumer interests. Further, the new law would have to maintain the 1914 law's ability to outlaw the use of deceptive advertising as a competitive weapon; yet reputable manufacturers must not be punished for the occasional piece of chicanery designed to stimulate sales. The Wheeler-Lea Amendment effectively balanced these competing considerations, and accordingly won the support of business groups. Suggestions were made in the course of the legislative debates that might have upset this delicate balance, but, as we shall see, they were not adopted.

The Wheeler-Lea Act in Congress

When the Wheeler-Lea Bill reached the House floor, it contained new sections providing for criminal penalties under very narrow circumstances. According to Section 14 of the Wheeler-Lea Bill, the F.T.C. could seek criminal penalties only if the food, drug, or cosmetic advertised was injurious to health when it was used under the conditions prescribed in the advertisement or if the Commission could prove specific intent to mislead.[36] Proof of specific intent is extremely difficult (as F.D.A. experience had shown), since a manufacturer is rarely careless enough to submit to a government agency documents that manifest a specific intent to defraud the public. The former provision, under which punishment would be imposed only when an advertisement's statements led to bodily harm, was attacked heatedly by a minority of the House Interstate and Foreign Commerce Committee because it would not deter most deceptive advertising of food, drugs, and cosmetics. This minority concluded that, given the agency's insufficient and weak enforcement powers (the cease-and-desist order) and its laggard pace in bringing matters to a conclusion, F.T.C. jurisdiction over such advertising would constitute a fraud on the consumer. "Unless the disseminator of a false advertisement knows at the time of the dissemination that he may at some time in the future be held accountable by a criminal or civil penalty action for the unlawful dissemination," said its report, "he will not be deterred from such dissemination. It is just this deterring effect that is lacking when dependence is placed upon the cease and desist order for enforcement."[37] And in support of its contention the minority noted that the F.T.C. had been active since its inception in opposing false advertising but that "the frequency with which false advertisements have been disseminated for the same products previously covered by cease and desist orders . . . would seem to demonstrate the ineffectiveness of the cease and desist order machinery in the case of false advertising."[38] Accordingly the minority proposed a provision under which substantial civil penalties could be assessed against the disseminator of a false or misleading advertisement of a food, drug, or cosmetic product. If such a provision were adopted, an advertiser would carefully consider the validity of his claims before making them, and thus consumers would be protected.[39]

Those who opposed F.T.C. jurisdiction first led a floor fight to strike from the Wheeler-Lea Bill those sections that dealt with advertising of food, drugs, and cosmetics. Failing in this effort, they then attempted to strengthen the criminal sections of the bill so that all false and deceptive advertising would be included. This move failed too, however, and the bill passed the House and then the Senate by large majorities. The measure was signed into law on March 21, 1938.[40]

During the course of the debates, proponents of the bill clearly indicated that under the Wheeler-Lea Amendment, business and the F.T.C. would be expected to cooperate in working out problems concerning false or deceptive advertising; deterrence was far from the sponsors' minds. Congressman Lea, for example, bitterly denounced the idea of subjecting businessmen to penalties, because that would "in effect largely destroy the usefulness of the Federal Trade Commission for ironing out difficulties with business instead of taking them into court."[41] In similar vein a Senate report on the bill stated that an F.T.C. proceeding, "unlike that under the Pure Food and Drug Act or the Postal Statutes, is merely preventative and cooperative rather than penal."[42]

Congressman Lea of course supported the imposition of criminal penalties on firms whose false or misleading claims resulted in injury to health, for this was the very kind of deception that would be discovered by consumers and would result in serious discredit to and financial loss for all drug manufacturers.[43] Thus the Wheeler-Lea Act trod a careful line between, on the one hand, the preservation of advertising flexibility and freedom from punishment for most transgressions and, on the other, the need to deter advertising that might lead to financial loss for manufacturers of a product because consumers' distrust of the claims made brought the whole drug industry into disrepute.[44]

When Will False Advertising Occur?

How effective has the Wheeler-Lea Act been in preventing deceptive advertising? The response almost uniformly offered is that it has been singularly ineffective. Before examining the reasons for this opinion and for the F.T.C.'s ineffectiveness, let us look at advertising from the perspective of competition to try to determine the scope of the problem. Specifically, which competitors are most apt to engage in deceptive advertising, and why? To answer these questions we must first try to delineate the incentives and disincentives for deception.

Richard Posner has listed three mechanisms, other than F.T.C. regulation and private litigation, that would tend to deter some false claims. The first "is the knowledge and intelligence of the consumer. Many false claims would not be worth making simply because the consumer knows better than to believe them."[45] The qualities of the product to which advertising relates can be divided into search qualities, experience qualities, and credence qualities. To make a claim about the qualities of a product readily available for inspection which even a superficial search will show to be untrue (search qualities) is an irrational thing for a seller to do. And it would be only slightly less irrational for him to make a claim that can be discovered at slight cost to be false after the product has been purchased (experience qualities), if the product is returnable or if repeat sales are hoped for. False claims can be rational only in the case of qualities that are expensive to judge after the purchase has been made (credence qualities).[46] Since large firms ordinarily display their consumer products in many outlets, where they may be readily inspected, claims pertaining to search qualities are economically irrational for such firms. Only smaller firms that lack outlets for the display of their wares and which seek a market of particularly gullible consumers have any incentive to make false claims about search qualities.

In most circumstances other competitive mechanisms operate to deter firms, especially the larger ones, from engaging in deceptive advertising concerning the experience and credence qualities of their goods. Most important is the cost to a seller of a reputation for dishonesty. As Posner observes,

a seller cannot expect a false claim to go undetected indefinitely. If the profitability of his business depends on repeated sales to the same customers, as is true of most established sellers, a policy of false advertising . . . is bad business: customers will take their business elsewhere after they discover the fraud. Even if the seller does not depend on repeat customers, prospective customers may hear about his fraud from his former customers and be deterred from patronizing him.[47]

This view is supported by an executive of one of the nation's largest advertising agencies (admittedly not an unbiased party), who argues that only fly-by-night outfits and others not interested in making repeat sales can rationally engage in deliberate deception. He points out that for "virtually all national advertising, the cost of making a sale through advertising is prohibitive unless the trial purchase results in a satisfied customer who comes back over and over again, thus amortizing the cost of the original advertising."[48] Whether we consider beer or automobiles, the danger of forfeiting a substantial market share certainly points a manufacturer away from deliberate deception. A declining or weak firm, on the other hand, is more apt to gamble on deception because it has less to lose. Finally, deception concerning the credence qualities of a product would be a sensible strategy if its discovery were near to impossible. This would be the case, for example, with the provision of highly technical services, such as medical or legal services.

A third factor that tends to deter deception in claims concerning experience and credence qualities is competition. Simply put, insofar as one firm's deceptive claims attract business away from another or prevent the other from gaining custom, the injured firm has a strong incentive to expose the deceiver. Firms in an oligopolistic industry are more likely than firms in an atomistic industry to engage in exposure exercises, first because they are more likely to have the resources to do so and second because they are more likely to perceive themselves as victims of deception. Moreover, as Posner hypothesizes, the injured firm is more likely to refute a falsehood than to commit a falsehood of its own, because exposing deception increases a firm's reputation for fair dealing and may gain for it not only the return of its lost customers but additional sales at the expense of its competitor.[49] It may also increase its immunity to attack on its own advertising.

Thus far, then, the indications are that there is less likelihood of deliberate deception on the part of large firms, particularly in oligopolistic industries that contain other large firms with retaliatory capabilities, than on the part of small firms in atomistic and unconcentrated industries. Moreover, in any industry small firms are more likely to practice deliberate deception than larger ones, since they have less to lose from the gamble and are more likely to be dissatisfied with their share of the market. But three important caveats should be entered. First, these arguments assume that firms operate rationally in pursuing such positive goals as increased sales and profits as well as the defensive goals of retaining current levels of sales and profits. That this is not always the case needs no demonstration. Second, we have been discussing deliberate misrepresentation. Any firm can negligently or inadvertently make a deceptive statement, although the chance is greater in the case of a small firm, since it is not likely to have available to it the host of advertising, marketing, and technical specialists employed by a larger firm, which *can* therefore (even if it does not necessarily) check more thoroughly the accuracy and implications of its statements. Third, and most important, there are situations in which every member of an industry benefits from misrepresentation or nondisclosure of material information. All cigarette firms, for example, suffer from revelation of the health hazards of their products. Similarly no dry cereal manufacturer benefits from exposure of the nutritional deficiencies of dry cereals in general. All benefit from claims espousing the virtues of their products, and comparative affirmative claims about such qualities are accordingly the competitive order of the day. A tire manufacturer's response to a claim made by a competitor concerning the safety of his product is likely to be not an attack on the safety of his competitor's tires but an exaggeration about the safety of his own. Some subjects, in a word, are competitively out of bounds; attacks that might arouse consumer doubts about the product class as a whole are outside the scope of competitive advertising.

Thus members of an industry are more likely to close ranks against disclosure than to be severally guilty of affirmative misrepresentation. For this reason, as we shall see, orders and trade regulation rules requiring disclosure of undesirable attributes that may be important to consumers constitute one of the most valuable parts of the F.T.C.'s work in the area of deceptive practices. Before we turn to the substance of the Commission's work, however, let us look at the scope of the problem it faces.

The Scope of Advertising

The extent, impact, and persuasiveness of advertising and other forms of communication about articles of commerce or services in American society can scarcely be exaggerated. Every level of trade, from manufacturer to retailer, uses advertising, whether through radio, television, magazines, daily newspapers, billboards, labels, in-store signs, or direct mailings. Many firms advertise a multitude of products and make a variety of claims about each of them. And each firm changes its claims and its advertising copy frequently.

A brief examination of the pertinent statistics will illustrate the extent and growth of advertising expenditures. Table 12 shows the

Table 12. Volume of advertising expenditures, 1940–1974 (in billions of dollars)

Year	Expenditures
1940	$ 1.691
1950	4.585
1965	12.297
1974	26.500*

Sources: Jules Backman, *Advertising and Competition* (New York: New York University Press, 1967), p. 189, and *Advertising Age,* December 16, 1974, p. 1.
* Approximate.

increase in the volume of expenditures between 1940 and 1974. The fact that total advertising expenditures by the 100 largest advertisers was $5.58 billion in 1973 (and presumably slightly more in 1974), or little more than a fifth of the total, is an indication of how wide-spread the use of advertising is throughout the economy.[50] Moreover, as Table 13 shows, expenditures are distributed among a number of

Table 13. Advertising expenditures in major media, 1956 and 1963 (in millions of dollars)

Year	Maga-zines	News-papers	Radio	Tele-vision	Direct mail	Total (including others)
1956	$ 795	$3,236	$568	$1,207	$1,419	$ 9,905
1963	1,034	3,804	789	2,032	2,078	13,107

Source: Jules Backman, *Advertising and Competition* (New York: New York University Press, 1967), pp. 178–179.

media, and the proportion going to each has changed over time. And, as we noted in Chapter 3, the number of advertising messages with which consumers are bombarded every day is in the billions.

The problem, of course, lies not in the extent of advertising but in the judgment that a significant but undetermined portion of it is either false or deceptive. Estimates of the proportion that is false or deceptive vary widely, but even if it is only a small percentage of the total, the problem for the consumer is, in absolute terms, substantial.[51] The prevailing view is that asserted in 1969 by the commission appointed by the American Bar Association at the behest of President Richard Nixon, which concluded that there was a "general conviction that marketing frauds against consumers are widespread and constitute a problem of major national concern."[52] The commission observed that the same conclusion had been reached by independent sources, various congressional committees, the National Advisory Commission on Civil Disorders, and the Federal Trade Commission itself.

National trade associations and other business organizations too have reached the same conclusion. The Pharmaceutical Manufacturers Association estimated in 1961 that "each year . . . 100,000 health phonies victimize 25 million Americans";[53] the F.D.A. concluded that $500 million is spent annually just on vitamins, minerals, and health foods, the need for which is misrepresented by sellers; and the American Medical Association has calculated that Americans spend $500 million each year on dietary preparations as a result of deception.[54] Congressional studies have concluded that deception is widespread in the marketing of such important commodities as weight-reducing preparations and tranquilizers.[55]

The problem of consumer fraud is further aggravated by the fact that its impact is not felt randomly by the population as a whole but is concentrated on such groups as the elderly and the poor—those who can least afford to squander resources on unneeded goods and services. The National Better Business Bureau has estimated that the elderly spend hundreds of millions of dollars annually on products that are deceptively advertised, while a Nader study group has concluded that the poor have been particularly susceptible to fraudulent advertising.[56] In short, the prevailing view is that losses resulting from consumer fraud, although difficult to measure, are enormous. Indeed, the Nixon administration, through its special assistant to the President for consumer affairs, characterized the problem as one that had reached crisis proportions.[57]

Has the problem been alleviated in the 1970s as a result of the widespread publicity on consumer protection that began in the mid-1960s? There is simply no way of determining whether a significant change has taken place. My own comparison of the 1970–1971 and

1975 advertisements in magazines directed at less educated, gullible consumers—such publications as *Movie Mirror, Screen Stars, Movie World, True Romance, True Confessions, Confession Time, Photo Screen,* and *Modern Romances*—led me to conclude that the tone had not changed in the least. While not necessarily deceptive, many advertisements in both periods made claims that were at least open to question. Among them were advertisements for lotions that would make hair "healthier," devices that would lead to greater sexual fulfillment, cosmetics that would make "wrinkles fade away in just 10 minutes," devices that would remove "ugly" hairs forever, creams and devices for bust development, and diet plans. Hundreds of advertisements in each of the magazines examined made questionable claims of this sort. And all of them were placed by small firms—in no case was a firm large enough to appear in the *Fortune* list of the 500 largest corporations. Since we are dealing here not with esoteric publications but with mass-circulation magazines, one is compelled to conclude, in the absence of better evidence, that the problem of deceptive advertising continues. We must ask, therefore, why the F.T.C. has made so little impact in this area. Is it because of misdirected output? Or is it because administrative regulation by the F.T.C. is an inappropriate means for attacking the problem of deceptive advertising?

The F.T.C. and the Wheeler-Lea Act

Both critics and agency personnel have concluded that the F.T.C. has failed to change the tone of advertising. In 1969 the Nader group charged the F.T.C. with devoting an inordinate amount of effort to cases involving marginal harm to consumers while ignoring the deception perpetrated by large firms advertising in mass media. They further concluded that the poor and other groups who are particularly vulnerable to fraudulent advertising are especially unprotected by the F.T.C.[58] This line was followed by the American Bar Association Commission, too, which complained:

While simultaneously asserting the lack of manpower and funds to initiate programs to combat ghetto frauds, monitor advertising, and secure effective compliance with orders, the F.T.C. has issued complaints attacking the failure to disclose on labels that "Navy shoes" were not made by the Navy, that flies were imported, that Indian trinkets were not manufactured by American Indians, and that "Havana" cigars were not made entirely of Cuban tobacco.[59]

These attacks, the most recent in a long line, received official acknowledgement in 1971 when the F.T.C.'s chairman admitted that the goal of truthfulness in advertising was nowhere near being achieved and that the existence of the agency and its statutes had not raised the tone of advertising, much of which was uninformative and treated consumers "like gullible dupes."[60]

These charges will be examined in the next chapter, where I shall seek to explain the Commission's output. It should be observed here, however, that the critics' charges have been greatly exaggerated. The F.T.C. has attacked the practices of large firms since its inception. It has entered orders, for example, against the Aluminum Company of America, General Motors, and the Ford Motor Company. And it sought to impose a trade regulation rule on cigarette manufacturers requiring health warnings well before the wave of adverse criticism. The explanation for the fact that few respondents have been large firms lies in the economic incentives and disincentives to false advertising discussed earlier rather than in F.T.C. timidity. Many orders have been entered, too, against firms making false medical claims.[61] As with other attacks on the Commission, the critics here used just some of the F.T.C.'s output to find an unwarranted nexus with its relative lack of impact on the problem of deceptive advertising.

A very different hypothesis concerning this lack of impact was offered in 1970 by Philip Elman, perhaps the F.T.C.'s most thoughtful commissioner since its birth. Pointing out that the agency was originally designed to guide business firms in their competitive methods and to enter cease-and-desist orders, Elman observed that such sanctions are

grossly inadequate for handling consumer frauds that involve fly-by-night operators to whom the Federal Trade Commission . . . and its voluntary compliance and cease-and-desist procedures are . . . meaningless and unthreatening. Such a swindler does not need to be told by a registered letter from Washington that he is violating the law—he knows it, and his sole purpose is to continue his frauds as long as possible. The cease-and-desist order, if and when it comes, will merely order the respondent to sin no more. . . . For such racketeers, this is virtually no sanction, and thus no effective deterrent.[62]

In other words, the F.T.C.'s inability to deal with consumer fraud lies in its statutory deficiencies, principally the ineffectiveness of the cease-and-desist order. The Commission has labored mightily to circumvent this limitation, especially in recent years through the trade regulation rule and other new techniques that will shortly be examined. But its basic tool remains the cease-and-desist order. Let us, then, look further at the agency's problems in this respect.

When the F.T.C. obtains an order against a firm engaging in deceptive advertising, the order enjoins only the kind of deception involved in the proceeding. The violating firm is thus free to use any other deceptive claim that it can devise. To take a hypothetical example, an automobile manufacturer may employ false horsepower claims, then false durability claims, then deceptive pricing claims, and so on and on; limitation lies only in the inventiveness of the firm's advertising copywriters. No wonder, then, that the F.T.C. has been unable to stop false advertising.

In addition, the facts of each case must be examined separately and investigated, even those involving alleged violations of trade regulation rules. Given the enormous potential for fraud, the F.T.C.'s output of orders and complaints is meager indeed, because public policy works through the cumbersome process of litigation. As Table 14 shows, the number of consumer-protection complaints and orders

Table 14. Number of F.T.C. complaints and orders concerning false and misleading advertising, FY 1963–1969

F.T.C. output	1963	1964	1965	1966	1967	1968	1969
Complaints	127	129	66	48	108	45	65
Cease-and-desist orders	118	161	67	51	96	53	68

Source: American Bar Association, *Report of the ABA Commission to Study the Federal Trade Commission* (Chicago, 1969), p. 20.

varies from year to year, but never reached 200 in either category in any year from 1963 through 1969. There was a spurt in 1971, but then the number of consumer protection orders dwindled again, as Table 15, showing consent and contested orders, indicates. The relatively small number of orders entered in 1974 cannot be explained on the basis of a shift to such new procedures as the trade regulation rule; from fiscal 1971 through the first three quarters of

Table 15. Number of F.T.C. consent orders and contested cease-and-desist orders, FY 1971–1974

Fiscal year	Consent orders	Contested cease-and-desist orders
1971	159	8
1972	116	4
1973	99	4
1974*	11	1

Source: U.S. House of Representatives, Committee on Interstate and Foreign Commerce, 93rd Cong., 1st sess., 1975, *Staff Report: The Federal Trade Commission, 1974,* p. 18.
* For first three quarters only.

fiscal 1974 the total number of proposed and final rules and industry guides was only twenty-four.[63]

In summary, then, the Wheeler-Lea Act provides the F.T.C. with singularly inappropriate instruments with which to deter fraud. As we saw in Chapter 3, the Commission has no means of detecting deception other than hit-and-miss monitoring—hardly a systematic mechanism to deal with the enormous volume of advertising messages radiated daily. Further, the agency has almost no technical facility for evaluating complex claims. Under the act, it must assess every conceivable kind of claim for every conceivable kind of commodity, and is given no specific tools for the job. So in the past it adopted the mailbag approach to gathering information on possible violations; and under this approach, as we have seen, letters from affected businessmen make up the most important class of complaints, for in most instances only competitors are sufficiently knowledgeable about a product to point out misrepresentations. Competitors carefully scrutinize their rivals' products, advertising, and other practices and have the knowledge to detect deception; consumers often remain deceived. Thus for most of the agency's career, the matters brought to its attention have largely reflected the priorities of affected businessmen, not those of consumers.

The Commission's personnel have been aware of the problem and have always sought to develop complaints from sources other than affected businessmen. Such public scandals as the "payola" controversy of the early 1960s have provided one alternative source of complaint. And monitoring, particularly of national television advertising, has been another. But as withering attacks on the mailbag

approach and scathing ridicule of some of its cases continued, the
F.T.C. sought new remedies.

New Remedies

Beginning in 1971 the Commission developed several new remedies
and a new technique to elicit information and deter extravagant advertising claims. The new remedies include orders of corrective or
retroactive advertising and orders of restitution or repayment; the
new technique is to treat a claim that an advertiser does not sub-
stantiate as an unfair act, thus apparently shifting the burden of
proof. Let us first look at corrective or retroactive advertising. One
case concerned several allegedly deceptive statements made by a
manufacturer of cranberry juice.[64] In the consent order Ocean Spray
Cranberries, Inc., agreed to devote 25 percent of its media time for
one year to a corrective advertisement stating in part: "If you've
wondered what some of our earlier advertising meant when we said
[our product] has more food energy than orange juice or tomato juice,
let us make it clear. We didn't mean vitamins and minerals. Food
energy means calories. Nothing more."[65] Another respondent agreed
to run a retroactive advertisement stating, in effect, that its tires were
of less than first quality.[66] Such consent orders have usually required
that a given percentage of advertising time be devoted to the corrective advertisement. Whether the firm advertises at all is its business. Some orders, however, have required respondents to advertise
corrections, as in the case of alleged false claims by trade associations,
which are under no necessary competitive compulsion to advertise
at all.[67]

Up to the end of the third quarter of 1975 the Commission had
not required a consumer warning in any contested case. All orders
of corrective advertising had been made either at the level of the
initial decision or through consent procedures. Nevertheless, the
F.T.C.'s statements on the subject leave no doubt that it was prepared
to enter such an order in a contested case.[68] Rejecting the argument
that an order demanding corrective advertising is both punitive and
retrospective, and therefore outside its powers, the F.T.C. concluded
that such an order might be necessary to dissipate the lingering effects
of a particular deception and is therefore both prospective and within
its powers.[69] But while the assertion of power is persuasive, the Commission does not tell us precisely when such a remedy is called for

and when it is not, or what guidelines it would use to ensure that its order did not go beyond dissipating the lingering effects of deception into the forbidden area of punishment. To take an extreme example, if a firm that had engaged in a single instance of innocuous deception in a local newspaper were required to announce that it was a liar over nationwide television for the next ten years, the order would probably be held to be punishment.

The question also arises of how effective a remedy corrective advertising will be in contested cases. Among the important factors about which the Commission would have to produce evidence in trying to justify an order and show that it was not punitive are these: (1) the length of time consumers remained aware of an advertisement after it appeared; (2) the size of the audience reached and its characteristics; (3) the frequency with which the advertisement ran; (4) the length of time it ran; (5) the blatancy of the deception; (6) the danger to health and safety raised by the advertisement; and (7) the effectiveness to consumer consciousness of the claims made in the advertisement. Put simply, corrective orders are an open invitation to prolonged litigation and therefore lose their deterrent effect for firms to which continuation of a deception is important. Nevertheless, preliminary research indicates that corrective advertising does affect consumers' attitudes toward a product, so some deterrent effect is indicated.[70] This type of order is not an answer to the fundamental regulatory problem of delay, however, or to the lack of a comprehensive strategy to thwart deception.

A more promising remedy is restitution. In a typical case, the F.T.C. charged a chain of drugstores with making certain claims in advertising relating to the safety characteristics of safety helmets. As part of the consent settlement, the respondent agreed to refund the purchase price in cash to any person who had relied on the misrepresentation and who returned a helmet within thirty days after publication of a notice.[71] In 1974 the Court of Appeals for the Ninth Circuit ruled that the F.T.C. did not have the power to order restitution when procedures existed for adjudicating private rights. Rejecting the Commission's argument that its order was prospective and tantamount to telling the respondent to cease and desist from holding misappropriated funds, the Court pointed to a recent bill that would have given the F.T.C. the power it was claiming because, in Congress' view, it did not already have it.[72] The issue became moot in 1975, however, when the Magnuson-Moss Act explicitly granted the F.T.C. authority to seek restitution in court proceedings on behalf of consumers in any instance that "a reasonable man would have known under the circumstances was dishonest or fraudulent." Such redress is to be compensatory and not punitive.

Again there is little question that the power to seek restitution on behalf of bilked consumers will have some additional deterrent effect; but it still does not answer the problem of delay—and indeed an even longer delay is now in prospect, since the F.T.C. must go through its own procedures and enter a final cease-and-desist order before it can commence a civil action in court. Nor does it provide a mechanism for the discovery of specific instances of fraud in the vast sea of possible fraud. Will the power of restitution have a significantly greater deterrent effect, then, than existing private remedies for consumer fraud, which, according to concerned investigators, have had precious little effect?

The problems of discovery and proof remain to plague the agency. But one ingenious new step has been taken to try to shift the burden of proof in some matters—the introduction of the advertising substantiation program, also known as the Pfizer doctrine. In the leading case the Commission held that it is unfair—although not necessarily deceptive—for a firm to make affirmative claims in advertising a product without having reasonable support for the claim. The argument applies even if the claim is true and the product performs as advertised. The unfairness lies in the imposition on the consumer of an avoidable economic risk that the product may not perform as advertised. Moreover, "fairness to competitors requires that the vendor have a reasonable basis for his affirmative product claims. A sale made as a result of an unsupported advertising claim deprives competitors of the opportunity to have made that sale themselves."[73]

What, then, is a reasonable basis for an affirmative claim? The Commission has stated that this issue is a factual one and consideration will be given to the type and accessibility of the evidence that is the basis for a particular claim. Would independent scientific tests be required for every claim, or could general knowledge of a product, technical literature, expertise, and some testing be sufficient? While the F.T.C.'s answer is by no means clear, its position has been rather stringent. In a case concerning the strength of tires, a retailer advertised its brand as having "polyester construction for added strength," relying on government standards and a letter from the manufacturer as the basis for its claim. The F.T.C. held these grounds to be insufficient, however, and the consent order required scientific tests with a 95 percent confidence level—that is, tests in which nineteen of each twenty tires tested supported the claim.[74] The issue arose in the first place because, while polyester construction undeniably does add strength, other factors also play a part in determining the strength of a tire.

While the legal theory of advertising substantiation is an ingenious one, aimed in part at shifting the burden of proof, the technique is subject to important criticisms and limitations. First, it may lead to the squandering of resources—resources that are already inadequate to cope with consumer fraud—on claims that are largely true and that cause the consumer no harm. Such, indeed, seems to be the trend in cases brought thus far by the Commission. Second, even if test results on technical claims are forthcoming, the F.T.C. must still devote considerable resources to ascertaining their accuracy and veracity. Third, as a leading advertising executive has observed, the consumer will have to pay the extra costs involved in stringent testing programs and may receive only marginal benefit, or none. Fourth, as another advertising executive has observed, since the program began, major advertisers have shifted the emphasis of their advertising away from the content of the message to acting and music: "It sounds good but it doesn't tell the consumer anything about the product. This is to me a form of deceit."[75] Fifth, as Richard Posner has observed, "The burden of the new policy will fall most heavily on new products and firms. By increasing costs to new entrants the policy will tend to thwart antitrust policies."[76]

Conclusion

The most important indication of the importance of advertising as a competitive weapon is the vast sums firms spend on it. These outlays can expand demand for the generic product, but they also help one firm to gain custom at the expense of its rivals. Advertising expenditures will not on their own bring about a large increase in sales, of course; other factors, such as price, the nature of the product, and follow-up sales effort, are also of major importance.[77] Nevertheless, advertising can play a major role in increasing sales when it artfully converts minor utilitarian differences into vast psychological differences.[78] In other words, advertising can be an important weapon to a firm that is seeking to increase its sales and profits. It is hardly the sole competitive device, and some advertising campaigns have failed in their purposes; but judging from the size of advertising expenditures in some industries, it is an important weapon.

Viewing advertising as a major means of competition, the F.T.C. used its original mandate to prevent unfair methods of competition by bringing cases against firms that engaged in deceptive advertising aimed at specific rivals and competing products. Yet even at this early stage the Commission tried to protect consumers as well as competitors, as the first Raladam case shows. Nevertheless, the principal focus was on cases of interest to competitors, not consumers.

The Wheeler-Lea Act did not alter this focus; it merely supplemented the older act in certain respects. The criminal provisions of the amendment applied to drug advertising that could lead to bodily harm. As we have noted, these are precisely the claims that will almost necessarily be discovered by consumers. And experience had shown that when consumers linked advertising with harmful results, sales of the whole product class suffered, and indeed sales of drugs generally. Accordingly, the concerned industries sought to deter this kind of conduct. At the same time the Wheeler-Lea Act's mild deterrent effect with respect to other kinds of advertising claims permitted firms to make extravagant statements with relative impunity. If the F.T.C. serves a complaint against one kind of claim, the firm can shift to another kind of statement in its continuing effort to boost sales.

The Wheeler-Lea Act was a compromise piece of legislation that reflected the conflict between preserving advertising as an important competitive weapon and preventing the damage to industry stability that could result if outlandish or dangerous claims destroyed consumer confidence in a whole industry or brought disrepute to the industry's products. Desire for some regulation on the one hand and fear of excessive measures on the other led to the structure of the Wheeler-Lea Act. But the act's weaknesses—in failure to provide for adequate means to discover wrongdoing, for quick and effective redress, or for technical means to evaluate claims—have had important consequences for agency enforcement. First the F.T.C. has largely, even if not entirely, had to rely upon the affected business community as its source of information about deception. And clearly the priorities of affected businessmen and consumers may diverge. Since the severe chastisements of 1969, however, the agency has sought to develop other sources of complaint.

Of even greater consequence than the agency's output is its apparent inability to prevent and deter consumer fraud. The weakness of the Wheeler-Lea Act is primarily responsible for the F.T.C.'s lack of impact. Both before and after 1969 the Commission developed ingenious legal theories and remedies in a valiant attempt to protect consumers. But given a statute that reflects hesitation about sharp curbs on advertising, its efficacy has necessarily been limited.

CHAPTER 8

The Control of Flimflam

The phrase "deceptive acts and practices" is, of course, susceptible to a wide range of interpretations and can cover virtually any advertising message or claim that is not entirely accurate. Where any ambiguity in meaning exists, someone may be deceived. The F.T.C. was therefore called upon early in its administration of the Wheeler-Lea Act to try to define its standards. What kind of person is to be the measure of deception: the informed consumer, the reasonable man, the person of average intelligence, or someone of thoroughgoing stupidity? In opting for the last alternative the F.T.C. claimed the broadest possible ambit for the concept of deception and was supported by the Supreme Court in the 1937 Standard Education case.

In that case the respondent had sold a set of encyclopedia volumes together with a series of loose-leaf supplements known as "the extension service," which subscribers were to receive quarterly for ten years. Salesmen always told buyers that the initial set was given away and that only the service was paid for. The Commission found this practice to be deceptive since in fact the price charged was expected to cover the costs of both the initial set of books and the extension service, plus profit. The Court of Appeals reversed the Commission's ruling, holding that "we cannot take seriously the suggestion that a man who is buying a set of books and a ten year 'extension service' will be fatuous enough to be misled by the mere statement that the first are given away, and that he is paying only for the second. Nor can we conceive how he could be damaged were he to suppose that that was true. Such trivial niceties are too impalpable for practical affairs, they are will-o'-the-wisps, which divert attention from substantial evils."[1] The Court of Appeals thus sought to restrict the application of the phrase "deceptive practice" by limiting the interpretation so that reasonably uninformed people would be protected but not those of colossal naiveté and stupidity. It assumed that only an extraordinary dullard would believe that a firm in business for profit would give away a significant part of its merchandise. Adopting a standard that would cover such a dullard, the Court warned prophetically, would lead the Commission to devote much energy to trivia that caused no objective harm to consumers and diverted attention and resources from substantial problems. But the Court of Appeals was reversed by the Supreme Court, which, in upholding the F.T.C., stated: "the fact that a false statement may be obviously false to those who are trained and experienced does not change its character, nor take away its power to deceive others less experienced. . . . Laws are made to protect the trusting as well as the suspicious."[2]

The Supreme Court thus gave its blessing to what has been called the Mortimer Snerd standard. Encouraged, the Commission tested further the boundaries of what could be reached under the heading of deceptive practices. As George Alexander stated, "General stupidity is not the only attribute of the beneficiary of F.T.C. policy. He also has a short attention span; he does not read all that is to be read but snatches general impressions. He signs things he has not read, has marginal eyesight, and is frightened by dunning letters when he has not paid his bills."[3] In short, even if most people would disregard a claim as patently absurd or mere puffery, the F.T.C. is free to proceed against an advertiser if a few extraordinarily naive persons may be deceived.

But just as the standard concerning the intellectual level of persons to be protected gives the Commission great latitude, so does the objective standard of deception. Obviously claims that misstate facts are deceptive, but equally deceptive are claims that "are capable of two meanings, one of which is false," and claims that "create a false impression although literally true."[4] Further, claims that are literally true but the proof for which is false have been held to be deceptive; for example, television mock-ups that give viewers perceptions that are different from studio reality may be deceptive even though the claim being made is literally true.[5] Finally, a claim may be deceptive when pertinent drawbacks are not mentioned. In brief, then, virtually any claim containing any ambiguity may be susceptible to an F.T.C. complaint of deception, regardless of the respondent's intentions or the degree of harm to the consumer's health, safety, or pocketbook. Only literal truthfulness, with no overtones of ambiguity or qualification, and simple puffery are safe. Given the brevity of most advertising messages in relation to the sum total of relevant facts about virtually any product, literal truthfulness is nearly impossible. There is almost always some ambiguity that may be misunderstood by a few gullible consumers, and almost invariably some information set forth is subject to an unstated qualification or drawback. Nor on inspection does puffery offer much more hope. Puffery is generally conceived of as enthusiastic descriptions that cannot be objectively disproved.[6] Yet the distinction between deception and puffery turns out to be illusory, or at best hazy; for virtually any general enthusiastic statement can be reduced to an objective claim susceptible of being tested under the Mortimer Snerd standard.[7]

We can illustrate the point by examining briefly some advertisements that appeared in the October 1975 issue of *Ladies' Home Journal,* a magazine long known for its high advertising standards and its refusal to accept questionable advertisements. Page 86 bears a picture of the hands of a mother and daughter holding dishes, and a statement that after years of using a detergent, "the mother's hands look almost as young as her own daughter's." To Mortimer Snerd this comment might suggest that the preparation being advertised retards the aging process. An advertisement for bananas (page 117) claims that they satisfy "snack appetites." Surely they do not in many cases. As a final example, page 121 speaks of a steak sauce that adds a "zesty flavor to *any* meatloaf you make" and promises that *"everyone* in your family" will "love" the taste. Little purpose would be served by further illustrations of the fact that the distinction between puffery and deception is more semantic than real. And one is inexorably led to the conclusion that under existing standards the F.T.C. could complain about virtually every advertisement in every medium.

At first blush these standards might appear to invite the Commission to fish randomly for examples of deception, since it will almost invariably find a statutory violation. But this conclusion neglects the important distinction between standards of proof and proof of violation. The Commission must prove the facts of violation, which are often complex, not merely suspect them. Therefore it relied in the past on knowledgeable letters of complaint, usually from affected businessmen who suffered some competitive disadvantage because of a claim and were in a position to bring sufficient information to the agency's attention to justify further investigation and ultimately a formal complaint. The insidious effect of the broad standards adopted is that virtually any claim brought to the Commission's attention in this way can be shown to be deceptive provided some supporting facts are mustered. So businessmen pursuing a competitive interest could show that deception had taken place even when the matter was of little objective consequence to the consumer's health, safety, or purse. The American Bar Association Commission's finding that the agency had devoted considerable effort to acting "at the behest of one group of industry members against another group" is thus not surprising.[8]

Those victimized by fraud are often ignorant of how they were bilked and unaware of where to complain; so the F.T.C. is often not supplied with information about fraud that affects the poor—as both the Nader group and the American Bar Association Commission complained. Somewhere out there are misleading credit terms, exaggerated earnings claims, and exaggerated utility claims for shoddy merchandise; the difficulties lie in finding the deception and then proving the facts.[9] I do not suggest, of course, that every case pursued by the Commission has originated with affected businessmen. Some have stemmed from consumer complaints and from the F.T.C.'s own monitoring service. Monitoring in particular has been a major basis of attacks on advertising by large firms, especially in cases that have employed the novel legal theory of advertising substantiation and the Colgate doctrine on television mock-ups. Advertising by large firms is widespread and thus very visible. Moreover, since complaints against very large firms have the effect of blunting the critics' charge that the Commission proceeds only against small firms, there is a strong incentive to monitor carefully claims made by giant advertisers and to employ a theory of deception against them. But unless one accepts as an article of faith the questionable but very popular view that bigness equals badness, one is likely to conclude that cases of this sort, like cases brought at the behest of affected businessmen, have no significant effect on consumers' safety, health, or income.

The problem, then, is not that the net impact of F.T.C. orders concerning deceptive practices has been harmful to consumer interests. Rather, as Judge Learned Hand predicted in the Standard Education case, the breadth of the concept of deception coupled with the manner in which the agency discovers violations has led to an em-

phasis on trivial cases—including those involving large firms and
novel legal theories—and little attention to substantial consumer
frauds. On the other hand, however, when matters of real import to
consumers have been brought to the F.T.C.'s attention—for example,
cases of land-sale fraud, false health claims, and home improvement
schemes—the agency has always acted, and not just since 1969. Nevertheless, as we noted in the previous chapter, the almost uniform impression is that its activities in such areas have had virtually no impact
on these problems in the aggregate.

Let us turn now to some of the cases to which the agency has devoted considerable attention and explore their implications. And, let
us compare the period 1956–1964—before the publication of the
major reports criticizing the F.T.C.'s output—with the 1970s to see
what differences can be discovered. For the later period we shall concentrate on the Commission's decisions on deceptive and unfair
practices under Section 5 of the F.T.C. Act in 1973, as published in
volume 82 of F.T.C. decisions. The Commission's emphasis can
change from year to year, of course, but some differences between the
pre- and post-1969 patterns may be discernible.

Many F.T.C. cases are sui generis and do not easily fit into any
category. I must also emphasize that this examination is not an attempt to discuss comprehensively F.T.C. cases involving deceptive
practices; such an effort would occupy many volumes.

Product Comparisons

F.T.C. action against product comparisons grows out of the common law tort of "palming off"—misrepresentation of another's goods
as one's own. If such conduct were permitted, the orderly operation
of the commercial system would be disrupted, because the incentive
to develop and market new products would be considerably lessened.
For this reason, and not primarily because of any adverse effect upon
the consumer, this kind of business conduct was declared under
common law to be unfair competition. Early in its life the F.T.C.
declared palming off to be an unfair method of competition, and it
expanded the basic concept to embrace related conduct as well.

A notable example of F.T.C. action to prevent comparisons involved the long-standing battle between oleomargarine producers and
dairymen, which culminated in the enactment of the Oleomargarine
Act in 1950. That act, sponsored by Senator Joseph McCarthy of

Wisconsin at the behest of dairy producers and farmers, amended
the Federal Trade Commission Act in such a way that any advertisement for an oleomargarine product that represented oleomargarine
as a dairy product or suggested in any manner that it might be considered one was deemed to be legally false.[10] The Oleomargarine Act
unambiguously outlawed from public advertising a certain kind of
statement. Under the act (which has been largely unenforced in recent years) a margarine manufacturer was enjoined from using the
trade name "Creamo" and retailers were forbidden to advertise
margarine with cheese, milk, and butter under the heading "dairy
products."[11] No extended discussion is required to suggest that consumers suffer no ill effects from this kind of deception and that the
principal beneficiaries of its prohibition are members of the dairy industry, who seek justification for higher prices for butter through
product differentiation.

The Oleomargarine Act is obviously intended to prevent competitive comparisons between two products. A great many other F.T.C.
orders under the Wheeler-Lea Act have the same aim. Usually the
firms against which such orders have been entered are small and the
dollar volume of advertising involved is not substantial. In almost no
case was the deception of major consequence to the consumer, and in
some cases there was no real difference in quality between the two
products. But the differentiation that complainants sought to preserve
was of significant pecuniary value to them.

Typical cases during 1956–1964 involved the use of such terms as
"porcenamal" to describe a finish for awnings that contained no
enamel; "Chatham Emeralds" to describe synthetic stones seemingly
identical to natural stones; "Atlas Rubber" to describe combs made
only in part of rubber; "charcoal" to describe briquets made from
lignite rather than wood charcoal; "Australian Oak" to describe euca-
lyptus; "Copy Calf" to describe ladies' handbags made of a synthetic
material; "Stone China" to describe dinnerware not made of china;
"Deerelk" to describe leather shoes made from neither deer nor elk
hides; "Bianco Marble" to describe trophies made of alabaster; and
"cultured" or "Cultique" to describe imitation pearls.[12]

All these cases involve new products with trade names that invite
comparison with older, established products. The trade names are,
however, distinct from those of the older products. The term "Copy
Calf," for example, explicitly invites comparison yet clearly indicates

that it is a copy of calfskin. The term is deceptive (although not false) because a very gullible person might confuse "Copy Calf" with calfskin. Usually such cases are brought to the Commission's attention by zealous trade associations, which also provide experts to aid the F.T.C. in proving deception.[13] Even statements explicitly indicating that a product is not what it is being compared with—"leather-like vinyl," for example—are unsafe under the Mortimer Snerd standard.[14]

The Commission not only has cast a sharp eye on interproduct comparisons but has enforced distinctions adopted within an industry, usually in the form of industry standards promulgated by a trade association at the behest of old established members. Whether the distinction is objectively important to consumers has been, for the Commission, beside the point. Typical 1956–1964 cases in which the F.T.C. placed its imprimatur upon certain industry standards or descriptions approved by a trade association involved such terms as "plateless engraved," "sterling silver," "jeweled," "down," "gem," "top-grain cowhide," and "pure bristle."[15] In these cases, it should be noted, the industry's objective standard is used; whether or not the consuming public has a clear understanding of what a particular term means is beside the point.[16] In instances of genuine dispute over the meaning of a term, moreover, the Commission has usually opted for the definition selected by the established firms whose products are more expensive than those of their newer rivals. For example, the F.T.C. ruled that the term "bristle" when used in the sale of paintbrushes may be applied only to coarse swine hair and not to cheaper horsehair.[17]

Another group of product-comparison cases comprise those involving the claim or implication that a product is new when in fact it is used or rebuilt. During the 1950s and 1960s the F.T.C. entered many orders of this sort, concentrating on two commodities, television tubes and motor oil. The television-tube cases were brought to the F.T.C.'s attention by small manufacturers concerned about the inroads being made in the market by rebuilders of tubes. No evidence was adduced to show that the rebuilt or reconditioned tubes were inferior to new ones, although the respondents' failure to disclose the fact that the tubes were rebuilt indicates that it was probably important to consumers.[18] In the cases focusing on reused motor oil, in fact, the Commission conceded that the reclaimed product (obtained from crankcase drainings) was of the same quality as new oil.[19]

All of these cases involved claims that sought to enhance one set of products by comparing them favorably to older, more established products. Additional cases have been brought involving firms that have disparaged or deprecated competitors and their products. The Commission devoted a great deal of attention to disparagement cases early in its career explicitly to prevent this sort of competition, whether or not deception or falsity were involved.[20]

Since passage of the Wheeler-Lea Act, the F.T.C. has acted against disparagement only when claims have contained elements of falsity or deception.[21] But, as we have seen, the change from the earlier standard is to some extent illusory, since proof of deception is relatively easy. As in other cases, the substantive deception usually has no effect on the consumer's pocketbook, safety, health, or welfare, but has significant competitive impact. For example, a leading shaving cream manufacturer ran a two-panel television commercial, one panel showing a man shaving with the respondent's shaving cream and apparently enjoying it, the other showing him in obvious discomfort as he shaved with a competitor's lather. The sound track asserted that ordinary lather dries out and that the respondent's does not.[22] The substance used to illustrate the pleasant shave was a mixture specially prepared to simulate shaving cream. The commercial was therefore deceptive, since the subjective perception (shaving cream) did not correspond to the objective product. The F.T.C. did not show that the message itself was false. There was no evidence that consumers were getting an inferior product for their money or that their health, safety, or welfare was being impaired. On the contrary, the evidence indicated that the respondent's shaving cream was an entirely adequate product; but the success of the commercial was a matter of great importance to rivals.

Since 1969 the number of cases that have involved product comparisons has sharply declined, though such cases have not disappeared altogether. Of the fewer than thirty orders entered under Section 5 relating to deceptive and unfair practices in the first half of 1973, only one involved product comparison. In 1973–1975, orders were entered in cases involving, for example, a manufacturer of imitation orange juice who compared his product with the real thing; an automobile company that claimed superior structural strength, quietness, and performance for its automobiles; a manufacturer who sold rewoven hosiery as first-quality hose; favorable comparisons between nonfat dry milk and whole milk; and a claim of uniqueness made for a brand of air conditioner.[23] Three major factors may account for the decline in the number of these cases that were brought against small firms—a change from the pattern of the past. First, the Commission claims to have adopted a cost-benefit approach to cases of deception, measuring the cost to the Commission against the possible economic or physical harm to consumers; if the benefits do not exceed the costs, the case will supposedly be dropped.[24] Second, the agency says that in light of the criticisms leveled against it in 1969, it has largely abandoned the mailbag approach to complaints. Third, the major thrust of its work against product comparisons has allegedly been shifted from individual cases to trade regulation rules.[25]

Reliance on the mailbag approach probably has declined in recent years, but considerable skepticism has been expressed about the zeal with which the cost-benefit approach has been followed. Posner, in his study of advertising orders, concedes that the number of "idiotic" cases declined in 1972–1973 but still concludes that "as before the bulk of the Commission's resources were devoted to marginal cases, to cases where private remedies would probably have been adequate, and to cases where the Commission's lack of punitive remedies prevented it from dealing effectively with the challenged practice."[26] As for the notion that emphasis on trade regulation has replaced the case-by-case approach, the paucity of final trade regulation rules—usually no more than two or three per year—makes the claim simply not credible, in this or any other area of deceptive practices.

There is little question that in the past, product-representation cases were often brought at the behest either of one industry group acting against another or of one industry acting against another that made close substitute products. And the group or industry against which the complaints were brought frequently produced newer or less costly products. Whether the consumer was economically or physically harmed by the "deception" was often not considered by the Commission. There is, in short, little doubt that the agency was taking action against a means of competition and was being used in complainants' attempts to maintain stability in what were usually very unconcentrated industries with many small producers. It has also been suggested that the F.T.C. supported traditional standards and obstructed the marketing of new products by preventing valuable comparative trade descriptions, even though the new products may have been as beneficial to the consumer as the old ones.

The more recent cases and those involving simulations in which product superiority is claimed (for example, the claim that a razor blade is so sharp it can shave sandpaper, when the "sandpaper" was in fact Plexiglas) have been criticized on several grounds: first, that although the orders involved were not brought at the behest of producers of substitute products, they had the same effect of thwarting competition; second, that they do not serve (or serve only marginally) consumers' interests in safety, health, or economic well-being, but concentrate on legal niceties, often against large firms, in an attempt to deflect the criticism of so-called public-interest groups; and, third, that they waste public resources because free competition or private legal action is the best means of dispelling deception. Let us examine these arguments. Posner, in line with the free-market school of thought, argues that the burden in these cases "might reasonably rest with the trade associations of the sellers of the substitute products to dispel the misrepresentation, either by advertising or by legal action against the misrepresenting seller."[27] Perhaps, but private tort remedies are not nearly so extensive as the concept of deception, and one who seeks to dispel deception might choose a strategy of greater deception rather than truth.

Second, while there is little evidence yet that the Commission will indeed apply a realistic cost-benefit test and evidence aplenty that these cases have been either of no benefit to consumers (the mock-up cases) or of only marginal benefit (the case of the orange juice substitute), and while the orders entered may have had the effect of thwarting competition, there is still something discomforting about this class of deception. Why should deception about a product be countenanced, even if no harm befalls the consumer's health, safety, or economic welfare? Not only is it unmitigated arrogance for the seller to decide what is good for the consumer, but it is bad public policy to encourage and reward corporate irresponsibility, which is already rampant.

But if we conclude that deception of this kind is unjustified, we are back to the question of whether the F.T.C., with its minimal abilities to discover and deter fraud, is the appropriate instrument with which to reach it. As I have argued earlier, this agency and its sanctions do not constitute an effective instrument. The same considerations and judgment apply in the area of misrepresentation of intangibles.

Misrepresentation of Intangibles

As a firm may misrepresent its product in an effort to increase sales, so too may it misrepresent some intangible aspect of a product. Such intangibles include the country of origin of the product, the trade status or affiliation of the seller, and the names of persons or organizations that endorse the product. Misrepresentation of these intangible aspects is as valuable a trade weapon as product misrepresentation, and with one major exception the same considerations apply to both categories. Whereas statements about the quality of a product may be made in an attempt to find new markets as well as to divert trade from competitors, misrepresentation of intangibles usually does not involve the kind of claims that expand demand for a generic product. False testimonials or misrepresentations about functional status (for example, a wholesaler's claim that he has manufactured the product he seeks to sell, implying that his prices are lower than those of other wholesalers) are not the same sort as those designed to stimulate consumer interest in a new product; rather, they boast about a particular version of a known product.

Like the product-misrepresentation cases, this category of F.T.C. action has usually involved small firms and unconcentrated industries. Further, the cases brought in the past have reflected the struggle for sales between established segments of an industry and newer firms seeking to make inroads on a market. Nowhere is this situation illustrated more clearly than in the "foreign origin" cases. The struggle between importers and domestic manufacturers has been a well-known and persistent theme in American history, particularly in the area of tariff laws. Less well known is the minor role the F.T.C. has played in the battle. During the 1950s and 1960s the F.T.C. entered a significant number of orders against importers for inadequate disclosure of foreign origin. In 1963, for example, 12 of the 146 orders brought under Section 5 of the F.T.C. Act against deceptive practices involved foreign origin.

Many of these cases concerned simple consumer goods (toys, sunglasses, and so on) manufactured in Japan or Hong Kong and priced below similar domestic products because of lower labor costs. Even if there were no markings on the product or its package, the F.T.C.

found deception, on the grounds that (1) consumers assume that goods are of domestic manufacture when there is no indication to the contrary, and (2) some consumers prefer domestically manufactured goods for patriotic or other reasons. Even if only part of a product was of foreign origin, the same principle applied.[28] No allegation or suggestion was made in these cases that consumers were being economically harmed by the "deception"; on the contrary, the imported goods were usually cheaper than their American counterparts. Nor was inferior workmanship alleged.

A peculiar twist was given to the foreign-origin principle in cases brought at the behest of perfume importers against newer domestic manufacturers that employed such French-sounding trade names as "Yvonne" and "Sydnee." Even such a mild and literally true phrase as "blended in the French tradition" was held to be deceptive.[29] The cases arose, of course, because the considerably lower price of domestically produced perfume was a threat to established importers of French perfume, who therefore sought to differentiate their products from those of domestic origin and thus justify a substantial price differential. The same principle explains the third subcategory of foreign-origin cases: those involving statements that goods made in one foreign nation were in fact made in another—"Swiss" watch cases actually made in Hong Kong, for example.[30]

Cases of this type had begun to disappear even before 1969, but orders involving deceptive endorsements and testimonials are still very much with us—indeed, they have a long history, for such cases had been brought even before the Wheeler-Lea Act. Essentially, testimonials suggest that one firm's product is superior to a competitor's because it has been endorsed by some well-known figure or organization. The Commission's grounds for enjoining endorsements have included (1) dishonest statements of belief by the endorser; (2) failure to reveal that the endorser has a financial interest in the endorsed product or company; and (3) publication of an endorsement without the permission of the purported endorser. The cases have covered testimonials by famous athletes, by private organizations, and by the United States government.[31] Perhaps the most famous testimonial cases were the payola cases; in 1960 the Commission entered orders against about one hundred small manufacturers and distributors of phonograph records because they had granted payments to radio disc jockeys in return for implied endorsement of their recordings. As in other testimonial cases, no harm befell the consumer; but testimonials are a useful competitive weapon, and the F.T.C. has been called upon to eliminate them.

The cases of misrepresentation of trade status involve the same considerations; cases of this sort, too, were brought even before the enactment of the Wheeler-Lea Amendment. Such descriptions as "manufacturer" and "mill" can lead consumers to believe that prices are low because distribution costs have been reduced. Usually such misrepresented trade status is used to highlight and explain what are in fact low prices. In cases brought to stop such misrepresentation the Commission does not show that consumers are dissatisfied or even that trade status is important to consumers.[32] Similar considerations govern cases involving the enhancement of status through deception. Claims that a firm is associated with a nationally famous concern, that a firm prepares tax returns on a year-round basis (instead of just during the income-tax season), that a firm's products have won "first prize," that a company is the oldest firm in a line of commerce, that a company's products have been advertised in a national magazine or given away on quiz shows, even that the size of the firm or its building is larger than it really is—all have been the subjects of F.T.C. orders.[33]

A brief review of cases involving misrepresentation of intangibles again leaves one in a quandary. On the one hand the deception involved has no apparent deleterious effect on consumer welfare. In fact, in some instances it is merely a technique to direct consumers' attention to bargains. The cases almost always involve small firms in highly competitive industries and are usually brought to the Commission's attention by disgruntled competitors who seek F.T.C. intervention to prevent rivals from making inroads on a market. Even when the cases are not brought to the agency's attention by affected businessmen—and the payola cases were not—they have the effect of stabilizing an industry and foreclosing a means of competition. One may therefore scoff at the Commission's work and sense of priorities. Yet—and here is the quandary—the consumer has a right to know the facts. The same considerations apply in cases involving pricing claims.

Pricing Claims

A firm's claim that its prices are lower than its competitors' will more quickly propel a rival into complaining to the F.T.C. than will any other kind of advertising statement, for no aspect of competition is more important than price. So if an advertisement suggests that consumers will receive a bargain by purchasing a particular product, the advertiser's rivals will carefully scrutinize the claim for possible deception. And deception, as we have observed, is not very difficult to find if one examines concise statements rigorously enough. Accordingly, and not very surprisingly, the F.T.C. receives a great many complaints concerning pricing claims. And in turn it has entered a large number of orders under Section 5 against deceptive pricing and related practices, and continues to do so. In the period 1956–1964 more than 150 such orders were entered, mostly (though not entirely) against small firms whose advertisements reached very few people. Table 16 shows the relative importance of cases of this type in three periods.

Table 16. Pricing orders entered by the F.T.C. compared with all orders against deceptive practices in three periods, 1963–1973

F.T.C. orders	FY 1963	July 1968–January 1969	June 1972–June 1973
Free goods, fictitious pricing, and "bait and switch" orders	21	12	15
Total deception orders under Section 5	146	47	97

Source: Richard Posner, *Regulation of Advertising by the F.T.C.* (Washington, D.C.: American Enterprise Institute for Public Policy Research, 1973), pp. 18, 22, 24.

Generally, though certainly not always, firms that boast of low or "lower" prices are seeking to compete in price. Most advertisers know well enough that a claim that a price is low when in fact it is inflated can be fairly easily disproved by at least a substantial minority (and perhaps a majority) of consumers. A firm that seeks to conceal high prices does not spotlight prices at all; it draws consumers' attention to some other facet of its product or firm instead. It is clear, then, why pricing orders are frequently entered against firms widely recognized as discounters or in industries in which price competition is particularly intense. Sellers who bring low prices to consumers' attention—perhaps through exaggeration—have always been a thorn in the side of higher-priced competitors, who in other situations have brought about enactment of state laws forbidding the advertising of prices of certain products or the use of such terms as "cut rate" and "bargain."[34]

The fictitious-pricing cases have covered a large range of statements at the manufacturing, distribution, and retail levels. At the retail level the F.T.C. has enjoined a number of claims, some of the more common of which involve comparative pricing. In a typical case, a supermarket operator in Washington, D.C., compared the manufacturer's list prices for appliances with its own selling prices, in order to draw attention to what the Commission conceded were the lowest prices in the area for such items. The agency held that "list price" may be understood by some consumers to mean the customary price charged for the product. Since other discounters and department stores in the area charged less than list prices, the claim was held to be deceptive. Not even a statement in small print at the bottom of the advertisement declaring that list prices were for identification purposes only could cure the deception. Of course, the fact that the consumer benefited from the low prices and was in no way injured by the deception was irrelevant.[35] "List price," it should be noted, is a particularly valuable comparative phrase since it enables a consumer to identify a product readily and to shop comparatively. Its value to the process of price competition is obvious.

Claims relating to "savings" have generally been subject to very stringent scrutiny. For example, statements quoting "regular" prices and telling what prices are "now" have often been proscribed when the merchandise has in fact been sold at the lower price for a long time. Similarly, statements claiming "extraordinary once-a-year savings" have been held to be deceptive when the price referred to was actually in effect either more than once during a year or for a long period.[36] Phrases like "Save up to . . ." are enjoined when the indicated percentage saving is not accurate, even if the prices are quite low; and the F.T.C. has also found deception in such cases by measuring a respondent's percentage claim against other low prices, not those generally charged in the particular trade area.[37] Finally, any ambiguity in language has almost always been construed against a respondent. For example, a discount firm offering automobile painting and body work advertised that its price for paint jobs was "special." The respondent argued that "special" meant that its prices were especially low compared to competitors', but the Commission rejected this interpretation, holding that "special" meant a variation from its usual price. Since the respondent's price was always low, the claim was deceptive.[38]

Whether at the retail level or at the manufacturing and distribution levels, cases have generally involved small firms in highly competitive industries selling at relatively low prices. Typically, cases brought against manufacturers or distributors arise from either claims in a mail-order catalog or inscriptions of selling prices above usual retail market prices on a ticket or label that remains on the product when it is sold to the consumer by the retailer. The Commission has rejected the argument that manufacturers or distributors are not responsible for the use retailers make of manufacturers' tickets on the grounds that the placement of an instrument of deception in the hands of another is an unfair or deceptive practice.[39] For this reason it found deceptive a manufacturer's use of list prices in advertising material given to retailers since price competition at the retail level usually results in retail prices that are below list.[40]

In one case a manufacturer of electric floor-polishing machines and similar articles that supplied its distributors and retailers with material showing list prices higher than the usual retail prices sought to justify its action by arguing that several benefits flowed from the use of this material: (1) it discouraged overcharging; (2) it provided a basis for trade-in negotiations; (3) it provided a guide to finance institutions; (4) it assisted retailers in determining the value of products; and (5) it helped consumers to identify the specific article offered for sale. The Commission rejected all of these probable benefits without discussion because, it said, some consumers would be deceived by the designation "list price."[41]

Not surprisingly, the F.T.C. employs an equally stringent test for the word "free." In the leading case, a paint manufacturer offered a second can of paint "free" if one can was purchased at the regular price. This offer had been made continuously for ten years, and the manufacturer, needless to say, took into account the cost of manufacturing and distributing the second can in setting the price of the first. Accordingly the Commission held that the offer was deceptive because the second can was not free.[42] The respondent's products were very cheaply priced and the claim made was clearly one that aroused price consciousness in consumers, thus arousing the ire of competitors who wanted to reduce price consciousness. The benefit to consumers from this and similar decisions is certainly marginal.

The use of the term "free" may indeed be deceptive, but it requires extraordinary naiveté on the part of prospective purchasers to believe that a firm is going to give away 50 percent of its merchandise unconditionally.

One is led to conclude that the Commission has been used by affected businessmen to harass discount sellers and others who desire vigorous price competition. These cases fall very clearly in the realm of promotion of stability and prevention of price competition. The firms involved are usually small and in very unconcentrated industries where price competition is rampant—to the dismay of the complainants. Perhaps more than in any other area, the F.T.C.'s actions against deceptive pricing justify the A.B.A. Commission's complaint that "the agency often acts at the behest of one group of industry members against another group."[43] Nor can these cases be justified by the criterion of economic harm to consumers. Yet when we examine the area of "bait and switch," the final subcategory of pricing cases, we may be left with a distaste for the dishonesty involved, even though the gravity of these practices may not justify the relatively high priority that the number of orders entered over the years implies they have received.

"Bait advertising" means advertising a product for sale at an attractively low price and then at the point of sale either telling consumers that the advertised product is not available or discouraging the purchase of that product. The point, of course, is to induce consumers to "switch"—to purchase a more expensive version of the product than the one advertised. One line of argument suggests that the practice is a nuisance to consumers, who are subjected to the deceptive implication that the advertised product is available. Nevertheless, it must be remembered that this practice does not necessarily involve deception with respect to the article consumers do in fact buy. Thus they may suffer no out-of-pocket loss or impairment to health because of the deception. The cases brought may, in short, be of very minor consumer interest.

An argument that can be advanced against this view is that consumer choice is very often not a rational decision-making procedure. Consumers are often subject to rash impulses, squandering money with which they can ill afford to part in response to the skillful appeals of talented salesmen. If a few days later a "baited and switched" consumer comes to regret his impulsive purchase, economic harm has indeed been done to him.[44] Posner replies that "evidently the Commission is unwilling to allow the consumer to shoulder any part of the responsibility for averting unhappy purchasing experiences . . . even in cases where it is plain that the consumer's only effective protection is self-protection."[45] In fact, self-protection is not the consumer's only protection, for some states have made bait-and-switch practices a misdemeanor.[46] In recent years, too, the Commission has included provisions for a cooling-off period in bait-and-switch cases; sellers who employ such tactics must allow customers a short time period (usually three days) in which they may cancel transactions.[47]

Orders in bait-and-switch cases have generally been brought in highly competitive industries where entry is easy—for example, against retailers of carpets and aluminum storm windows. The practice is not simply a competitive device, but one especially harmful to low-income consumers; nevertheless, the question remains whether F.T.C. orders and discovery procedures are effective in dealing with what may be a very widespread practice. The few cases brought each year are trivial in comparison to the number of selling schemes that may use the tactics. Nor, as we have observed, is the deterrent likely to be effective against people who know full well that they are engaging in an unlawful practice. Much the same conclusion must be reached with respect to F.T.C. regulation of food and drug advertising.

Food and Drug Advertising

In its attempts to control false advertising of food and drugs the F.T.C. has used three major tools: trade regulation rules (TRRs) and Sections 5 and 14 of the F.T.C. Act. We shall begin with one of the more dramatic and innovative events in the F.T.C.'s history: the promulgation of the famous cigarette rule. The first major scientific study linking smoking and lung cancer was published in 1939, but it was not until January 1964 that the surgeon general's advisory committee brought out its widely respected and publicized report. In June 1964 the F.T.C., acting on its own initiative, issued a TRR for all cigarette advertising and labeling requiring disclosure that cigarette smoking "is dangerous to health and may cause death from cancer and other diseases."[48] The Commission's argument was essentially that nondisclosure was deceptive "in light of the appearance, nature, or intended use of the product."[49] Offering the product for consumption implied healthfulness. Here, then, was an instance of nondisclosure in which every member of an industry would suffer from revelation. Congress responded initially by depriving the F.T.C. of power to compel health warnings for cigarettes, but in a later series of enactments it required the warnings itself and banned cigarette commercials on television.

In view of the popularity of cigarettes and the wide dissemination of information about the relationship between cigarette smoking and lung cancer, this is an excellent case with which to evaluate the policy of requiring warnings and disclaimers in advertising and labeling. If warnings do not work in the case of cigarettes, they will probably have even less effect in connection with other products, even allowing for the fact that cigarette smoking is addictive. Cigarette smoking continued to increase each year through 1974, and much of the additional consumption each year was accounted for by new smokers. These increases have occurred despite the ban on television advertising (a ban that, it should be added, came about largely because the manufacturers themselves wanted to withdraw from competition in television advertising, which they felt to be of questionable worth).[50]

The agency has issued a few other TRRs relating to food and drugs, and proposed still others. Certainly there can be no quarrel with the claim that they constitute beneficial output, but substantial questions must be raised about their impact. If cigarette warnings have thus far been ineffective, how useful, for example, is the considerably less publicized rule requiring disclosure of the lethal effects of inhaling the quick-freeze aerosol sprays used for frosting cocktail glasses?[51] Moreover, as we have observed, if a firm wants to disobey a TRR, the Wheeler-Lea Act makes a lengthy litigation process possible. Finally, attention must be drawn again to the length of time that elapses between an investigation and the final promulgation of a rule and to the small number of rules that exist—the inevitable result of the time required for rule making and the complexity of the procedures.

While the F.T.C. has emphasized the TRR as an enforcement tool since the late 1960s, its powers of injunction under the Wheeler-Lea Act have been virtually unused. Section 14 of the F.T.C. Act makes false advertising (a narrower concept than deceptive advertising) of food, drugs, and cosmetics a misdemeanor if use of the product under the conditions specified in the advertisement, or under customary conditions, "may be injurious to health" or if there is specific intent to mislead or defraud. As we observed in connection with the legislative history of the Wheeler-Lea Amendment, the former contingency covers only a small portion of drug advertising, while the latter is extremely difficult to prove. Predictably, therefore, there have been very few criminal actions, and most F.T.C. cases in this area have been approached in the same manner as other kinds of deceptive-practice cases.

Whether or not the new injunctive powers granted to the agency under a 1973 amendment to the Trans-Alaska Oil Pipeline Act will increase the Commission's capacities remains to be seen. Under the new statute the F.T.C. must still show that it has properly weighed the equities in seeking an injunction and must show the probability of ultimate success.

There remains the case-by-case approach, which the agency has traditionally followed. As we noted in the last chapter, the F.T.C. has been uniformly criticized for its lack of impact on food and drug advertising. Yet its output has been relatively high. During 1956–1964, for example, it entered more than 150 orders in food and drug cases. In the following years, however, the number dropped precipitously; in the first half of 1973 only three orders were entered. The same number, however, was entered just in the first three months of 1975. An examination of these orders reveals that virtually all respondents have been very small firms that made their deceptive representations in media with limited circulations. Further, while nothing good can be said for deception in food and drug advertising, there are degrees of danger associated with various claims, and more often than not the Commission proceeds against firms making claims that involve only minimal risk to health or safety.

Clearly some of the 1956–1964 cases were brought in response to competitors' complaints. Several cases involved small manufacturers who claimed that their preparations would remove foreign matter that caused dandruff and would also retard baldness or hair loss.[52] The ingredients in the preparations have, in fact, been used by dermatologists in the treatment of scalp conditions, and the respondents produced medical experts to testify to the virtues of their products. Other experts, however, testified that the claims were exaggerated, and the hearing examiner believed the Commission's witnesses rather than the respondents' and therefore found the respondents in violation of the F.T.C. Act. Many of these cases were brought at the behest of trade associations representing the manufacturers of hair-care and beauty products, who objected not only to the competitive advantage that the firms making such claims might gain but also to the financial harm that might accrue to the industry as a whole if consumers discovered the claims to be untrue. Actions against firms advertising hair restoratives and hair implantings continue, indicating the near futility of attempting to clean up this easily entered and highly competitive industry.[53]

Also typical of the F.T.C.'s preoccupation with interindustry problems of marginal import to consumers during the 1956–1964 period were the more than twenty orders entered against contact lens manufacturers and retailers who sought to show by exaggeration that their product was superior to eyeglasses. The claims involved in these cases were usually statements that were true in general but subject to qualifications not ordinarily made in concise advertising messages. For example, one respondent claimed that (1) everybody can wear contact lenses, (2) they never cause irritation or discomfort, and (3) a wearer can entirely dispense with eyeglasses.[54] These claims, although largely correct, should have been qualified, for a few people cannot wear contact lenses, and under some unusual circumstances they can cause eye irritation or discomfort—so they cannot *always* replace ordinary eyeglasses. Cases of this type have, again, continued to be brought.[55]

Not all F.T.C. orders in the area of food and drugs, however, have involved small firms and problems of competition, and not all have been of little benefit to consumers. The agency has continually acted both against ghastly frauds perpetrated by small firms and against very large firms that have made questionable advertising claims. In the first category, it has entered orders and obtained injunctions against quacks who promise miracle cures for cancer, arthritis, and other tragic afflictions.[56] And it has entered orders against small firms that have deceptively claimed that their products alleviate or cure such lesser ailments as insomnia and stomach distress.[57] The persistence of such cases, however, points to the ineffectiveness of F.T.C. orders in stamping out such cruel and harmful frauds, a conclusion supported by the congressional and public-interest opinion cited in the last chapter. Given the ease of entry into the quack-medicine business, the minimal requirements in both capital and technological skill, and the promise of quick profits, F.T.C. regulation is hampered by two major problems: (1) its inability to discover the potentially numerous purveyors of quack medicines and (2) the ineffectiveness of either a cease-and-desist order or a temporary injunction as a deterrent to outrageous fraud.

Orders against large firms have generally involved relatively minor infractions (except, of course, in such situations as cigarette advertising, when an entire industry has an interest in concealing or deceiving, in which case a trade regulation rule rather than an individual order is appropriate). The temptation to shoot an elephant has been too great for the F.T.C. to resist; for if nothing else, such action deflects the criticism of those who claim that the agency attacks only small firms.

The flavor of orders brought against large firms in the 1956–1964 period may be gauged from the Colgate-Palmolive and Carter cases. In the former, one of the largest tooth paste manufacturers claimed in nationwide television commercials that its product contained an ingredient that formed a "protective shield" around teeth, thereby giving complete protection against tooth decay. The commercial stated that the tooth paste fought tooth decay—apparently a supportable claim. But under F.T.C. standards the advertisement was deceptive because the product did not literally form a protective shield around teeth and did not afford *complete* protection against tooth decay.[58] Similar hairsplitting took place in the almost interminable case against Carter Products (thirteen years from complaint to order), which was brought in large part to compel the respondent to remove the word "liver" from the product originally named Carter's Little Liver Pills because some consumers might be deceived into believing that the product was a cure for liver ailments.[59]

Orders against large firms for relatively harmless infractions in food and drug advertising have persisted. In 1973, for example, orders were entered concerning (1) an analgesic, because the claim was made that it was more effective in relieving pain than aspirin or Bufferin when in fact the question of its superiority was subject to scientific dispute (there was no question that it was at least as effective); (2) a gelatine protein drink, because slightly exaggerated nutritional claims were made; and (3) a brand of oleomargarine, because statements made by its manufacturer on the relation of cholesterol to heart disease were a subject of scientific dispute, and the advertisement did not say so.[60] In none of these three cases, the only ones brought in the first half of 1973, was there a question of economic or bodily harm to consumers. Moreover, in each instance the manufacturers of close substitutes were more than capable of dispelling any deception in the advertisements in question. Butter products, for example, may be expected to counter the claims of margarine manufacturers. But even if we assume for the sake of argument that the claims made by these large manufacturers were serious ones, worthy of the F.T.C.'s attention, the Commission's enforcement mechanisms are still ineffective. Large firms can and do change their advertising messages and emphasis with great frequency. By the time a complaint—or even an application for preliminary injunction—is entered, the firm has abandoned the questionable claims and made many others. And of course the claims that could be made for the products are numerous, limited only by the ingenuity of copywriters. The Commission's pursuit of false and misleading advertising by large firms is as inevitably destined to failure as the greyhound's chase after the mechanical hare.

For a number of reasons, then, the Commission's impact on food and drug advertising in both atomistic and oligopolistic industries has been slight, even though its output has been high. Only TRRs against industry-wide concealment or deception appear to be fruitful. But even here two caveats must be entered. First, the efficacy of a warning is very much open to question in view of experience with both cigarette warnings and credit disclosures under the Truth-in-Lending Act (which will be discussed in Chapter 10). Second, the TRR procedure has been so slow and cumbersome that very few such rules have been established, and the provisions of the Magnuson-Moss Act have not speeded things up.

Deception, Unfairness, and Public Values

Early in its career, when its jurisdiction was limited to prohibiting "unfair methods of competition," the Commission interpreted the phrase to include acts that were contrary to social values as expressed either in federal law or in the weight of state laws: commercial bribery, harassment of competitors by the threat of suit, interference with contractual relations, malicious spoliation of a competitor's property.[61] The unfairness lay in the fact that such practices, if allowed to continue, could disrupt the commercial system's smooth functioning. Obviously, therefore, the use of such competitive methods would have to be prevented.

Of the many unfair methods proscribed in the early cases, selling goods through a lottery device turned out to be the most important in spelling out the practices the Commission might prohibit. A lottery sale is defined as consisting of three elements: prize, consideration, and chance. A typical lottery sale occurs when a customer, upon purchase of a product, is permitted to punch a square in a punchboard. Some squares offer prizes, others do not. While moral attitudes toward gambling clearly play a signficant role in the law's disapproval of punchboard selling, commercial factors enter into it as well. In one of the more thoughtful lottery decisions, the highest court in Utah pointed out that the justification for commercial rivalry lies in its welfare function. Firms should therefore compete on the basis of business methods, product superiority, and advertising (which presumably disseminates information about the product and the manufacturer's business methods). To allow competition to be based upon the thrill of acquiring something for nothing would patently subvert these higher goals.[62]

The F.T.C. felt similarly as it anxiously awaited the Supreme Court's decision on the 1934 Keppel lottery case after a rather bad track record with the Court in previous years. The Court upheld the Commission's decision on both moral and competitive grounds, observing that lottery selling is unlawful in many states and that competitors who refuse to engage in the practice are at a competitive disadvantage. Moreover, continued the Court, even if lottery selling were not explicitly criminal, it would still be contrary to public policy as expressed in the law's general view of gaming. Finally, the Court observed, this competitive method is prohibited under Section 5 of the F.T.C. Act not in an attempt to censor the morals of businessmen, but as a matter of policy.[63]

Enactment of the Wheeler-Lea Amendment added to the original Section 5 language, as we have observed, prohibitions against deceptive and unfair acts and practices. Since the amendment was passed, the Commission has prosecuted certain kinds of case as blends of unfair competition, deceptive practice, and unfair practice, or of two of these. The essence of the charge in such cases, however, has been the same as the rationale in the Keppel case: that the practice went against public values as expressed in state and federal legislation. If an act violated either the letter or the spirit of such legislation, it could be prosecuted as unfair and/or deceptive.

Until the late 1960s the Commission took little advantage of the

Keppel principle, confining its activities in this area to only a few kinds of case. Foremost among them were cases involving lottery selling: during 1956–1964 the F.T.C. entered twenty lottery orders. The respondent firms, many of which were small even by Commission standards, sold such highly competitive light goods as candy, toys, dolls, clocks, cameras, and cheap watches. Almost all of them were engaged in assembling purchased merchandise and lottery devices and selling the packages to operators, who then sold them to the public.[64] To justify these lottery cases in terms of consumer protection is hard on any but the most abstract legal grounds. Lottery selling in these highly competitive industries is nothing more than a promotional device akin to trading stamps, contests, and other lures. The reduced prices were a boon to some lucky consumers, but even the less lucky ones paid no more than they should have for the products they bought. Yet the cases can be understood on the ground that to allow competition to focus on gaming is to divert attention from those aspects of competition that are central to its purported welfare function.

Other types of public-value cases brought before 1969 were clearly intended, however, to serve at least some consumers. Consider, for example, the skip-tracer cases; more than thirty orders were entered between 1956 and 1964 against firms that traced evading debtors (skippers) by employing either deceptive statements promising some reward on forms addressed to debtors or true statements made without any indication that the addresser was in the business of locating delinquent debtors.[65] Complaints have been brought in such matters both by debtors who have succumbed to the lures of skip tracer and by credit bureaus anxious to retain what remains of shaky reputations in their unpopular business.[66] The firms involved in skip tracing are invariably small, fly-by-night, and sleazy. To their contention that they perform a public service by locating delinquent debtors the Commission and the courts have answered that the persons engaged in such a business are themselves cheap swindlers who frequently harass people who either are not debtors or have good reason not to pay questionable debts. Legitimate means exist for obtaining payment of debts, both through the courts and otherwise, and the integrity of these processes should be protected.

The sleazy operator or common swindler figures in two other staples of Commission consumer protection activity: cases involving frauds perpetrated on homeowners and frauds based on phony employment prospects. Typical of the former category are cases in which salesmen make false statements in attempts to sell such products as aluminum siding, storm windows, freezers, and furnaces. While there is no way of knowing the real incidence of deceptive claims made to homeowners, the available evidence indicates that the Commission is highly ineffective in curtailing this sort of fraud. The F.T.C. enters, on average, approximately five orders a year against such practices; the National Better Business Bureau received 20,717 complaints in 1965 and 1966 alone and has estimated that consumer losses incurred through home improvement sales amount to between $500 million and $1 billion a year. The Nader group has similarly asserted that home improvement frauds cost consumers "millions" each year. While such estimates of consumer losses may be viewed with some skepticism, the size of the problem is clearly enormous. The number of complaints received by the National Better Business Bureau, the fact that in 1963 there were 66,223 organizations in the United States engaged in direct selling, and the strong incentive to fraud that exists for sellers unconcerned with repeat sales and capable of deception about experience and credence qualities all point to considerable fraud in this area.[67] And again the F.T.C.'s output, regulatory processes, powers of deterrence, and discovery mechanisms hardly measure up to the problem created by take-the-money-and-run con men.

The available evidence suggests F.T.C. failure not only in control of homeowner fraud but also in the area of fraud connected with employment prospects. There are two categories of cases in this latter group: those involving instruction through correspondence when the seller promises excellent training and high earnings if the course is successfully completed and those involving sale of franchises and provision of supplies when the seller assures franchisees of substantial profits. The cases involve, once again, small firms in atomistic industries. And the relatively few orders the F.T.C. enters each year are, once again, hardly a deterrent to these shady operations—though one wonders whether criminal deterrence has done a better job.

F.T.C. action in such cases of public concern as gambling and fraud continue. Since 1969, however, the agency has expanded the range of public values it seeks to protect, partly because of the attacks made on the Commission's alleged attention to trivia and party in response to the Supreme Court's expansion and reiteration of the Keppel rationale in the 1972 Sperry and Hutchinson (S & H) case. The Court invited the F.T.C. to be like a court of equity, considering "public values beyond simply those enshrined in the letter or encompassed in the spirit of the antitrust laws."[68] The S & H case was brought to establish the right of operation of trading stamp exchanges (which were forbidden by S & H to its trading stamp users) on the theory that restricting the right of redemption to the issuing firm's own exchange was unfair to consumers. In keeping with this value, the Commission also promulgated a trade regulation rule in 1971 forbidding retail food stores to advertise products without having a sufficient quantity available to meet the demand that might reasonably be anticipated,[69] and then brought several cases that focused on the availability of products in supermarkets.

The F.T.C. has also acted to protect the public value of product safety. Although it had entered a few orders before the 1970s which involved either failure to disclose the fact that products were unsafe or affirmative disclosures that were deceptive, the respondents were invariably small.[70] The cases brought in the 1970s have been few, too, but they have involved large firms.[71] The F.T.C., it should be noted, is not the agency primarily charged with guarding consumer safety; that task has devolved upon the Consumer Product Safety Commission. Nor, obviously, are the hit-and-miss procedures of the Commission designed to attack the problem of consumer safety in a comprehensive manner.

Except in these areas, the F.T.C. has not taken advantage of the mandate provided it under the S & H doctrine to protect public values. But even if it were to expand its output into new areas, could we expect any substantial impact? The F.T.C.'s record in areas to which it has devoted great attention offers little hope.

Summary

Over the years the F.T.C. has expended considerable effort in seeking to control deceptive and unfair practices. Yet, if one may judge by the enormous volume of complaints that consumers and businessmen continue to make and the conclusions drawn by experienced and attentive observers, impressionistic though most of them are, the agency's impact has not been great. One of its major shortcomings has been its inability to obtain accurate, reliable marketplace information. In the past it relied largely on complaints submitted by affected businessmen. The cost of this approach, as we have seen, has been a good deal of attentiveness to matters of little moment to consumers' safety, health, or economic priorities but of importance to affected businessmen. Most cases involved small firms and unconcentrated industries.

Yet, as we have seen, the Commission has been by no means inactive either in matters of importance to consumers or in relation to large firms. The cases involving large firms, especially in recent years, have usually been based on the Mortimer Snerd standard. Deception will inevitably be found if the agency looks hard enough for it, and the pressure from self-appointed spokesmen for the consumer, convinced that bigness equals badness, has been too great to resist. Some very silly cases, memorable only for their legal niceties, have been the result. But even if we were to concede that the cases against large firms were correctly brought, we would still have to conclude that F.T.C. regulatory procedures are insufficient to curb deception, for the large firm can change its advertising slogans, campaigns, and claims much more quickly than the F.T.C. can enter orders or muster enough facts to get an injunction against it. Moreover, the overriding problem of large-firm advertising is not met by the notion of deception. The large firm's advertisements employ psychological and subliminal appeals that make surreptitious, if unstated, promises. Advertisements for perfumes and cosmetics implicitly promise sexual success without ever really saying so.[72] Other advertisements appeal to the desire for enhanced social status. If the object of public policy is to assure rationality in consumer purchases, it has not even begun to meet the problem raised by the new psychotechnology.

The older problems of fraud, concealment, and notorious deception are usually encountered in highly competitive industries in which entry and exit are easy and which are populated by many small firms, as the mass of the F.T.C.'s cases so well illustrates. When one looks at F.T.C. orders against the perpetrators of home improvement frauds and the like, one might conclude that smallness is badness. An exaggeration, perhaps, but the enormous number of potential perpetrators of fraud, the lack of effective deterrence in the F.T.C.'s cease-and-desist orders, and the unlikelihood of discovery by the agency render its impact in this area minimal, no matter how great its output of orders against such practices. But one wonders whether the more stringent penalties proposed by former Commissioner Elman and others would be much more successful. After all, criminal penalties have not stopped crime rates from rising. As long as a society places high value on individual accumulation of wealth, we may rest assured that unscrupulous con men will exist—and thrive. We shall examine this idea more closely in the last chapter.

The area of deception in which the agency has registered its greatest success is the collusion engaged in by members of an oligopolistic industry when they have something to conceal. The F.T.C. has met this problem with the trade regulation rule, designed to impose uniform standards on the members of an industry. While the cigarette rule may have been the Commission's finest hour, the TRR procedure is so slow and cumbersome that very few matters of this sort have been reached in comparison with the potentially large body of information that large-scale industries may have an interest in concealing. Moreover, as we have observed, the policy of requiring warnings appears to be relatively ineffective. Nevertheless, the TRR procedure comes closest to the statutes the agency administers in imposing explicit standards. Are such statutes the answer?

CHAPTER 9

Standards and Labeling

Max Weber suggested that under capitalism, public law tends to eliminate discretion and impose clear, explicit legal standards.

These modern businesses with their fixed capital and their exact calculations are much too sensitive to legal and administrative irrationalities. They could only come into being in the bureaucratic state with its rational laws where . . . the judge is more or less an automatic statute-dispensing machine in which you insert the files together with the necessary costs and dues at the top, whereupon he will eject the judgment together with the more or less cogent reasons for it at the bottom; that is to say where the judge's behavior is on the whole predictable.[1]

While this may be the tendency of legislation that affects business—though for a large body of other statutes there is reason to doubt the hypothesis[2]—the goal is never fully realized; for, as Weber observed, insofar as evasion of statutory requirements is advantageous to a firm, it will seek to evade them. And it can often succeed, for no matter how clever legislators may be in drafting laws that they think will cover all cases and all market situations, the businessman's market knowledge allows him to circumvent them. In short, a firm looking for loopholes can usually find them. For example, the framers of the Sherman Act sought to ensure "competitive" prices by outlawing what they conceived to be the two conditions that prevented competitive pricing, collusion and monopolization. Yet, as we have seen, a third alternative, oligopolistic coordination, has to some extent allowed firms to prevent realization of the act's goals. Regulatory conduct becomes under these circumstances a fencing match in which administrators seek to develop innovative means within a statute's framework to achieve statutory goals, while regulated firms seek, insofar as evasion fits perceived corporate needs, to avoid the behavior these goals demand. The process builds up a large body of case law, although the legislators' original choice was a regulatory rather than a judicial scheme of enforcement, precisely to prevent this result. And through it all, the business community usually remains at least one step ahead of the regulators.

Weber's hypothesis forgets, too, that legislation often reflects not a single statutory purpose, but, as in the case of the 1914 F.T.C. Act, contradictory purposes. The net effect may be that an agency, in pursuing these contradictory purposes, achieves stalemate as the output directed toward one goal effectively cancels the output directed toward the other. Or, as in the case of the Wheeler-Lea Act, the contradiction between desire for regulation of others and fear that such regulation may limit one's own competitive capabilities can lead to an inherently ineffective statute. Again the regulatory dynamic involves the enforcing agency in a desperate attempt to utilize its statutory tools to realize legislative goals.

If enforcement fails to have a significant impact, despite increasing output, one solution is to enact new legislation specific enough to achieve the goals of the group seeking it. New enforcement mechanisms and techniques for discovering wrongdoing can be incorporated within such a new statute so as to ensure that it does not suffer the defects of the older, broader one. Two models of this solution can be isolated in statutes enforced by the F.T.C. In the first, illustrated by the older labeling laws, one group of businessmen seeks to gain an advantage over another through a statute that imposes burdensome requirements on the other group and thus inhibits its ability to compete. Thus minimum safety or health standards may impose burdensome costs on marginal or small producers,[3] and labeling requirements that set up quality standards by definition may be used to differentiate one group of products from another and so justify a wide price spread. In the labeling case the "lower quality" product is classified as inferior by government imprimatur. The wool, fur, and textile acts are good examples of the way imposition of standards through labeling can act to the detriment of rivals. Whatever the motivation behind such legislation, the consumer *may* still benefit considerably from it.

Not all consumer legislation, of course, comes about as a result of the action of producers. In the second model (to be discussed in detail in Chapter 10), illustrated by some of the more recent statutes enforced by the F.T.C., legislation is enacted over the opposition of business groups at the behest of other groups. But, as we shall see in the case of the newer labeling acts, this legislation has been achieved only when original proposals have been modified in ways satisfactory to important business groups. The new consumerism has not seriously disadvantaged important business groups, despite the antagonistic intent of the groups that favored the new legislation. In this model, important industry groups are at first vehemently opposed to the new legislation but then move to modify the bill, either to reduce it to a symbolic, "harmless" piece of legislation or to make it work to the advantage of at least some segments of the affected business community. The law finally enacted is quietly accepted by powerful segments of the business community, which discover virtues in it. As we observed in the last chapter, the cigarette industry welcomed the statute banning cigarette commercials on television because major firms in the industry had been squandering large sums of money on such commercials without receiving commensurate benefits.

We shall begin our examination of the first model with the Wool Act. This statute's importance lies not in the substance of its jurisdiction but in its breakthrough role as legislation that explicitly imposes standards.

The Wool Products Labeling Act

The first of the labeling statutes, the Wool Products Labeling Act of 1939 (the Wool Act), illustrates the differences between the older statutes that impose standards and the new ones. The act not only declares affirmative misbranding to be unlawful but also requires stamps, tags, and labels attached to wool products to show the percentages of wool, reused wool, reprocessed wool, and other fibers used as well as the name (or assigned number) of the manufacturer. Failure to provide this information is deemed to be misbranding. Every manufacturer of a wool product is also required to maintain and preserve fiber-content records for three years; failure to maintain such records can lead to civil penalties. If a party continues to violate the Wool Act after receiving notice from the F.T.C. that it has reasonable cause to believe that a violation is taking place, his wool products are subject to confiscation and condemnation. Importers of wool products are required to specify the fact that the products are imported and name the country of origin on labels and tags. Failure to disclose this information, or disclosure of false information, constitutes an unfair method of competition and can subject the importer to an order prohibiting importation of wool products unless he files a bond with the Secretary of the Treasury equal to double the value of the wool products and import duties. Finally, willful violation of the statute is punishable by both a heavy fine and imprisonment.

The Wool Act thus differs from the F.T.C. Act and the Wheeler-Lea Act not only in its specificity but also in its apparent ability to deter. It may not be so effective a deterrent as a criminal statute would be, but it certainly has more teeth than the Wheeler-Lea Act. Naturally enough, interests that stood to gain from enforcement of the statute eagerly sought its enactment as a supplement to the Wheeler-Lea Act. The stringency of the Wool Act reflects, as we shall see, the almost complete victory of one group of affected businessmen over another.

According to Congressman Lawrence Lewis, a principal spokesman for the Wool Act, the major purpose of the new legislation was to protect consumers from deception by carefully distinguishing among virgin wool, reprocessed wool, and reused wool. (Reused wool is wool that has been fashioned into a product that has then been worn or otherwise used by a consumer and subsequently torn down into the fibrous state; reprocessed wool is wool that has been fashioned into a product that has been torn down into its fibers without ever having been used in any way by a consumer.) Lewis likened the bill to the Food and Drug Act and asserted that the Wheeler-Lea Amendment was insufficient to protect consumers from the evils arising from nondisclosure of pertinent information; failure to reveal the specific kind of wool fibers contained in a wool product would not constitute a deceptive practice under the Wheeler-Lea Act.[4]

But if this were the statute's rationale, why should its coverage be limited to wool products? The same argument could apply to every other fabric and fiber from which garments are made. The limitation leads one at least to suspect that the legislation was promoted by special interests and was not the product of a concern for consumer interests. This suspicion is reinforced by the House minority analysis of some of the bill's inadequacies. The minority report pointed out that the bill did not require labels to carry any of the information that would be of real concern to consumers—how long the garment would probably last, its abrasion strength, its color-fastness, its probable shrinkage, the tensile strength of its fibers, the length of the fibers, the insulation value of the fabric against heat or cold, the workmanship in the garment, or the strength of the weave.[5] Further, the minority pointed out, the classification of wool into the categories of new, re-processed, and reused was entirely arbitrary and meant nothing to most consumers. In fact, the classification scheme was itself deceptive in that a superior-sounding term was being applied to fabrics that were not necessarily superior; in the hearings all witnesses had agreed that the processes of manufacture were vastly more important to the quality of a wool product than the kinds of fiber used.[6] The mere statement that a garment is made of new (or virgin) wool may be misleading, since, as Senator Elbert D. Thomas noted, the fiber may be the tag of very poor sheep and greatly inferior to much reprocessed or reused wool.[7] Indeed, as Senator Thomas pointed out, producers distinguish among fourteen different grades of virgin wool, categories of which the bill took no notice. Congressman John Hinshaw noted that wool prices varied between three and fifteen cents a pound, de-pending on quality, and that some reprocessed wools could be worth several times the price of some of the virgin wools. But even this fact, he observed, was peripheral to the central point that the kind of wool a garment contains is a minor factor in its value and that the Wool Bill disguised this important fact. Hinshaw also noted that the bill's opponents would welcome legislation that was truly designed to pre-vent deception in the sale of all clothing. To these objections the bill's proponents made no reply.[8]

If consumer protection was not the principal purpose of the Wool Act, what was? One way of approaching the question is to ask which groups were actively promoting the bill's enactment and what they sought to accomplish through it. The evidence is clear that domestic woolgrowers were most active in supporting the bill. *Business Week,* usually well informed about such matters, reported that domestic woolgrowers and a few "top-notch" manufacturers were the chief backers of the bill and had sought such legislation for many years. According to Congressman Hinshaw, the domestic woolgrowers had spent a great deal of money lobbying for the bill, which was intro-duced by a senator from Wyoming, a key woolgrowing state.[9]

Opposition to the bill came from clothing manufacturers that uti-lized substantial amounts of reprocessed or reused wool as well as from manufacturers of clothing that contained other fibers, who feared that the labels required by the statute would enhance the status of virgin wool relative to other fibers in many consumers' minds. The Clothing Manufacturers Association charged that the Wool Act would create an artificial demand for virgin wool at the expense of other fibers. The National Retail Dry Goods Association, a large clothing retailers' association, opposed the bill because of the record-keeping requirements that would be imposed on its members.[10]

What, then, did the woolgrowers and their allies seek to gain from the statute? A clear answer was provided by Congressman Robert Secrest, one of the bill's leading proponents: "Those of us from wool-producing areas . . . have been vitally interested in securing passage of a truth in fabrics bill, realizing that it would result in a much greater use of virgin wool, with a consequent rise in price to the producing farmer."[11] In other words, the domestic wool producers hoped for economic advantage from the product differentiation that would result from the Wool Act's labeling requirements. In effect, the government's stamp of approval would be placed on virgin wool. And the bill was under consideration at a critical time: not only was the wool industry suffering as a result of the Great Depression, but there was a serious threat that the industry's conditions would worsen. In 1938 approximately one-third of the woolen fibers used in producing garments was reused, and the amount might well have increased because a recent reduction in tariffs on woolen rags had led to a marked rise in the rate of their importation. (The tariff had been reduced as a result of reciprocal trade agreements covering a number of commodities exchanged between Great Britain and the United States.)[12] The urgency of the woolgrowers' drive for new legislation is thus obvious.

The Wool Act is typical of statutes whose central substantive purpose—in this case the differentiation of virgin wool from other fibers—is built into the structure of the statute. There can be little (if any) discretion in its enforcement; the major significant variable is the amount of money to be expended on enforcement. And the identity of the principal sources of complaint concerning violations is reasonably clear from the statute and its legislative history. First, persons and firms in the various branches of the wool business would have the interest and knowledge to discover and keep track of products that were either not made of virgin wool or were only partially fashioned from wool, and which were improperly labeled. Second, F.T.C. inspection procedures would discover violations of the act's technical requirements.

The American Bar Association commission appointed to study the F.T.C., which asserted that the wool, fur, and textile acts were designed primarily to protect producers rather than consumers, complained in 1969 that the F.T.C. "has given inordinate attention to these areas. Moreover, the F.T.C.'s enforcement effort again has been focused on trivial matters." The commission further charged that "literal minded enforcement" was hardly relevant to serious consumer interest.[13] And what was true in 1969 about enforcement of the Wool Act was equally true in the years 1956–1964, when the F.T.C. entered approximately 200 cease-and-desist orders, almost all of them against small firms. In the 1970s, however, the act was enforced less frequently, as Table 17 shows.

Table 17. F.T.C. output under the Wool Act, 1970–1973

F.T.C. output	1970	1971	1972	1973
Complaints issued	31	9	9	4
Cease-and-desist orders	29	10	8	4
Inspections	3,386	1,675	970	513

Source: U.S. House of Representatives, 93d Cong., 1st sess., 1973, Committee on Interstate and Foreign Commerce, *Wool Products Labeling Act Amendment, 1973,* p. 15.

As might be expected with such an explicit statute as the Wool Act, the factual statements and legal considerations of most of the cases brought were very simple. The largest number involved claims that overstated the wool content of fibers and understated the amount of reprocessed or reused wool or other fibers; the products involved ranged from hats and coats to fabrics and men's socks.[14] In a few cases concerning materials composed of reprocessed and reused wool, the amount of reprocessed wool was overstated and the amount of reused wool understated.[15] Thus the pecking order of product differentiation that the statute's supporters sought was indeed established. No further proof is needed beyond the large number of orders entered against firms that overstated the wool or reprocessed wool content of their products; obviously these firms perceived a competitive advantage in this kind of differentiation.

The Wool Act's relative administrative effectiveness derived not only from the power it gave the F.T.C. to order a stop to mislabeling, but from its affirmative requirements on labeling and invoicing. Failure to supply information on fiber content, even when no misstatement, either explicit or implicit, is made, can result in the entry of a cease-and-desist order.[16] In this way the statute flushes out information on fiber content and virtually forces a firm to make a choice between accurate and inaccurate information.

The Wool Act's specificity makes it much easier to enforce than the Wheeler-Lea Act; the requirement that accurate records be kept on fiber content considerably eases the Commission's burden in proving a violation. In addition the Wool Act performs, in its subject-matter jurisdiction, the traditional Wheeler-Lea function of enjoining deceptive statements. In the "traditional" cases, however, as well as in those previously discussed, the F.T.C. has acted to protect the product differentiation of wool. For example, an importer of sweaters used the trade name "Cashmera" on tags attached to its products, thereby allegedly implying that the sweaters contained cashmere when in fact they did not. The respondent argued that its sweaters could not be confused with sweaters made of cashmere because (1) their price was one-third the price of cashmere sweaters; (2) the actual wool content appeared on the labels; and (3) no consumer had ever complained about being deceived. The Commission ruled, however, that these defenses were beside the point because the term "Cashmera" could possibly deceive prospective purchasers, and pointed out that in passing the Wool Bill the House had sought to dissociate wool in the public mind from "fabrics and articles which simulate wool or part wool products."[17]

In this and similar cases, even though apparently no consumer complained about deception, the Commission acted to prevent possible competitive comparisons with wool and to reinforce the implication of wool's superiority by protecting its product differentiation. Thus these cases, like others brought under the Wool Act, fulfilled the central purpose of the statute by enhancing the prestige of virgin wool at the expense of other fibers.

Two general conclusions can be reached about the Wool Act. First, as with so much else in trade regulation policy, output has been considerable but impact minimal; the nature of competition in the fiber industry has been little changed. From the perspective of its proponents, the act has failed to do the job. Since the end of World War II, wool production in America has declined markedly. In 1940 total production was 434 million pounds; by 1960 it had fallen to 298.9 million pounds, and by 1964 to 237.4 million pounds. Over the same period, production of noncellulose synthetic fibers grew at a remarkable rate, partly at the expense of wool.[18] To counter the competition from lower-priced substitute fibers, the various wool trades had sought to project an image of virgin wool's superiority in order to justify their higher prices. Enforcement of the Wool Act was seen as an important means to this end, since it would help to distinguish virgin wool both from reprocessed and reused wool and from other materials that entrepreneurs sought to compare favorably with wool by saying, in effect, that their products were the equal of woolen products but much cheaper. The woolgrowers' strategy did not work, however.

Second, the ease with which the Wool Act could be enforced and the special relationship that developed between an industry group and a federal agency were bound to be attractive to groups in other industries confronted with competitive problems. Even if the Wool Act had failed to have the desired impact, a similar statute might work in another industry, especially if its regulatory standards were even more explicit than those of the Wool Act. Further, a new statute might be more successful if, unlike the Wool Act, it really did cause information vital to consumers to be supplied. And so the setting was prepared for the Fur Products Labeling Act of 1951, which had even more stringent standards and explicit regulatory tools than the Wool Act.

The Fur Products Labeling Act

The Fur Act was passed in 1951 and became effective one year later. Consequently the act's protagonists had ample opportunity to reflect on the structure and operation of the Wool Act. This reflection is manifested in the considerably greater explicitness of the Fur Act. Like the Wool Act, it declares false or deceptive advertising, invoicing, or branding to be unlawful; but the list of activities that constitute falsity or deception is far more explicit and comprehensive than the earlier act's. A fur product is considered to be falsely or deceptively advertised (or misbranded) if an advertisement (or label) does not show (1) the generic name of the animal from which the fur was produced; (2) whether the product contains or is composed of used fur; (3) that the fur product is bleached, dyed, or otherwise artificially colored, when such is the case; (4) that the fur product is composed in whole or in part of paws, tails, bellies, or waste fur, when that is the case; (5) the name or other designation issued and registered by the F.T.C. in the case of a firm that manufacturers, distributes, or sells the product in interstate commerce;[19] and (6) the name of the country of origin of any imported furs used in the product.

The Fur Act then goes on to require the same information on each invoice in the chain of distribution, except that the name of the person issuing the invoice is required rather than the name of the manufacturer or distributor. Failure to supply such information is deemed false invoicing. Failure to maintain all invoices and other records showing the information required by the act for all fur products and furs handled subjects the offender to a civil penalty of $100 for each day of failure.

The F.T.C. may enter cease-and-desist orders against firms that violate any of these provisions, and in addition it is granted powers of confiscation and condemnation if it has reasonable cause to believe that a fur or fur product is being manufactured, held for shipment, shipped, or sold in violation of the act after it has given notice to the violator. If the Commission has reason to believe that a firm has violated or is about to violate the act, it can seek an injunction. Any person who willfully violates the act is guilty of a misdemeanor and can be fined and/or imprisoned.

The information the Fur Act requires manufacturers and subsequent handlers of the product to divulge is not only more detailed than that required by the Wool Act, but more beneficial to consumers. Whereas the Wool Act divides products into three arbitrary categories that would in fact tend to mislead consumers, the Fur Act legislates for provision of information of real value to consumers. In this instance, the interests of consumers and the producer group that wanted the new legislation were identical.

The Fur Act was passed as a result of vigorous activity by the domestic fur farming industry, which was deeply concerned about the problems of misleading descriptions and imports. Retailers often sold fur products under a variety of misleading and ambiguous names, and consumers were so confused that considerable distrust was engendered in the public mind. The reputation of the whole industry had suffered, and the producers of superior furs suffered most because the public could not readily tell the difference between their products and inferior, cheaper ones.[20] A seller of an inferior fur might describe his product as "Australian mink," for example, when in fact it was Canadian muskrat. True mink, of course, would sell for considerably more than "Australian mink"; the reason for the concern felt by dealers in good-quality furs, and for their need for mandatory identification of all fur products, is thus clear.

An executive of the National Board of Fur Farm Organizations stated in the course of Senate hearings on the Fur bill: "Stability of the fur industry and full confidence of the ultimate consumer in fur products is of vital interest to us as producers of fine raw materials. It is the type of pelts produced on our ranches which are most commonly imitated."[21] And he went on to assert that "the honest furrier is entitled to and can benefit from a fur labeling act which will protect him from that small minority who abuse and misuse customer confidence."[22] Thus, while consumers would unquestionably benefit from strict requirements for provision of generic names, the fur farmers' principal concern was with their own economic well-being. Further evidence of this central purpose is provided by the testimony of the director of the National Board of Fur Farm Organizations, who asserted that confusion over trade names "causes many women to refrain from buying furs because they might make a foolish deal"; the new act would "stimulate sales of furs in the long run."[23]

The second problem that concerned the Fur Act's protagonists was imports. The major weapons that can be used against foreign competition are, of course, tariffs and import restrictions, and the domestic fur industry has been successful with both weapons, especially the latter. As a close student of the fur industry notes, although a total embargo on all Chinese and many Russian furs "was ostensibly imposed for international political reasons, actually it was passed at the urging of the United States fur farmers who thought that a ban on furs which competed with their production would result in higher prices for their pelts."[24] The Fur Act was also expected to restrain imports through its labeling requirements: "An important part of the Act is identification of country of origin. Fur farmers hope that the consumer will prefer to buy American furs."[25] Both the House and Senate reports on the bill explicitly stated that a major purpose of the new legislation was to grant protection to the domestic fur industry. The Senate report, in particular, confidently predicted that the new legislation would contribute substantially to the domestic industry's economic well-being.[26]

The Federal Trade Commission, too, noting that the skins produced by the domestic industry were often of higher quality than many imports, observed in a letter to the Senate Interstate and Foreign Commerce Committee that the bill would shield domestic fur farmers and their distribution networks from competitors who use "false and glamorized designations for cheap imported furs."[27] The Commission's statement links together the two major reasons for enactment of the Fur Bill: the domestic fur farming industry produced, in general, high-grade skins and therefore favored mandatory identification of generic names; foreign competition came allegedly from lower-grade skins whose producers sought to make them more appealing by giving them misleading trade names.

Who opposed the act, and what were their reasons? The opponents were the importers of foreign furs and manufacturers who fashioned furs from foreign skins. The reasons they advanced against enactment were, it must be admitted in all candor, feeble indeed. First they argued that deception in the retail sale of furs to consumers was a local problem. The act's proponents easily countered this argument by noting that local merchants could be deceived by the labels attached to fur products; the problem therefore involved interstate commerce, for which local protection was inadequate. The opponents' second contention, advanced on the basis of the paucity of complaints about misbranding of fur received by Better Business Bureaus, was that the problem was not serious. But, as we have noted in connection with enforcement of the Wheeler-Lea Act, the deceived often do not discover the falsity of a well-designed misleading claim, and this pattern would surely apply in the case of furs.[28]

The arguments advanced against the act during the hearings were not repeated on the floor of Congress, and the Fur Act passed easily in both chambers without a roll-call vote. There can be little complaint about an act that clarifies for consumers in a rational manner the kind of article offered for sale, but in some respects it did not go far enough. The act does not require that the grade, quality, or wearability of the fur product be divulged, though these characteristics may vary within each species of animal.[29] A demand for labeling of this kind, however, would probably have split the coalition of domestic fur farmers that supported the bill.

In summary, much of the information required to be divulged under the Fur Act is useful to consumers, but consumers need even more information to make proper buying decisions. In this respect, the interests of consumers conflict with the interests of the groups that supported the act. On the other hand, most of the categories of information required by the act are sensible and relate to important aspects of quality.

The Fur Act has been a bonanza for those in the F.T.C. who are interested in the numbers game. Approximately 475 orders were entered under the act between 1956 and 1964, almost all of them against small firms. The trend continued through 1972; but in the first half of 1973 only one order was entered, and this change marked the beginning of a new pattern that continued through 1974 and 1975. The small number of orders entered in these years probably reflected the introduction of new statutory responsibilities for the F.T.C. and the Commission's desire to change its image as a nit-picking watchdog over small firms and petty matters, rather than any feeling that the fur-labeling problem had been solved. This interpretation appears to be confirmed by the F.T.C.'s 1972 Annual Report, which states that only 10 percent of the man-hours of the Division of Textiles and Furs was devoted to enforcement of the wool, fur, and textile acts.[30] Little purpose would be served by a detailed analysis of these cases. Suffice it to say that most have involved small local retailers who have either failed to provide required information on invoices, labels, and advertising, misstated names of animals or countries of origin, or failed to identify furs that had been artificially colored. The great number of orders entered each year during the period when the act was being vigorously enforced suggests that the act's objectives were not being completely met. The act was not an effective deterrent to small retailers bent on deceptive practices. On the other hand, if one may judge by the frequency of inspection and the paucity of complaints against them, more visible retailers and manufacturers have probably abided by the act's requirements. The high percentage of fur advertising placed by these firms which can be assumed to have shown proper generic names has probably benefited consumers as well as differentiated products of high quality from cheaper furs masquerading as their betters.

As we have seen, the wool and fur acts mark a step forward from the Wheeler-Lea and F.T.C. acts as far as enforceability is concerned. Yet one must still doubt whether they have achieved the purposes of the business interests that sponsored them. The Wool Act, for example, has clearly not prevented the erosion of wool's market position relative to other fibers. This failure is attributable in part to the manner in which standards are imposed. Essentially, these statutes are intended to serve business groups by placing the imprimatur of the federal government on product differentiation, which theoretically justifies price differentials. But the cheaper products may still sell, no matter what names are used to describe them. The third act we shall examine escapes this difficulty by banning products below a certain standard.

The Flammable Fabrics Act

In January 1952 a series of incidents known as the "torch sweater episode" occurred. In the short span of one month a large number of persons wearing what turned out to be highly flammable sweaters were seriously burned. While the tragic events of January 1952 catapulted the problem to national attention, it was not new; there had been a long series of similar incidents in which sweaters, jackets, playsuits, and other textile products exploded or burned rapidly after contact with heat or flame, causing injury and sometimes death to the wearers.[31] The manufacturers responsible for the products involved were invariably very small operators either in the United States or in the Orient, and the fibers used were always largely synthetic rather than natural wool or cotton. Public action was forthcoming in 1953, enthusiastically supported by a number of substantial business interests that sought to deal a blow to their fly-by-night competitors. The Flammable Fabrics Act was endorsed by, among others, the National Cotton Council of America, the Retail Dry Goods Association, and the Tufted Textile Manufacturers Association.

In addition to expressing what must be assumed to be genuine feelings of outrage and concern over the torch-sweater episode, businessmen were quite frank about their economic interest in the legislation. The Textile Distributors Institute, for example, stated that there was "also a selfish consideration on the part of the members of this association to the extent that their good will and prestige might be seriously affected by a recurrence of the disasters resulting from highly flammable apparel."[32] Thus the same kind of fear that played a significant part in the enactment of the Wheeler-Lea Act—fear of possible sales losses for a whole product class because of the activities of a few unscrupulous operators—had a role in this legislation. One trade association executive after another stated the theme, pointing out that fly-by-night manufacturers were exclusively responsible for production of highly flammable wearing apparel. Given the ease of entry into the industry, voluntary standards were of no avail; only government action could meet the problem. As a J. C. Penney executive pointed out, long-standing voluntary standards on flammability had not deterred many small textile manufacturers from producing flammable merchandise.[33]

With nearly universal support from producer groups and others, the act passed both houses without any substantive amendment. Initially the act covered all articles of clothing except hats, footwear, and gloves, but in 1967 it was extended to cover not only all articles of clothing but interior furnishings, such as rugs, as well. In essence the act made the manufacture and sale of commodities that do not conform to an administrative standard of flammability unfair methods of competition and unfair and deceptive acts. The F.T.C. was authorized to conduct inspections and tests and to bring injunction and/or seizure proceedings against producers of substandard merchandise. The Commission was further authorized to establish procedures for receiving from manufacturers and others guarantees that their products met the minimum standards.

Unlike the Wool Act and the Fur Act, the Flammable Fabrics Act has continued to be enforced, indeed with increasing vigor. Between July 1955 and June 1956 eight orders were entered; in just the first three months of 1964 an equal number was entered; and in the first six months of 1973, thirty-four such orders were entered. (More recently responsibility for enforcement of the act has been transferred from the F.T.C. to the Consumer Product Safety Commission.) Almost without exception, the orders entered before the 1970s were directed against importers of oriental fabrics and wearing apparel and enjoined the respondents from importing, selling, and transporting dangerously flammable fabrics. These orders also required the respondents to notify customers of the dangerous nature of the products they had purchased.[34] The 1973 orders included some of the type just described and some directed at relatively small manufacturers of carpets that failed to meet the Department of Commerce flammability test for carpets and rugs developed in accordance with the 1967 amendment.

Evaluation of the impact of the Flammable Fabrics Act is difficult. Ralph Nader has asserted (without proof) that the act has not been enforced,[35] yet a substantial number of orders have been entered each year, and there has certainly been no repetition of the torch-sweater episode. Indeed, in fiscal 1972 only seventy-nine cases involving injury through burns that might possibly have been connected with violations of the Flammable Fabric Act were brought to the F.T.C.'s attention.[36] On the other hand, the very fact that there has been no decline in the number of orders entered over the years suggests that the problem has not yet been licked. Nor, judging from the names and descriptions of the more recent F.T.C. orders, has the act cleansed the garment industry of the kind of fly-by-night operators that originally caused the statute to be enacted. Like the wool and fur acts, and, as we shall see, the Textile Act, the economic impact of the statute has not been very noticeable.

The Textile Act

As we noted in connection with the Wool Act, the end of World War II saw dramatic changes in the domestic textile industry as a result of the dual impact of cheap imports and synthetic fibers. These developments led to a sharp decline in the proportion of natural fibers used in making clothing, floor coverings, and other products previously composed largely of wool and cotton. Cheap imports and the plethora of new fibers led, too, to overproduction and sharp declines in prices; prices of all textile products declined by about 11 percent between 1950 and 1962, while the composite price index for all industrial commodities rose by 21 percent.[37] Not only the domestic natural-fiber industries but also the domestic synthetic-fiber industry was subjected to intensive competition from foreign manufacturers, often of shoddy (and sometimes dangerous) fibers and fabrics. The affected industries responded by seeking tariff protection, agricultural price supports (in the case of natural fibers), and regulatory protection. One of the results was the Flammable Fabrics Act, directed at cheap Oriental products.

While there can be no quarrel with the Flammable Fabrics Act, whatever the underlying motives of businessmen who sought to benefit by its enforcement, considerable controversy attaches to the 1958 Textile Fiber Products Identification Act (Textile Act). The new act was both broader in coverage and more ambitious than previous labeling statutes. Its provisions covered all fibers, fabrics, yarns, and household textile articles except those covered by the Wool Act. The Textile Act required labeling that showed the percentage by weight of all natural and synthetic fibers used in production, each to be described, in order of predominance, by the generic name assigned to it by the F.T.C. Tags or labels were also to contain the name or identification number of the product's manufacturer and the country of origin if the article was imported. The act required somewhat less information in advertising but imposed stringent record-keeping requirements on manufacturers (and others who substitute their own labels for the manufacturer's); failure to keep such records constituted an unfair method of competition. The Commission's powers under the act included cease-and-desist orders, inspections and tests, and, in some circumstances, injunctions, import prohibitions, and criminal penalties. A number of products were exempted from the requirements of the act, among them upholstery stuffing, furniture coverings, structural linings, sewing thread, bandages, footwear, luggage, and diapers.

The hearings, held in 1957 and 1958, were notable for the absence of any nongovernment witnesses other than affected businessmen. The act was sponsored by a number of legislators from cotton-growing states, chief among them Senator John Stennis (Mississippi) and Congressmen Kenneth Roberts (Alabama) and Frank Smith (Mississippi). Support came from both cotton growers and such major domestic producers of synthetic fibers as Du Pont. Congressman Roberts, who presented the principal arguments in favor of the bill, began by showing that the cotton industry was in bad shape as a result of imports and a growing trend toward blends of cotton and other fibers. Cotton farmers lost in two ways when cotton was blended with cheaper fibers: "First when rayon is 'slipped in' a product which is traditionally all cotton, farmers lose part of their markets through unfair competition. On top of this, they lose prestige for their product from consumers who are dissatisfied with blends they purchased in the belief they were all cotton."[38]

The act's proponents made no attempt to conceal the benefits that were expected to accrue to cotton growers from the new law. Point-

ing out that woolgrowers had received the benefits of special legislation, Congressman Roberts suggested that fairness should allow the
cotton growers to get theirs. Congressman Charles Wolverton explicitly stated that the bill was designed to promote the interests of
cotton growers and manufacturers—as well as (of course) consumers.[39] Essentially the legislation was designed to thwart a form of
competition in the highly competitive industries that used fibers as
their basic material. Textile manufacturers, seeking to cut costs, had
been reducing the proportion of cotton in their fabrics and increasing
the proportion of such lower priced synthetics as rayon. Without the
labeling requirements that the new statute was to impose, these manufacturers could truthfully claim that their products contained cotton
and, say, rayon, without differentiating blends that contained a large
proportion of rayon from those that were largely cotton. Congressman
Smith charged that "there has been a concerted drive by some rayon
producers to persuade textile mills to blend rayon with cotton in traditionally cotton articles. Unfortunately a percentage of rayon in a
cotton fabric doesn't generally change the appearance or even the feel
of the fabric. . . . The manufacturer can substantially increase his
profit because his product is made of a substantially cheaper fiber."[40]
Congressman Smith forgot to add that the manufacturer might, alternatively, reduce his price in this highly competitive industry. Since
manufacturers who reduced the cotton content of their products could
still advertise that they contained cotton—a more highly regarded
fiber than rayon—the solution, from the perspective of the cotton interests, was to require percentage labeling. And this solution, as an
opponent of the bill observed, had an added benefit to cotton producers: labeling an article "100 percent cotton" supported the not
necessarily correct impression that pure cotton was superior to a
blend, just as a pedigreed dog is "better" than a mutt.[41]

Similar reasons motivated such large domestic manufacturers of
synthetic fibers as Du Pont to support the Textile Act vigorously.
These large firms had invested considerable sums in promoting the
new fibers they had developed, which they considered far superior to
rayon. It became quite important, therefore, to differentiate these
newer fibers—which, according to a Du Pont executive, "impart
truly remarkable properties when used in sufficient quantities in
blends"—from the cheaper, older synthetic fibers, especially rayon.
If not blended in sufficient proportions, these higher priced, heavily

promoted synthetic fibers imparted "none of their properties," yet any blend could be unfairly promoted by reference to the highly regarded name, thereby "implying properties" that the fabric did not have.[42] The manufacturers of these new fibers therefore favored textile labeling legislation to prevent garment manufacturers from enjoying a free ride on the basis of manufacturers' promotional campaigns while actually using only small amounts of synthetic fibers. Besides, the use of the new fibers in quantities insufficient to impart unique qualities created a negative image for these fibers.

The statute's sponsors made it eminently clear that they approved of this reasoning and intended the domestic synthetic-fiber producers to benefit from the bill. Congressman Smith stated: "It seeks to protect the producers of the quality synthetics against the reputation-damaging producers of textiles advertised as containing those quality fibers when in fact they do not contain them."[43]

Opposition to the bill was led by garment manufacturers interested in continuing a form of competition in which percentages of fibers were juggled to reduce costs and/or prices. Percentage-labeling requirements might make it more difficult to alter the fiber composition of garments rapidly. As for consumer interest, trade associations representing these atomistic industries (dress manufacturers, coat manufacturers, infant-wear manufacturers, and so on) argued that the labeling requirements of the act were misleading, since they implied that fiber was the sole or most important determinant of product quality, whereas in fact the grade of the particular fiber and the construction, finish, and fabrication are of at least equal importance. Furthermore, the consumer was to be given no information on the strengths and weaknesses of various fibers and blends and the reasons for particular mixtures. A small percentage of a well-publicized synthetic fiber might impart more strength to a garment than a larger percentage, yet percentage labeling might create in the consumer's mind a false impression of inferiority. And the consumer might well believe that 100 percent of one fiber was necessarily superior to any blend. Finally, as Congressman Leo O'Brien argued, under the proposed legislation the consumer would be confused by a long list of fibers and would turn away from bargains in favor of something that could be fully understood, such as cotton. The bill's proponents made no reply to these arguments, either during the hearings or in the congressional debates.[44]

After enactment of the statute, the F.T.C. promulgated its Rule 7, setting forth sixteen generic names of textile products (to which a seventeenth, Anidex, was added in 1969). Manufacturers may use trade names but only in conjunction with the generic name, such as "Orlon-acrylic." The act was amended in 1969 to provide for explicit labeling of fibers constituting 5 percent or less of a product if the fiber has functional significance; under the original act fibers constituting less than 5 percent needed only to be labeled "miscellaneous fibers."[45]

Since the act came into effect, on March 3, 1960, the F.T.C. has entered, on average, between ten and twenty orders a year, most of them developed through inspection procedures. The number has varied from year to year, apparently as a result of nothing more than changes in the emphasis placed by the Division of Textiles and Furs on the various labeling statutes. Orders have been entered against firms at every level of trade and have usually involved such technical deficiencies in labeling, advertising, and invoicing as failure to reveal generic names and percentages. Other cases have involved nothing more than failure to maintain all of the records required by the act. And other orders have been entered because tests have shown the percentages of various fibers used in a product to vary slightly from the percentages claimed on labels or in advertising. Almost all of the firms against which orders have been entered have been small, many of them minuscule. But even during the most vigorous period of enforcement the Commission inspected only 20 percent of textile mills and between 10 and 15 percent of retail outlets—and the proportion has dropped sharply since 1969. One wonders, therefore, how effective a deterrent to deception the act is, if we assume for the moment that its purpose is largely to benefit consumers.[46] The steady stream of orders, year after year, suggests that the perceived risk of being caught is fairly low for the unscrupulous and the careless.

Nor has the act been the boon to cotton producers that they anticipated, as Table 18 shows. During 1965–1970, a period of vigorous enforcement of the Textile Act, domestic cotton production declined by one-third. And despite the hopes of the act's proponents and the fears of its opponents, cotton production (and therefore, we may assume, consumption) has been lower in the 1970s than it was when the act came into effect. Comparison of the production figures for the three fiber groups suggests that competitive factors rather than regula-

Table 18. Domestic production of cotton, rayon and acetate, and noncellulose fibers, 1960–1973

Year	Cotton (millions of bales*)	Rayon and acetate (millions of lbs.)	Noncellulose Fibers (millions of lbs.)
1960	14.2	1,028.5	854.2
1965	15.0	1,527.0	2,062.4
1970	10.2	1,373.2	4,053.5
1973	13.0	1,357.0	6,997.9

Source: Economic Research Service, U.S. Department of Agriculture.
* A bale weighs approximately 500 pounds.

tion have had the major impact on the division of the market. This observation leads to the final point to be made about the Textile Act: the consumer attitudes that it was hoped (or, from the opposite point of view, feared) that labeling information would foster apparently did not take root. The limited technical information conveyed to consumers under the provisions of the Textile Act and other labeling statutes is apparently easily counteracted by other aspects of advertising and by price considerations.

Conclusion

Under the impact of technological development and foreign competition, the traditional sectors of the fiber industry—wool, cotton, and animal fur—have lost ground to foreign competitors and the producers of synthetic fibers. The four pieces of legislation examined in this chapter have constituted attempts by the traditional sectors to stem the competitive tide. With affirmative disclosure of the generic names of a garment's component fibers and furs, wool, cotton, and fur interests hoped to differentiate what they perceived as their superior products from products of lower quality, and thereby to justify their higher prices. At the same time they hoped that the government's imprimatur on generic names would aid sales of their products and discourage sales of close substitutes. After all, everyone knows that mink is superior to rabbit. Similarly, pure wool should be more desirable than reprocessed or reused wool. Cotton, too, is a known commodity, whereas "saran" and "anidex" are terms relatively unknown to consumers and therefore to be distrusted. The hope was, then, that consumers would not take a chance on purchasing presumably inferior, tainted, or unknown products and would stick to the tried and true.

When an opportunity has arisen to ban or restrict competing foreign merchandise, traditional-sector interests have seized upon it. In 1967, for example, partly as a result of the Five-Day War in the Middle East, the House and Senate sought to remove the long-staple cotton quota assigned to Egyptian producers and transfer it to American producers.[47] That bill failed to survive the President's veto, but the theme of tariff protection and quotas for foreign textile fibers and products has persisted in the post–World War II era. The Flammable Fabrics Act, laudable as it may be, was a footnote to the theme. Taking advantage of the dangerous flammability of certain fabrics imported from the Orient, the domestic textile industry happily supported the act, knowing that it would be directed at cheap foreign competition.

These four acts represented attempts to lessen competition by imposing standards. In the case of the wool, fur, and textile acts, the standards were those of definition. In the case of the Flammable Fabrics Act, the standards were of minimum product quality. But, one may ask, what does it matter that these statutes were enacted to serve producers' interests if they help the consumer? As far as the Flammable Fabrics Act is concerned, one can have no reservations about its aims. The lesson to be learned from it, however, is that small fly-by-night firms have a much stronger incentive to violate the law than do large visible firms whose reputation could be demolished overnight by a torch-sweater episode. Regulation is considerably easier and more effective, too, if regulators have to consider only a few large firms and not thousands of small ones. In the most simple terms, an atomistic industry is the natural enemy of effective consumer protection, a lesson already clear from the last chapter.

While the aims of the Flammable Fabrics Act are uniformly considered laudatory, the other three statutes have many critics. Specifically, they are charged with promoting deception, in that they require disclosure of only a few relatively unimportant facts about a product, but the fact that this information must be disclosed leads consumers to believe that it is most important to consider when they decide on a purchase. Thus the critics of the Textile Act argue that construction and finish, for example, are more important factors than fiber, and the critics of the Wool Act argue that the distinctions made in that statute are irrelevant. Perhaps the critics are right; but it does not necessarily follow that these acts should be repealed. Perhaps the statutes should rather be amended to require further and more relevant disclosure. It might be argued that for consumers the information that must be disclosed is trivial compared to the rest of the promotional message. If this is so, all labeling legislation is more or less futile unless extraneous material is banned from advertisements. The F.T.C.'s administration of the three statutes certainly does not indicate that the agency's considerable efforts have had much impact on consumers' purchasing decisions.

Perhaps the most important effect of the three statutes is that they have provided a new outlook on regulation, one that could be employed in other statutes. Statutes tailored to meet specific problems might be useful in advancing the consumer's cause in other contexts, even if the three early labeling statutes failed in that purpose. To this subject we now turn.

CHAPTER 10

Consumerism and the F.T.C.

In 1967 Colston Warne, for many years an officer of Consumers Union, caustically described the labeling statutes discussed in the last chapter as far more concerned with producers' than consumers' interests: "The Textile Labeling Act, for example, fits the Du Pont competitive need far more snugly than the consumer need for product information."[1] As we have seen, the principal supporters of the various labeling acts were business groups. The legislative history of the next set of consumer-oriented regulations to be enforced by the F.T.C. is very different: groups purporting to represent the consumer interest played the leading role in advocating new legislation, while business groups were, *at first,* almost uniformly hostile. This significant new pattern is popularly described as "consumerism."[2] Why did consumerism develop, and what is its significance?

The Rise of Consumerism

The development of consumerism is usually attributed to the catalytic work of one man, Ralph Nader, and more explicitly to the 1965 publication of his exposé of automobile safety.[3] Closer analysis shows, however, that the phenomenon is related to important sociological and ideological changes that have taken place in the United States since the end of World War II, most notably since the end of the 1950s. Before World War II the ambiguous phrase "middle class" was likely to evolve the image of a small businessman or a managerial employee in a large enterprise. Professionals were medical doctors or dentists—small entrepreneurs in their own right—or lawyers, most of whom functioned in conjunction with business, large or small, national or local. The postwar era, and especially the period since the beginning of the 1960s, has seen the growth of what Paul Weaver terms the "New Class." The nexus between this class and business is considerably looser than the ties that bound the prewar middle class to business.[4] The events that triggered the formation of the New Class were the enormous expansion of higher education and parallel growth in public employment and institutions (such as foundations) that, though established with corporate funds, operate relatively free of business control. Though the number of people employed in education, government, and the social services is small in relation to the total work force, the expansion of employment in these areas meant the expansion of a highly articulate, relatively well-off segment of the population.

During the postwar era, three other developments contributed to the political consciousness of the New Class, and hence to the development and support of consumerism. First, with the advent of the Cold War, public officials at all levels took part in a massive propaganda campaign to emphasize the virtues of the "American way of life," with its ability to deliver quality products to consumers, in contrast to the Soviet system. Second, the business community vastly expanded the amount of money it spent, through advertising and promotion, on proclaiming the virtues of its products.[5] Third, this advertising placed such heavy emphasis on alleged improvements in previously marketed products that "new, improved" became a household cliché. For many products, however, improvement meant an increase in complexity—and thus an increase in the number of functional parts that might require repair. Consider the refrigerator, a relatively simple appliance. In the 1950s the refrigerator had two operational units; by the early 1970s the simplest model had at least seven and the most complex sixty-three.[6]

The result of all this self-congratulation was a great rise in expectations about product quality, performance, durability, and reliability—and, in general, exceedingly high expectations about the quality of the "American way of life," especially in the area of physical well-being. Yet as consumer goods became increasingly complex and novel, they acquired the reputation, if perhaps not always the reality, of increasingly frequent breakdowns and repairs. Americans became increasingly intolerant of the external costs of high rates of growth, technological change, and consumption, as well as of product imperfections. The former led eventually to the development of the antipollution crusade, the latter to consumerism.

In most quarters consumer dissatisfaction led to nothing more ominous than grumbling, but in the highly articulate New Class, people began to organize and to campaign for new legislation and more effective administration of existing laws. The surgeon general's staff, for example, was principally responsible for legislation to restrict the promotion of cigarettes; the role of public-interest lawyer Ralph Nader in automobile safety legislation is well known; less well known is the contribution of product-liability lawyer Edward Swartz, who was the prime force behind the movement for toy safety. Behind such people lie well-financed organizations, composed of members of the New Class, which carry out investigations and testify before public bodies on every relevant policy issue. Such organizations include the Public Interest Research Group, the National Consumer Law Center, the National Consumers' League, and many others.

Faced with concentrated demands for new legislation and the New Class's articulated hostility to big business, large firms have reacted with surprisingly little antipathy. A 1974 survey of managers of leading firms found that 89 percent felt that business could capitalize on consumerism as a competitive marketing tool; only one of ten perceived consumerism as a threat. The report concluded: "So businessmen see consumerism basically as an ally, a tool through which profits can be generated."[7] The strategy is, of course, to appear to accede to proposals for product modification and market a new "new, improved" product that answers at least some consumer demands. Thus can consumer confidence be restored or maintained. As President Nixon observed in a message to Congress on consumer protection: "Most businessmen in recent years have recognized that the confidence of the public over a long period of time is an important ingredient for their own success and have themselves made important voluntary progress in consumer protection."[8] In an economy that demands for its successful operation a high volume of sales to consumers, the urgency to business of maintaining consumer confidence cannot be faulted. Since consumers' confidence in large corporations and in their products has been eroded in recent years,[9] rational business strategy is not to pretend, ostrich-like, that this erosion has not taken place, but rather to capitalize on it.

Other advantages may accrue to large firms as a result of consumerism. First, high product standards may impose an overwhelming cost burden on smaller firms. The managing director of the U.S.A. Standards Institute has observed, "I can get G.E. and Westinghouse to reduce current leakage. But the standard would put fifty manufacturers out of business."[10] Second, the costs of innovations relating to safety and quality can often be passed on to consumers, though of course the manufacturer's freedom to transfer costs in this way will vary with the rise and fall of demand for the product, and with the elasticity of demand.[11] The postwar experience of the automobile industry in passing on the costs of style changes and new devices added to cars voluntarily suggests very strongly that additional costs have been transferred easily in oligopolistic industries.[12]

But if consumer demands are to be met, the government must impose uniform standards. A firm will not often lead the way in making a costly change, because it could not pass on the additional cost if a price increase put it at a competitive disadvantage. Whole industries therefore try to act together on new standards through government intervention (voluntary agreement without public approval might violate the Sherman Act in being a collusive agreement to restrain trade). A statute that imposes standards acceptable to an industry represents, then, another advantage of consumer legislation: it forecloses competition in the area that is the subject of legislation. But while such a prospect might seem attractive in one respect, it is disturbing for businessmen to be barred from using a particular mode of competition. Uneasiness over this contradiction may account for the peculiar business attitude toward consumer laws.

Most of these laws are initially proposed by organized groups from the New Class and sponsored by legislators who sympathize with them; sometimes the process is reversed. Industry at first opposes the legislation but is insufficiently aroused to do much about it; then, when there appears to be a serious possibility that a bill will be passed, important business interests successfully act to modify it to their advantage. Once these changes have been made, the business interests responsible for them support the bill in its final stages. After enactment they discover that the new law does not hurt at all, and indeed has some advantages. Let us examine in the light of this analysis the three most important additions to the F.T.C.'s statutory obligations in the area of consumer interest: fair packaging, truth-in-lending, and warranty legislation.

Fair Packaging

The problem of "slack-fill" had been conceptually recognized as deceptive by the Commission before enactment of the Fair Packaging (sometimes called Truth-in-Packaging) Act, but very few orders were entered on these grounds. Between 1956 and 1964, for example, only two orders involving deceptive packaging were entered, although a similar theory of culpability was involved in five orders entered against paperback book publishers for failing to give adequate notice that their editions were abridgements.[13] The slack-fill theory argues that the shape and appearance of a product's package implicitly make certain claims, just as surely as words do. Seeing a box or a can, consumers infer that it is filled nearly to the top; if half the space is occupied by air, they are deceived. Similarly, the purchaser of a book assumes that it contains the entire work whose title it bears, unless it carries an explicit notice to the contrary. While the Commission's theory of slack-fill is undoubtedly sound, the problem is not so simple as it may initially appear. Many products shrink during transit from the manufacturer to the retailer; others require some empty space for technical reasons.

Competition in packaging has two distinctive aspects. First, putting into a container a smaller quantity of a product than is contained in a competitor's identical container can lead to either cost savings and higher profits or price cutting without a reduction in the margin between price and costs. In either event, this form of competition can disturb the stability of an industry. And since it is so quantifiable, it can also lead to retaliation, either through price cutting or through the reductions in cost that can be achieved by a lowering of quality.

Historically, trade associations have responded to the problem either by promulgating voluntary grade, size, and quality standards or by supporting standards imposed by Congress or an executive agency. Before World War II the Canners League of California established specifications and grades for nine kinds of fruit and five sizes of cans, and the Northwest Canners Association developed similar standards for several vegetables. In the same period the California Olive Association developed explicit grade-labeling requirements and even standards governing the number of olives that each of four standardized cans should contain. The other side of the coin is represented by the failure of the National Canners Association and others to simplify can sizes and shapes, "because producers want to vary dimensions and capacities of cans slightly from those of their competitors."[14] Trade associations seeking to escape from the limitations of voluntary standards have supported such statutes as the 1930 McNary-Mapes amendment to the original Food and Drug Act, which empowered the Secretary of Agriculture to establish quality and minimum-fill standards for canned goods. The McNary-Mapes Act, in fact, drew its major support from large canners, who sought government protection from the competition posed by low-quality canners.[15]

Why, then, did no affected industry support the original Fair Packaging Bill? Obviously the conflicting desire to compete in terms of fill and container size played a part; but of at least equal importance was the question of the impact that standardization would have on the construction of packages. For a second kind of competition in packaging had begun in earnest in the 1950s, when the number of alternative packaging materials proliferated. Where once the tin can was standard, it now competes with aluminum, paper and foil, plastic, and other materials. Clearly the ability to shift from one material to another in pursuit of the best price and lowest shipping cost is in the interest of the canners. Equally clearly, promulgated standards *may* inhibit quick shifts from material to material.

In addition, packaging design and graphics have become a major tool in the sale of consumer products. This trend is most noticeable in the area of perfumes, cosmetics, and toiletries, but it can be found in other product areas as well. Among firms that have achieved substantial increases in sales as a result of novel packaging are the Welch Grape Juice Company, which put jams in drinking glasses; General Foods, which marketed its Log Cabin Syrup in glass pitchers; and the Borden Company, which packaged its pickles in apothecary jars.[16] Packaging has thus become an important new competitive weapon, used both as an attention-catcher for the ever increasing number of new products and as a means of achieving increases in sales of established products whose performance may not be meeting manufacturers' expectations. Manufacturers are sometimes able to capitalize on variations in size, too, by imputing qualitative virtues to particular variants. Large containers, for example, may be promoted as "family size" or "large economy size," smaller ones as designed to prevent waste. Because competition through packaging has become increasingly important in the postwar era, many firms are loath to see restrictions placed on this form of rivalry. Yet historically industry has built up considerable momentum in establishing standards to prevent price competition.

The bill introduced by Senator Philip Hart in 1966 had been debated in committee in previous sessions of Congress but had never reached the floor of either chamber. In 1966, however, it received for the first time the strong support of the executive branch. Commentators have surmised, without any hard evidence, that President Lyndon Johnson was looking for a popular issue to balance against the twin debacles of the War on Poverty and the Vietnam War. Consumerism was, in this analysis, precisely the right issue because it could regain liberal support lost as a result of the administration's failures and because, in comparison with other programs, it would cost little.[17] Whatever the underlying reasons, President Johnson recommended to Congress on March 21, 1966, that it enact fair packaging legislation in order to protect the consumer in the marketplace.[18]

The bill as initially introduced would have given the federal government the right to standardize package sizes and shapes, thus effectively prohibiting odd shapes and sizes. The food industry adamantly opposed the bill because this provision, in their judgment, would have effectively ended competition in attractive packaging.[19] Spokesmen for large food manufacturers did not emphasize this point, however. Rather, they pointed out that they had voluntarily developed adequate standards and that the need for repeat sales constituted a strong disincentive to deceptive packaging. Moreover, sharp curtailment of product sizes and shapes would impose enormous costs on food manufacturers, since they would be forced to close down many production lines and install new ones. These costs would ultimately be borne by the very consumers the bill was intended to protect. The representatives of small business complained that mandatory standards would be hardest on them. Small firms, it was urged, must try to offer something more than, something different from, the products of their larger competitors. Moreover, small firms were less able financially to retool and purchase the new equipment required to meet mandatory packaging standards.[20]

The government's witnesses took a clearly conciliatory tone, arguing that through reduced costs industry as well as consumers would benefit from standardization. Moreover, since the voluntary standards adopted through trade associations were unenforceable, public action was necessary to protect the overwhelming number of honest manufacturers from their few unscrupulous competitors.[21] The conciliatory approach initially met with rebuff from leaders of the food industry, who refused the offers of Senator Hart and others to discuss compromises on the main parts of the bill. Industry's aim was simply to kill the bill. A key change in tactics occurred during the House hearings, however, when industry leaders entered into discussions with some committee members and administration officials. A compromise was reached which *Fortune* concluded "is one that industry can live with. It requires no more than changes in most labels which are frequently revised in any event." Instead of mandatory packaging standards, industry was given a one-year period in which to develop voluntary standards on packaging sizes and standard weights where "undue" proliferation impaired product comparisons.[22]

Congressman Harley Staggers described the bill as imposing requirements that were no more onerous than those that business had been meeting voluntarily since 1926; under the aegis of the Department of Commerce it had already arrived voluntarily at more than 500 standards.[23] The bill pleased virtually everyone and passed the House by an overwhelming vote of 300–8. The change in the food industry's attitude was so complete that in 1969 the Grocery Manufacturers' Association strongly recommended to the House that sufficient funds be appropriated for adequate enforcement of the statute.[24]

Authority under the act was divided between the F.T.C., the F.D.A., and the Department of Commerce. The F.T.C. was empowered to prepare regulations governing the terms that manufacturers could use to describe the size of a package. Thus it could standardize terms like "giant" and "family size"; but it was expressly forbidden to place any limitations on size, shape, weight, or dimensions. Second, the agency was empowered to issue regulations governing the use of such promotional phrases relating to price as "cents off." Third, the F.T.C. could issue rules requiring that the common or usual names of commodities be affixed to packages. In the case of a commodity with two or more ingredients, it could require a listing in order of predominance. Fourth, it could make rules pertaining to slack-fill, provided that it took into consideration in each case the functional necessities of the product. Violations of the act and of regulations promulgated under it were deemed violations of Section 5 of the F.T.C. Act.

In accordance with its authority under the act, the Commission has entered a number of regulations—and proposed others—of which the so-called economy-size rule is the most interesting. Under F.T.C. regulations such terms as "giant" and "family size" can be used only when the manufacturer offers packages of at least one other size. The term "economy size" can be used on only one size of package, whose unit price is considerably less than the unit price of other sizes.[25] A regulation of importance proposed in 1974 would require disclosure of ingredients on detergent containers.[26] Very few orders have been entered in recent years involving slack-fill or related practices.[27]

The original version of the Fair Packaging Bill was viewed in some quarters as another Magna Carta. Affected industries, initially intransigent, later accepted a modified version of the bill which allowed federal agencies to restrict competition in some areas that might involve intensive price competition, such as slack-fill, but did not make inroads on competition in packaging shapes and designs. The act thus reflects the contradiction between stability through standardization and competition through innovative packaging. A similar uneasy compromise is reflected in the Truth-in-Lending Act.

Truth-in-Lending Legislation

Like the Fair Packaging Act, the Truth-in-Lending Act (formally known as the Consumer Credit Protection Act) had languished in Congress for a considerable period before it became part of President Johnson's legislative program. First introduced by Senator Paul Douglas in 1960, it was reintroduced in every congressional session until Douglas' defeat in the elections of 1966. In 1967 Senator William Proxmire and Representative Lenore Sullivan, with strong administration backing, reintroduced modified, and different, versions of the bill. This time a version passed both houses and was signed into law at the end of May 1968.

The intended purpose of the Truth-in-Lending Bill was the protection of consumers by "full" disclosure of the annual terms and conditions of finance charges. It received the enthusiastic support of the National Consumers League and similar organizations, while lending institutions (with the exception of credit unions) uniformly opposed it during its initial stages. The opposition of banks and small loan companies, which had never been more than lukewarm, gradually shifted to support or indifference. By the time the bill reached the House floor, Representative Sullivan could observe that "the support from legitimate business has been most heartening and also very effective. . . . This industry, like all responsible industries beset by fringe operators who give a bad name to an essential service, has demonstrated a willingness to accept a significant number of long overdue reforms which can be accomplished only through legislation."[28]

What had changed the initial hostility into feelings of harmony? Essentially it was the widespread conviction among lenders that the act did *not mean* a thing and would not alter consumers' purchasing or borrowing patterns at all. This conclusion was in keeping with the reasoned projection of President Johnson and his economic advisers. In his 1966 message on consumer interests the President asserted that the legislation would not reduce the volume of credit, dampen consumer spending, or regulate the cost of credit.[29] More important, lenders had seen that state truth-in-lending statutes had neither reduced the volume of loans nor forced down interest rates. Particularly relevant in this respect was the Massachusetts truth-in-lending law, which had been in effect for more than a year by May 1968.[30]

Let us examine some of the more important provisions of the act to see why lenders had so little to fear and why Homer Kripke, a leading expert on consumer credit, has described truth-in-lending legislation as a put-on. The heart of the Consumer Credit Protection Act lies in two major requirements. First, creditors must tell consumers in writing all the costs assessed when credit is extended—that is, not only interest but also loan fees, charges for credit investigations, and premiums for credit life insurance. Second, the lender must disclose the "true" annual rate of interest on the transaction. This seemingly simple provision was a major point of controversy in the hearings. The first Senate version, prepared by Senator Douglas, provided for no tolerance of error, even though in some financial situations a simple, accurate rate cannot be calculated by a retailer in advance. The Proxmire version allowed tolerance for error of one quarter of 1 percent in irregular installment situations.[31]

The question of tolerance was but one aspect of the controversy surrounding the true annual rate of interest. Under then-common lending terminology, if one borrowed $100 and agreed to repay the loan plus a $6 charge in one year, the arrangement would be described as a 6 percent loan. Under Section 107 of the Truth-in-Lending Bill, however, the true rate of interest was based on the amount a debtor could use over the repayment period. Thus if a repayment schedule calls for equal monthly payments of $8.83, the amount left in use decreases each month and the true rate of interest therefore increases. Calculated on this basis, the true annual interest rate on that $100 loan would be approximately 11 percent. The system, developed by the Treasury Department, has the merit of making comparisons among different kinds of lending institution simple. According to the vice-chairman of the Federal Reserve Board, such a system of computation would strengthen competition by allowing consumers to compare credit costs accurately.[32] The bankers objected that banks might appear to be violating various state usury laws. Accordingly the statute allowed interest rates to be cited in terms of dollars per hundred until 1971, on the assumption that the states would by then have revised their laws to embrace the new system of computation.[33]

The bankers, already tightly regulated at the state level with respect to both interest charges and disclosure, did not object, then, to the principles involved. Indeed, they had contributed substantial time and money to the Uniform Credit Code Project of the National Conference of Commissioners on Uniform State Laws. Their principal objections were to overly rigid computational requirements and the possible conflict with state usury laws.[34] And in these respects they were accommodated. Moreover, since bank rates of interest are generally lower than the rates of other lenders, a uniform system of comparison makes them "look good against the 18 percent to 36 percent that loan companies usually charge."[35] As for the notion that a uniform system for stating interest rates would somehow produce more competition than is usually found in the credit market, that was a pipe dream at best. During periods of credit shortage, lenders will operate as any oligopoly does, seeing little point in reducing rates to accommodate small customers. During periods of surplus funds, competition will produce rate reductions.

Another important class of lenders, retail merchants, also were opposed to the bill initially but ultimately supported it. Their major concern was over the provisions governing "revolving credit," a form of credit extension employed by department stores and the issuers of credit cards, such as Master Charge. Under this system creditors assess a monthly interest charge on the balance outstanding. Obviously the dollar amount owed can vary from month to month, depending on the cardholder's purchases and payments during the previous accounting period (usually one month). The Senate's truth-in-lending bill required a statement of the monthly interest rate applied plus a dollar figure on money owed, a formulation acceptable to department stores. The House bill, however, required translation of the monthly rate into annual terms. Thus where the Senate bill allowed a statement announcing an interest rate (or service charge) of 1.5 percent per month, the House version required a statement to the effect that interest was being charged at the annual rate of 18 percent.

Those who extended revolving credit made three arguments against the House bill.[36] First, they claimed that the peculiarities of revolving credit precluded an accurate comparative method of calculating interest to individual customers. Ordinarily in a revolving-credit scheme, interest is calculated as of a specific date; for example, all persons whose last names begin with S may have their interest calculated as of the twenty-fifth day of each month. But suppose S_1 was extended credit on the first day of the month and S_2 was extended credit of an equal amount on the twentieth day. Since interest, by definition, has a time dimension, the real rates paid by S_1 and S_2 would be different. When this notion is extended to the great number of persons who make purchases through revolving credit accounts, these creditors argued, a simple true rate of interest, applicable to all customers, becomes impossible to state.

The second objection stemmed from the so-called free-ride provisions of most revolving credit plans. Under these provisions the customer is granted a period—usually thirty days—after a purchase is made during which no interest has to be paid. Creditors argued that the period over which interest is measured should begin from the date of purchase, not the date from which interest charges accrue, on the ground that credit is extended at the time of the transaction. Obviously the longer the time period of measurement, the lower the interest rate, and hence the preference for the longer period.

Third, those who extended revolving credit argued that the yield to them was considerably less than the 18 percent that would be stated on bills under the House bill, since under revolving credit plans interest is computed on outstanding balances, not the sum originally borrowed. Under an installment plan, a customer who purchased $100 of merchandise would be required to pay $118 (18 percent per year). But under a revolving credit plan, since interest relates to outstanding balances, the yield can be considerably less. If one pays $10 principal plus $1.50 interest during the first accounting period, the payment during the next accounting period will be $10 principal plus $1.35 interest; then interest payments, on an annual basis, will amount to considerably less than under the installment plan, and the effective rate of interest, these creditors argued, will be much less than 18 percent.

The Senate accepted these arguments but the House did not. Meanwhile, other extenders of credit objected strongly to the fact that they were to be required to state interest in annual terms while those engaged in revolving credit were not. What happened, they asked, to the principle of comparability? Associations of stores that usually enter into installment contracts (in which interest was required to be stated in annual terms) were particularly incensed at the alleged favoritism shown to their larger competitors.[37] The compromise that resulted required the extenders of revolving credit to state both the annual rate and the periodic rate, but permitted them to state the lower "effective rate" as well. It is not absolutely clear what changed the minds of such large extenders of revolving credit as Sears and Montgomery Ward and led them to support the compromise, but two factors may plausibly be argued to have been crucial: experience with the Massachusetts law's general lack of impact on consumers' spending and credit habits; and a feeling that the welter of shorthand credit information required to be disclosed, on billing statements and elsewhere, would tend to confuse and bore customers more than inform them.[38]

The law has fulfilled the expectations of lenders who anticipated that its effects would be minimal. A survey conducted in 1971 revealed that 82 percent of borrowers had no interest in the law and that it had had no effect on the volume of loans. Moreover, consumers showed less interest in and familiarity with the fine points of lending than before the law was enacted. The only major change observed was a drop in credit advertising.[39] Nor has the act done much for the poor, on whom a great deal of testimony centered during the hearings. Many poor people cannot understand the written disclosures required; others understand full well that they are being overcharged but know they will receive credit only from merchants and credit agents who charge high interest rates. Finally, these consumers are concerned more with the total charge for a product than with the relative proportions of sales price and finance charge; the ghetto merchant can therefore shift part of his finance charge to the sale price with relative impunity.[40]

More affluent consumers who can shop around will be far more interested in comparing total prices and terms of payment than in naked statements of interest charges. In Posner's illustration of the process, a consumer shopping for a color television set is quoted two prices: (a) $450 cash, (b) $20 a month for 36 months. "He will have to compare the advantage of paying a lower price all at once with the advantage . . . of paying a larger amount in monthly installments. He will not be helped in this comparison by an interest-rate figure unless he is in the habit of saying to himself: 'my personal discount is __ percent.' "[41] Finally, in requiring retailers and other competitors to publish interest-rate information, the act permits them to keep close watch on each other's moves. Since a reduction in one department store's interest-rate charges can usually be readily matched by others, there is no incentive for rate reduction.

Although the impact of the statute has been minimal for consumers, the F.T.C. has entered many orders under it. Enforcement is divided among several agencies under regulations prepared by the Federal Reserve Board. Generally speaking, the F.T.C.'s jurisdiction does not include banks, other financial institutions, or industries, such as airlines, that come under the jurisdiction of other regulatory agencies. Its major jurisdiction is over retail establishments. During the first half of 1973 the F.T.C. entered fifteen orders under the act, almost all of them against small retailers. In the first three months of 1975 alone, twenty such orders were entered, again involving very small firms. The charges vary somewhat from case to case but they typically concern failure to disclose certain information required by the act, such as unpaid balance or "deferred payment price." In addition the Commission has challenged violations of such highly technical requirements as provision of duplicates of contracts and use of the term "financial charge."[42] Many minor violations, however, are corrected by Commission staff through informal procedures.[43]

The Truth-in-Lending Act was heralded as a great advance in consumer protection; yet, as we have seen, it has had little impact on the credit decisions of either middle-class or poor consumers. Nor has it had any impact on lending institutions, the volume of credit, or interest rates. The F.T.C.'s efforts in the area have been substantial since the statute was enacted, but to little avail. It may have entered a relatively large number of truth-in-lending orders, but the task of supervising the enormous number of retail establishments that grant credit is formidable. To an establishment that wishes for some reason to violate the statute, the deterrent effect is minimal. The Truth-in-Lending Act, then, is one of those "laws which have been enacted under promising consumer protection titles [but] come close to being name only bills."[44] Let us now examine the warranty provisions of the Magnuson-Moss Act to see whether they promise to be as ineffective as truth-in-packaging and truth-in-lending legislation has been.

Warranties

The Magnuson-Moss Warranty–Federal Trade Commission Improvement Act became law on January 4, 1975. Long before that—indeed, before the Wheeler-Lea Amendment—the Commission had entered orders against deceptive guarantees and warranties as unfair methods of competition.[45] In the 1960s the Commission was active in the warranty area, especially with respect to watches. Typical cases involved failure to give prominence on a guarantee slip to the information that handling charges would be levied for postage and insurance, and claims of "unlimited" warranty when in fact there were limitations.[46] Why, then, in view of the F.T.C.'s activity in the area of warranties and guarantees, was new legislation needed? And why did large manufacturers and retailers support the new legislation?

In order to answer these questions, we must first review the use of warranties and guarantees as a form of competition and then examine the problem of product reliability in this context. Obviously for some products durability is as important a competitive consideration as price. Indeed, price and durability may be closely connected in purchasers' minds in that they compare not just the actual price of a product, but the price averaged over the lifetimes of alternative products. When buying a wristwatch, for example, the consumer takes into account not only the fact that watch A costs $100 and watch B $50, but also the probability that watch A will last twenty years and watch B only five years; thus the cost of watch A, averaged over the years of its useful life, is lower than that of watch B.

The index of durability is the guarantee or warranty by which a seller (manufacturer or retailer) effectively promises that if a product fails to perform its intended function for a certain period, the price paid by the purchaser will be substantially reduced. Warranty considerations are, of course, far more important in the acquisition of products intended for long-term use than in the case of goods intended for rapid consumption, such as food. And the more complex a product is, the more importance the purchaser attaches to the warranty or guarantee. Both the problem and the opportunity of competitive advantage lie in the fact, observed earlier, that products have become increasingly complex. *Fortune* has estimated that repair vans make at least 100 million calls per year.[47] This pattern has sharpened purchasers' awareness of the importance of warranties, and hence producers' attentiveness to their possible use as competitive weapons. Their importance, then, may entice some sellers to practice deception in warranties. As Congressman John Moss succinctly put it, "What the bold print giveth, the fine print taketh away."

Two problems are raised by crafty warranties that do not mean what they apparently say. First, consumers can become reluctant to purchase new appliances. The potential importance of such a development becomes clear when we realize that appliance purchases do not involve simply the few basic machines we all depend on and replace from time to time, for the number of new products is continually increasing. *Fortune* lists more than fifty appliances that have been marketed for the first time since 1951, among them electric typewriters, electric toothbrushes, and electric carving knives.[48] In view of the importance to producers of selling such new products, many of them unnecessary if not downright frivolous, consumer resistance based on the suspicion that warranties do not mean what they say can be an important problem. Nor can it be solved either by individual instances of forthrightness or by such joint endeavors as the Major Appliance Consumer Action Panel, set up in 1970 by three major trade associations to review the complaints of appliance owners, for the unscrupulous can still provide deceptive warranties.

The second major problem arising from unrestricted language in warranties is that it can lead to outbreaks of intense warranty competition. For example, from 1930, when the automobile dealer franchise system developed, until 1960, automobile manufacturers uniformly offered a warranty in force for ninety days or 4,000 miles, whichever came first. Then from 1960 to 1967 the four largest automobile manufacturers competed in their warranty terms. When the competition was over, the firms were offering almost identical warranties, but the terms were far more generous than those that had prevailed before 1960.[49] Thus while a firm has an obvious economic incentive to increase warranty protection, there is a countervailing incentive to prevent competition in warranty terms.

On balance, manufacturers desired some standardization of warranties to limit competition, but did not want so much uniformity that all competition disappeared. Clearly what they did not want was what the F.T.C. proposed in 1970 for automobiles—high minimum standards of quality, durability, and performance for new automobiles, including all parts. Under the F.T.C. proposal, manufacturers would have had a statutory obligation to provide defect-free automobiles and to repair defects free of charge for a considerable period of time. Legislation of this sort might have imposed such high costs that either profits would be eroded if automakers absorbed the costs or prices would be increased to the point where demand fell if costs were passed on to the consumer. The consumer groups advocating such a law were gravely disappointed that the Magnuson-Moss Act did not contain these provisions.[50]

Business spokesmen, however, were by no means entirely satisfied with the final warranty bill. Among the especially dissatisfied were those concerned with the survival of small manufacturers of consumer goods. In order to understand their position, let us look at the provisions of the act as they pertain to warranties. The law does not require that warranties be given; but if they are, thirteen specific pieces of information must be set forth:

1. A clear identification of the names and addresses of the warrantors.
2. The identity of the party or parties to whom the warranty is extended.
3. The products or parts covered.
4. A statement of what the warrantor will do in the event of a defect, malfunction, or failure to conform with such written warranty, at whose expense, and for what period of time.
5. A statement of what the consumer must do and what expenses he must bear.
6. Exceptions and exclusions from the terms of the warranty.
7. The step-by-step procedure that the consumer should follow in

order to obtain performance of any obligation under the warranty, including the identification of any person or class of persons authorized to perform the obligations set forth in the warranty.

8. Information concerning the availability of any informal procedure offered by the warrantor for settling disputes, and a recital, where the warranty so provides, of the fact that the purchaser may be required to resort to such procedure before pursuing any legal remedies in the courts.

9. A brief general description of the legal remedies available to the consumer.

10. The time at which the warrantor will perform any obligations under the warranty.

11. The period of time within which, after notice of a defect, malfunction, or failure to conform with the warranty, the warrantor will perform any obligations under the warranty.

12. The characteristics or properties of the products, or parts thereof, that are not covered by the warranty.

13. The elements of the warranty, in words or phrases that would not mislead a reasonable, average consumer as to the nature or scope of the warranty.

The second major provision of the warranty law in effect precludes the use of a warranty to effect a tie-in sale between the warranted product and other products or services identified by trade or corporate name. But it was the third major provision that aroused the major controversy during the hearings. The act divides warranties into two categories: "full" and "limited." In order to qualify as a full warranty, a warranty must specify that the warrantor will repair the product within a reasonable time free of charge, provided only that the consumer has not damaged the product, used it unreasonably, or failed to maintain it properly. Further, the warranty cannot place any limit on the duration of a product's implied warranty[51] (in most states four years) either to the initial consumer or to subsequent owners. Finally, after a reasonable number of attempts to repair the product, the warrantor must allow the consumer to elect either a refund (minus an amount for depreciation) or replacement. The F.T.C. is empowered to rule on what constitutes a reasonable number of attempts to repair in various circumstances. Unless all of these conditions are met, a warranty must be described as "limited."

The F.T.C. is required to help warrantors set up informal procedures for settlement of disputes and make sure they are fair and effective. If informal procedures fail, consumers may sue individually and,
if successful, may recover attorneys' fees as well as damages. Class
actions may be brought if there are at least one hundred plaintiffs
each of whom has at least $25 at stake and if the total value of the
controversy is at least $50,000. But class actions cannot be brought
until the warrantor has had a reasonable opportunity to comply with a
warranty's terms. Finally, any violation of these statutory requirements, or of rules promulgated under them, can be a violation of
Section 5 of the F.T.C. Act.

Most major trade associations and firms that took the opportunity
to testify at the congressional hearings on the bill supported the new
warranty provisions. The Gas Appliance Manufacturers Association
claimed that much of the bill's informational requirements originated
in the association's guidelines for industry members, which had been
developed in part to assure successful competition with manufacturers
of electrical appliances. The association also observed that the law
was far less stringent than other proposals, which would have been
onerous to manufacturers.[52] Strong support came also from large retailers. Sears, Roebuck, for example, enthusiastically endorsed the
legislation, as did the National Association of Food Chains.[53] The
only breach in the ranks was caused by an electronics industry trade
association, which objected to the term "partial" warranty—which in
any event was changed to the more innocuous "limited" in the final
version of the bill.[54]

Most hesitant to approve the act was the Department of Commerce,
in its role as spokesman for small business. While expressing support
for the statute, Commerce noted its fear that small manufacturers
would be unable to provide a nationwide network of service and repair centers. Small firms would be unable to offer full warranties, and
the costs to them of checking on compliance with limited warranties
serviced by contracting firms would rise considerably. Insofar as warranties were an important competitive device, Commerce concluded,
"there is considerable concern that small manufacturers may not be
able to compete and many may be forced out of business."[55]

The act's proponents claimed that four principal benefits would
follow from this law: (1) improved consumer understanding; (2)
assurance of minimum warranty protection; (3) assurance of war-

ranty performance; and (4) improved product reliability.[56] While the act, like other F.T.C. statutes, requires information to be set forth in a given form, it does not follow that all consumers understand the mass of information contained in a warranty. Since a limited warranty may be very flexible in its terms and conditions, confusion can still result. But the provision allowing the F.T.C. to promulgate rules to ensure that "average" consumers will not be misled does serve to curtail egregious deception in warranties. This provision, then, and the standardized information required tends to promote warranty uniformity. So far as the second, third, and fourth benefits are concerned, the act may have less effect. Since no minimum warranty requirements are set forth, the warrantor may theoretically give virtually no protection at all. Only competitive forces—unchanged by the statute—can determine the level of warranty protection; the statute neither adds to nor subtracts from the protection that firms may choose to give. About the same can be said of the claim that the act tends to improve performance. Private remedies under state laws and competitive pressures toward reliability are supplemented only marginally by the hard-to-assemble class-action suit. Finally, it is hard to see how pressure for product reliability could be increased as a result of the law. Clearly no firm offers a full warranty unless it is close to certain that defects will not occur. If it offers a limited warranty, as most firms do, its warranty need offer nothing more under this law than it did before, and the quality of its product therefore need be no higher or lower than it was earlier.

The act's requirements seem indeed to have had a chastening effect on those warrantors who do not mean what they purport to say. To this extent firms that used warranties deceptively as a competitive device by making lavish promises that they did not have the capacity to fulfill are restrained. Thus, although consumers are generally aided, warranty competition has tended to be stabilized. And many observers seem to have concluded that smaller manufacturers are at a serious disadvantage because it is difficult or impossible for them to set up widely dispersed repair facilities. The problem for small firms is compounded by the fact that consumers must be given both advance and sufficient notice of warranties, which enhances consumers' awareness of warranties. Warranty wars have not resulted, and there is no reason to think that they will; the automobile warranty war has probably educated manufacturers in this respect. Rather, the trend seems to be toward a minimum warranty standard within each industry, with some competitive flexibility within the "limited warranty" format. Firms that cannot meet industry standards can be seriously disadvantaged— although of course they may compensate by competing in other ways. If a firm believes it has a decisive advantage, however, it may offer more generous warranty terms than its competitors, just as it could before the act.

In summary, then, the warranty provisions do not require a high, rigid standard of warranty service. Consumer proposals along these lines, which might have imposed substantial costs on all manufacturers, were largely ignored in the proceedings. The provisions of the bill were acceptable to leading firms, which sought to eliminate the destabilizing effects of deceit in warranty offerings by imposing standards. Competitiveness in warranties remains, but on a considerably reduced scale. Yet the statute's requirements impose a substantial burden on those small firms that offer warranties but do not have the facilities to live up to their obligations. Since consumers have come to expect at least some warranty for a product, firms offering none are at a disadvantage. In these respects, then, both consumers and larger firms derive some benefit, but the benefit to consumers of improved product quality is far less than might have been obtained through the establishment of high minimum product standards.

Conclusion

The three consumer-oriented statutes over which the F.T.C. has been granted jurisdiction have had similar histories. Demands for the statutes arose from legitimate complaints of business shortcomings. Members of the New Class, whose hostility to business is directly proportional to firm size, sought legislation that leading firms perceived as punitive or unworkable. Business elements were initially hostile to the proposed statutes but then successfully modified them in important respects. The laws finally enacted have been either innocuous or even beneficial to leading business firms. Each of the new laws inhibits unacceptable forms of competition yet is sufficiently flexible to permit some competition to remain in the problem area. Consumers are marginally aided, but the new laws fall far short of the goals initially sought by the consumerists.

The very fact that such a clamor has been raised for new laws is a telling comment on the F.T.C.'s previous inability to shape the outcome of events in the problem areas. These new laws do not grant the F.T.C. jurisdiction over substantial new areas—it could deal with slack-fill or warranties in the past. But their enactment constitutes a recognition of the minor impact that the F.T.C. has had, despite its considerable output. Will the new laws allow it to have more impact? The evidence indicates that here, as in nearly every other area of F.T.C. jurisdiction, little change can be expected. Thus the more fundamental question is raised: Is there some defect in the nature of regulation itself? Is the notion that regulation will have a beneficial impact for consumers equivalent, in Milton Friedman's image, to an expectation that cats will bark?[57]

PART FOUR

CONCLUSION

CHAPTER 11

Barking Cats,
Roaring Lions

At various times in this century—in 1914, in the mid-1930s, and most recently in the 1970s—many people have placed their hopes for "fair" competition and consumer welfare on the F.T.C. Yet the almost universal conclusion of persons both sympathetic and hostile to the F.T.C.'s supposed missions has been that it has failed continuously. Among those friendly to the regulatory process, hope is always born anew; if only the agency had new personnel or new powers, all would be well. Conservative critics hostile to any interference in the market process charge that regulation necessarily interferes with consumer welfare and can never work effectively. This group also argues that the costs of regulation exceed the benefits that can accrue from it. Other views of regulation have been put forward, and have been ably presented elsewhere.[1] It is not my purpose here to develop a full-scale theory of regulation, but rather to attempt to show what the F.T.C. experience can teach us about regulation and its alternatives.

The proper starting point is the realization that different persons and groups have expected different results from the agency's output. And as I have sought to show, one group may have two conflicting purposes in mind, neither of them very clearly illuminated. If there is one conclusion that may safely be drawn, it is that any statement beginning "The F.T.C. was created for the purpose of . . ." must be arrant nonsense, no matter what is put into the blank. The F.T.C.'s statutes reflect a host of divergent interests and contradictions. Yet it would be wrong to jump to the conclusion that a kind of canceling-out process is necessarily at the root of the F.T.C.'s ineffectiveness. The Wool Act explicitly reflects the single-minded interests of wool-growers, yet it has failed to stem the decline of wool products. On a

broader scale, the Robinson-Patman Act, despite intensive enforcement efforts by the F.T.C. over a long period, failed to retard the
changes in food distribution that began in the 1920s.

The strange conclusion that emerges from an overview of all the
perspectives on all the F.T.C.'s statutes—from the general, such as
Section 5 of the Federal Trade Commission Act, to the narrow, such
as the wool, fur, and textile acts—is that nobody has been satisfied.
Neither producers nor consumers are pleased with the impact (or
lack of it) of the F.T.C.'s actions. I hope, however, that I have shown
that the agency's lack of success has not been altogether a matter of
inactivity, bad personnel, or bad judgment. Certainly it has suffered
from all of these shortcomings on occasion, but at other times, both
before and since 1969, the Commission has been innovative and
courageous.

Why, then, has regulation failed to have the desired impact in the
case of either specific or general statutes? Why has failure occurred
both when weak remedies (cease-and-desist orders) have been used
and when more stringent means (injunction, divestiture, penalties,
seizure) have been employed? Finally, why has the F.T.C. failed both
when discovery techniques have been reasonably good, as with inspection under the Fur Act, and when inadequate discovery techniques
have led the Commission to rely for information on the very persons
who are supposed to be regulated?

Let us look first at some of the reasons traditionally given for
regulation's failure. First, the resources—both time and money—
available for carrying out the Commission's designated tasks have been
limited. And the resources that would be required for effective policing of the areas under the F.T.C.'s jurisdiction amount to many times
the sum that could ever reasonably be expected to be appropriated.
Consider, for example, the number of people the F.T.C. would need
just to examine all questionable advertising or all instances of parallel
pricing to see whether collusion exists. The problem is compounded
by the fact that resources must be allocated not only to the discovery
of violations—which firms do their best to conceal—but also to the
policing of orders and rules already entered. The problem has a political dimension too, for the idea of any vast increase in the policing
presence raises, in the judgment of many, grave questions of civil
liberties. The incremental increases in resources appropriated for the
F.T.C., the Antitrust Division, and similar enforcement agencies are

not likely to allow these bodies to cope with their problems. Steady increases in the number of policemen have not reduced the rate of serious crime or the rate at which crimes are solved. Indeed, crime appears to increase as the number of policemen rises. Short of totalitarian measures, regulation tends to be ineffective as long as strong incentives exist for violating the law.

The defects apparent in the regulation of business stem in part, too, from the fact that the system of private litigation has been taken as a model. The result is enormous delays. A significant lapse of time is likely to occur between an undesirable event and its discovery by the enforcement agency. Additional time then elapses before the agency's enforcement arm can muster and order the facts sufficiently well to issue a complaint or propose a rule. Then the respondent must be given a reasonable amount of time in which to answer and prepare its case. Next the pretrial procedures designed to reduce the number of cases affords additional occasion for delay; and in this process respondents are afforded ample opportunity to raise procedural side issues. Then the case goes before an administrative judge for trial, often lengthy as both sides present their arguments and quarrel over the admissibility and relevance of testimony and exhibits. The administrative judge must then spend time reflecting on the evidence and arguments presented by both sides and write a decision, explaining his reasons for it. But we are not through yet, for appeals and arguments before the full administrative agency, the courts of appeal, and sometimes the Supreme Court follow before an order is made effective. Given the enormous amount of time taken up in litigation, a great deal of harm—sometimes irreversible—may be done.

We have already noted that the trade-regulation-rule procedure in force before the Magnuson-Moss Act improves the situation only marginally. What difference does the new statute really make? Under the new rule-making procedures set forth in Section 202 of the Magnuson-Moss Act, the F.T.C. must still discover the alleged wrong that calls for promulgation of a rule and still investigate the activities in question to determine whether they constitute wrongdoing. If the Commission is satisfied that wrongdoing exists, and on a scale large enough to justify a new rule, it must publish notice of the proposed rule, stating the precise reasons for it. Then sufficient time must be allowed for interested persons (not simply affected persons) to submit written data, views, and arguments. After that the agency must provide opportunity for an informal hearing, allowing time for oral presentations, some cross-examination, and some rebuttal. (And here ample opportunity exists for interested parties to raise procedural issues over whether they were denied ample opportunity for cross-examination and so forth, and hence to create further delay.) Next the F.T.C. must review all of the material assembled and promulgate a final rule. Again appeals are permissible. Whether this new procedure will be more or less time-consuming than the case-by-case method (which will still apply for less general practices) remains to be seen. But it is already clear that it will still allow enormous delays between the occasion of the presumed wrong and the entry of public relief.

Nor would it appear that the time problem can be significantly alleviated within such constitutional requirements of due process as notice and a fair opportunity to be heard. Only an injunction proceeding offers any hope of significantly reducing the time that elapses between transgression and relief. But even then the event must first be discovered, and discovery may not take place until long after great harm has been done; and the agency must still prepare its case and muster facts and argument to persuade a court that continuation of the practice in question would probably result in such harm to the public interest as to outweigh the respondent's interest in continuing the activity. Only rarely is such a showing likely to persuade a court that relief should be entered before full trial, and even then considerable time is bound to have elapsed between initial transgression and injunctive relief.

If the regulatory process is not likely to reach a practice until long after it has taken place, can the practice be deterred effectively through sanctions? Virtually all observers agree that the cease-and-desist order has been an ineffective sanction. The Magnuson-Moss Act adds to this mechanism an action against a respondent on behalf of consumers after a cease-and-desist order or rule has been violated. The relief in such cases may include damages, money refunds, and return of property. For the action to be sustained, the Commission must show that a "reasonable man" would have known that the practice was dishonest or fraudulent. Merely to show deception, in other words, is insufficient. Nor does the provision apply to practices encompassed under the antimonopoly aegis. In short, these new provisions appear to be aimed at the activities of the multitude of small fly-by-night con men.

Yet even outright criminal penalties imposed on the perpetrators of specific activities by various state laws have apparently not reduced the scale of these activities. In an era when the effectiveness of deterrents to the commission of proscribed acts is increasingly questioned in the area of criminal law, those concerned with trade regulation still cling to a simplistic set of notions. The con man is likely to calculate, reasonably, that he can still get away with prohibited actions. Justice, he knows, will not be swift and sure; in fact, the likelihood that his acts will escape the notice of the F.T.C. is strong. And besides, even if he is caught, the Magnuson-Moss Act requires only that he give back what he gained by fraud; he will not be subjected to criminal penalties. Finally, unlike those who engage in most forms of criminal conduct, a defrauder may hide behind the facade of the corporation with its limited liability for individual shareholders. All things considered, the unscrupulous man may well decide that it is worth his while to deceive.

An additional and crucial defect of legislation, though one not usually considered, is embraced within the concept of discretion—not the discretion of the statute or of the administrative agency, but the discretion that remains to the firms to be regulated. Put simply, Alfred Chandler's conclusion, based upon meticulous research, that antitrust policies have played little part in shaping the structure, conduct, or performance of industries[2] can be explained more readily by the wide discretion available to firms, even after regulation, than by any other factor. And even if one firm, or an entire industry, is regulated, considerable discretion remains to rival firms or industries selling close substitutes.

Let us look more closely at this notion. If one limits the discretion of cigarette firms by requiring health warnings on packets or by banning television advertising, many ways remain for these firms to get their selling message across. Moreover, the warning plays a very small part in any cigarette ad. A clever advertising copywriter can produce a message that is attractive to consumers—psychologically, subliminally, or otherwise—by focusing on those parts of the message over which the firm exercises considerable autonomy. Similarly, the disclosure requirements of the Truth-in-Lending Act can be overwhelmed by the attractiveness of the product, appeals related to it, or the ghetto merchant's ability to shift what might have been interest payment to the selling price. Truth-in-lending legislation has not, in short, come close to stopping the exploitation of a particularly vulnerable group of consumers. Nor do truth-in-lending provisions face up to the fact that oral representations by sellers, which are extremely hard to discover, can completely defeat the written word.

Not all regulations, of course, can be defeated, particularly those concerned with minimum standards. Yet the public can be defeated in other ways that stem from the firm's discretion to impose costs or penalties. The most obvious case is that of costs passed on to the consumer, but there are other, less obvious examples. Since 1962, for example, pharmaceutical firms have been required to demonstrate the safety and efficacy of newly marketed drugs. The costs of testing and documentation have risen so sharply that the number of new drugs marketed has declined sharply, particularly among smaller firms.[3] Spokesmen for drug firms and the free-market proponents of deregulation claim that the 1962 amendments "forced" the drug firms to curtail their research activities. In fact, of course, they were not forced at all; rather, they collectively, although probably not collusively, exercised their discretion in changing their behavior.

Similarly, the allegedly overzealous regulation of natural gas rates by the Federal Power Commission has led to similar distortions. The F.P.C. tends to restrain prices during inflationary periods, causing the regulated industry to curtail exploration, which in turn has led to the severe shortage of natural gas in the mid-1970s.[4] But here again firms are not, strictly speaking, forced to stop exploring for natural gas; they choose to do so because they attach more importance to enhancing or at least maintaining their profit and growth rates than to any other social value.[5] In addition, when regulation limits discretion to the point where profitability is impaired, the firm or industry may be denied the capital either to furnish or to improve the service or good it is expected to provide. Thus costs and penalties can be imposed by the exercise of discretion by firms and industries with which the regulated firm or industry must interact, in this case capital-raising and lending institutions.

To summarize this line of argument, the impact of regulation may often be nullified because of the wide discretion left to the firm, or, if the regulation is stringently enforced, undesirable costs or penalties may be imposed on the public that is supposedly to be served. The critical variable is not so much the discretion vested in a regulatory agency by an operating statute as the discretion remaining to the firm. Meanwhile, regulation is a costly process for the consumer. Public expenditures alone are estimated to be approximately $2 billion a year. Far more insidious are the costs that firms pass on to consumers. I have never found a convincingly calculated estimate of total regulatory costs passed on to consumers, but guesstimates are frighteningly high. The Goodyear Tire and Rubber Company announced, for example, that it expended $30 million in 1974 in complying with federal and state regulations. If we assume that regulatory costs represent the same percentage of sales for the top 500 manufacturing firms as for Goodyear (.0057), total regulatory costs for this group of firms alone were in excess of $4.75 billion in 1974.[6] While we have no way of knowing what proportion of the total is passed on to consumers, it seems probable that most is. Thus, while the sum arrived at is clearly suspect as an accurate calculation of the private-sector costs of regulation to consumers, it suggests that the total amount is quite substantial and raises two specific questions: Are the purported benefits from regulation worth the direct costs? And if they are, can these benefits be realized through the process of regulation? My conclusion, based on the arguments developed here, is that, on balance, the kind of business regulation we now have is not and cannot be an effective instrument for the promotion of public values.

Several alternative models to the standard regulatory ones can be advanced. But before examining alternatives, let us try to pinpoint the values that regulation, or for that matter competition, is supposed to protect and enhance. It is sometimes forgotten that competition and regulation are not ends in themselves, but are expected to serve human well-being. Adam Smith, for example, considered himself not a technocratic economist but a moral philosopher, and argued for free and unrestrained competition, in the famous "invisible hand" passage, on the grounds that the most effective way to promote society's interest was to allow each individual to pursue his own selfish interests. Most people today have less faith in the free-market solution, and many values have changed since *The Wealth of Nations* was written, but there is still a surprisingly high degree of concurrence on a core of values that a political-economic system should promote. Let us list some of these values and then see how alternative models would serve them.

The first two values are safety and health. Consumers have a right to expect that products and services offered to them will be reasonably healthful and safe if they are put to their intended use—not that they will be safe and healthful under all circumstances, but that they will be so under reasonable conditions of use. No matter how well automobiles are constructed, for example, they can destroy their drivers and others if they are carelessly used. But they should be as safe as reasonable production costs can make them. A caveat must be entered, however, that leads us to the third major value. A consumer may decide to forgo safety and health in order to satisfy other cravings. The history of mankind teaches us that often we cannot be saved from our follies. We may decide to smoke cigarettes even if we fully understand the proven risks; or we may decide to buy aluminum siding even if we cannot afford it. Under these circumstances we expect to be told the truth about a product and not to be deceived. This means, first, that we are entitled to all important information about a product; second, that we should not be deliberately misinformed; and third, that we should not be manipulated into acquiring any product.

The latter point is the most troublesome. No demonstration is needed to show that the amount of relevant and impartial information currently conveyed in advertising messages is small compared to the sum of statements of a psychological, subliminal, or simply nonrational nature contained in the mass of advertisements with which consumers are bombarded. Moreover, although we cannot be certain on this point, it seems likely that as far as impact on the consumer is concerned, the nonrational parts of the message may effectively nullify the portions that convey information.[7] Consumers are not "free" to choose or not to choose to smoke cigarettes. Essentially they are manipulated to choose to do so. Consumer sovereignty, which rests on the assumption that consumers choose rationally, is the central premise of F.T.C. advertising regulation; yet the assumption has become increasingly questionable, as the F.T.C. implicitly recognizes in bait-and-switch cases. Alternative models must therefore face up to the enormous problem of truth, the crucial underpinning of the theory of consumer sovereignty.

At first blush these values seem to bear no real relationship to a set of values more narrowly focused within the economic realm. These latter values have been articulated in a number of post–World War II documents (and some from before the war), most notably the Employment Act of 1946. One of the most important of these values is the provision of services and goods adequate to meet the demand for them. Obviously the implications of such a notion are elastic, and equally obviously the demand for services and goods varies from nation to nation. American expectations are among the highest in the world; the American consumer demands the provision not only of railroad transportation, abundant energy, and pharmaceuticals, but also of toasters, television sets, door locks, and so on—goods beyond the immediate dreams of the inhabitants of most of the world. When the provision of these services and goods is inadequate, we perceive performance as inadequate. We also expect the range of prices of most goods and services to be within the reach of most consumers; not everyone will be able to buy a Cadillac, or even a new compact car, but virtually everyone should be able to acquire a used car that can perform reasonably well.

These considerations lead to additional values. While profits are certainly permissible, they should not be "excessive"; that is, they should not reflect prices that are higher than necessary. Low prices, however, require low costs, which ordinarily can be achieved only through innovation and progressiveness. The value of innovation and progressiveness relates to another demand—the demand for improvement in the quality of goods and services. Passenger railroad transportation in the United States, for example, is generally regarded as both expensive and of low quality. The two ideas of "reasonable" price levels and innovation lead us on to another set of values, somewhat harder to define. We demand that a firm's prices not reflect a commitment to frills and unproductive expenditures. The pharmaceutical industry, for example, has been sharply criticized for pushing up the prices of drugs beyond reasonable bounds by employing a veritable army of detail men, who do not, in any event, convey much accurate information.[8] Detergent manufacturers have been criticized for spending approximately 10 percent of their sales revenue on advertising that tells us almost nothing about their products.

The final set of values to be considered is less consensual, especially in its application, than the ones we have considered so far. These values concern what economists term "externalities"—the intended, unintended, or incidental by-products of some otherwise legitimate activity.[9] Among the most important externalities are air and water pollution, caused both by firms' activities and by high levels of consumption. While difficulties attend any attempt to set forth a universally acceptable public value on undesirable externalities, it is probably fair to say that most of us wish to balance the cost of the externality against the benefits that would be lost if the activity that creates it were reduced or altered. Thus most of us object to the pollution of the air by emanations from steel mills, but we are not willing to forgo steel production entirely; so we grope for a balancing strategy that will allow steel production to continue, but at a reduced rate, or at the increased cost associated with the installation of control devices to reduce air pollution, or through some other compromise.

This enumeration by no means exhausts the list of public values, even those pertaining to the economic sphere. It does, however, provide a framework for a critical look at the various models of business control that have been advanced. The discussion that follows is not intended to do more than open the subject of alternative models of corporate control, a full treatment of which would require a volume unto itself. Finally—and perhaps this sentence should be in big, block letters—I do not mean to imply either that any model can solve all problems or even that anything can be done about some forms of undesirable behavior. I suggest, rather, a cost-benefit analysis of alternative models of economic control.

The free-market and regulatory solutions are only two of several models that can be applied to the problems that have been raised. Others include (1) atomistic restructuring of industry; (2) restructuring of industry at a lower level of oligopoly; (3) the full-scale public utility model, in which a firm's discretion is sharply reduced and shifted to public institutions; and (4) public ownership. Let us look first at the free-market solution advocated by various academics associated with the "Chicago school." The first two alternative models may be employed in conjunction with either the free market or public regulation.

The free-market model depends ultimately on the assumption that the free market will best satisfy public values through the instrumentality of the invisible hand. Yet the evidence is overwhelming that public values and the goals of firms diverge sharply. Cigarette firms, for example, felt no need to warn consumers of their product's dangers, nor did automobile manufacturers voluntarily make cars safer. Indeed, the enormous volume of fraud that the F.T.C. and various federal, state, and local bodies have uncovered points to the inescapable conclusion that when profit and sales goals conflict with public values, the latter must yield in business calculations. To cite still another example, firms do not attempt on their own the kind of balancing exercise suggested earlier in relation to externalities.

The reasons for corporate inattentiveness to public goals have been well stated by Neil Chamberlain:

Even in these limited exercises in social responsibility the individual corporation must recognize two constraints. First, it must show a profit that compares favorably with the profit positions of other major corporations. This is necessary for several reasons. The legal framework vests ultimate corporate authority in a board of directors nominally elected by the stockholders, and incumbent managements must perform well enough to forestall a challenge to their position. . . . Further, although internally generated funds provide much of the capital needed by large corporations, it is occasionally necessary to resort to the capital markets for new financing. Whether in the form of equity issues or long-term loans, the terms on which that capital can be secured depend on the price at which the corporation's stock is selling, which in turn reflects its present and prospective profit position. Moreover, a strong profit position is necessary to discourage an attempted takeover by a less socially conscious corporate raider who sees a return on assets that is not being fully realized by a management that may have followed its "corporate conscience" with excessive zeal.

Second, a corporation must maintain a size (preferably a rate of growth) that permits it to continue those facilitating activities—advertising, research and development, personnel policies, public relations—on at least the scale that has brought it to its present position. A decline in size, even a declining rate of growth, creates problems of holding onto and recruiting high-quality talent and of finding places for or dismissing older employees. . . .

Such a fixation on profit and size does not arise because these are necessarily the most desirable objectives that can be imagined . . . but because the company is driven to them by the requirements of its position.[10]

In summary, then, profits and growth are the supreme values for corporations. If firms' discretion were further enlarged through the operation of the free-market principle, we might expect that in some areas their derelictions would expand correspondingly, even if some market distortions attributable to regulation disappeared. Natural gas would flow again, and new drugs would be produced again. But the costs of the free-market approach might very well outweigh the benefits; if nineteenth-century experience is any guide, snake oil and placebos would join new drugs in the marketplace.

We turn next to approaches that seek a restructuring of American industry either on an atomistic basis or at a lower level of oligopoly. As far as the atomistic model is concerned, advocates of small-scale enterprise, such as the late Senator Kefauver, point to the presumed social and political benefits that would flow from such a restructuring and to the helplessness of the individual before the large-scale organizations he must confront in all areas of modern life. Yet the notion that smallness is goodness is belied by the numerous orders entered by the F.T.C. against small firms, many of which have involved vicious frauds. Further, a great increase in the number of enterprises would make regulation much more difficult. Finally, as Robert Heilbronner said in answer to proposals for atomization, industries characterized by small units

> have also been the models of industrial backwardness, characterized by low research and development, low wages and long hours, antiunionism, company towns, etc. I see no reason to believe that an IBM cut down to size would spend its fragmented profits in a more socially beneficial manner than its master company. . . . The power of the corporation to work social good or evil would not be lessened by fragmenting it. It would only be made less visible and hence, in the end, less accountable or controllable than by bringing it out into the open at the top.[11]

Smallness of scale might indeed be counterproductive with regard to research and development. While small firms have, in the past, unquestionably been responsible for a considerable amount of innovation, they do not spend proportionately more than large firms. Moreover, the threshold sums required for significant innovation are sufficiently high in many industries to effectively rule out the possibility that small firms might engage in significant research activity.[12] At best, then, smallness can make no difference in the development of cost-cutting and quality-improving innovations, and at worst, because of the threshold effect, it might greatly retard innovation.

If a policy of restructuring American industry into small-scale units appears both impractical and costly, can the same be said about restructuring it into less concentrated oligopolies? Aside from the arguments already considered in our discussion of mergers and oligopoly—that the largest firms are more efficient than smaller ones and that prices in highly concentrated industries rise more slowly than those in less concentrated industries—other considerations render this model problematic. First, a long time must elapse between a dissolution action and the actual completion of the spin-off. Buyers are not easy to come by. If such dissolutions were to be contemplated over large segments of the economy, we would be fantasizing if we expected an adequate number of buyers. Successful sales of acquired firms that have had to be divested under antimerger decrees have been infrequent enough; yet the scale of the problem has been minor compared to what would happen under the F.T.C.'s proposals on shared monopoly. Who could buy the large units to be unloaded except already substantial firms or financial institutions, neither of which would be likely to act any differently from the existing members of an industry? Finally, during the long period between a dissolution action and a decree, a firm would have a strong incentive not to innovate or expand, since such action could be interpreted as aggressive conduct. In any event, why should a firm develop some new product or process if the innovation might have to be shared with a spun-off competitor or be taken away altogether? In short, application of this model, even if it could be achieved on a large, meaningful scale, would invite stagnation.

Finally we reach the full-scale public utility and public ownership models. In the former, almost all of a firm's discretion is transferred to a public authority, which effectively makes almost every major decision for a firm. But why, one may ask, should private ownership continue after all justification for the entrepreneurial function is removed? In any event, it is only reasonable to believe that as a firm's discretion is more and more reduced, and as profit considerations are made subsidiary to other, "public interest" considerations, needed capital will not flow toward it. Capital will gravitate instead toward industries and nations in which the profit motive is not thus fettered. The government will then have to become the principal source of funds.

If the public utility model raises problems too, we are left with public ownership, the great merit of which is that conflict between public goals and corporate profits can disappear since theoretically the latter have no further role. This is not by any means to say that accounting disappears, but rather that turning a profit becomes only one of several goals for an enterprise. But the public enterprise model raises the question of whether an alternative system of effective incentives can replace the pecuniary system of incentives under capitalism. For public ownership is not necessarily a panacea, as the U.S. Postal Service and the French matchbook industry attest. And public ownership has been associated with so many repressive regimes that one must wonder whether public ownership and totalitarianism are inexorably linked, as F. A. Hayek and others argue. The dangers associated with a concentration of economic and political power in a few hands need not be belabored; several nations provide dramatic illustrations.

Yet it would be erroneous to equate a socialist solution with a productive apparatus controlled by a bureaucratic class. For in the public ownership of the means of production envisioned by Karl Marx and other socialist theoreticians, the public plays a part in the decision-making processes of industrial enterprises, and is not simply told which of many alternatives will be taken, as it is under the Soviet five-year plans. This scheme does not require, of course, that every industrial decision be subject to a referendum, but it does require some measure of public participation. Although the complexity of the problem should not be underestimated, the public can certainly have far more impact on the shaping of what we regard as the private sphere than is currently the case in either capitalist or state bureaucratic economies.

I recognize that these are grave questions. Perhaps the logic of the argument leads to pessimism, no matter which road is taken. Yet the attractions of a solution that appeals to our finer instincts rather than our baser ones are too great to throw away simply because a number of bad examples can be cited.[13] Why did the Soviet Union and China become totalitarian? Can it not plausibly be argued that their political excesses sprang from their underdeveloped status rather than from their economic system? Could not widespread public ownership operate in the United States, or in any other developed society, within a democratic framework? These questions require exploration and deserve not to be ignored. All of the models that operate within a capitalist framework have glaring deficiencies. To expect any of them to play a major role in upholding public values is like asking a cat to bark; we can be assured, though, that public and private decision makers will roar like lions in proclaiming their devotion to the public interest.

Bibliographical Note

The volume of material published on the subject matter of the F.T.C.'s jurisdiction is so enormous that a bibliographical listing would cover twenty or twenty-five pages. Such a list would be of little benefit to the reader who desires to pursue further the matters raised in this book. Instead I shall briefly discuss the most important writings; this procedure will enable the reader to delve further into the area of trade regulation in an orderly manner. The reader who wishes more bibliographical material is urged to consult such standard reference works as the *P.A.I.S. Service* and the *Index of Legal Periodicals*. An additional source of paramount importance is the quarterly *Journal of Economic Literature*.

A convenient starting point is earlier books on the F.T.C. The major works are Thomas C. Blaisdell, Jr., *The Federal Trade Commission* (1932; New York: AMS Press, 1967); Gerard C. Henderson, *The Federal Trade Commission* (1924; New York: Agathon Press, 1968); American Bar Association, *Report of the ABA Commission to Study the Federal Trade Commission* (Chicago, 1969); and Edward C. Cox, Robert C. Fellmeth, and John E. Schulz, *"The Nader Report" on the Federal Trade Commission* (New York: Richard W. Baron, 1969).

One of the major drawbacks of all of these works is that they treat the agency in isolation from the development of regulation generally and the important changes that occurred in American capitalism during the last two decades of the nineteenth century. The reader who wishes to explore these topics should begin with Werner Sombart, "Capitalism," in the *Encyclopedia of Social Sciences,* 1930 ed., vol. 3. The most important of the works that place the origins of the F.T.C.

in the context of the changes in capitalism and developing concepts of regulation is Gabriel Kolko, *The Triumph of Conservatism* (New York: Free Press, 1963). But Kolko's revisionist account should be contrasted with Harold U. Faulkner, *The Decline of Laissez-Faire* (New York: Harper & Row, 1951); William H. S. Stevens, *Unfair Competition* (Chicago: University of Chicago Press, 1917); and John B. Clark and John M. Clark, *The Control of Trusts* (New York: Macmillan, 1912).

There are several notable histories of specific statutes enforced by the F.T.C. The most important are Joseph Palamountain, *The Politics of Distribution* (Cambridge: Harvard University Press, 1962), on the Robinson-Patman Act; Charles O. Jackson, *Food and Drug Legislation in the New Deal* (Princeton: Princeton University Press, 1970), on the Wheeler-Lea Amendment and related legislation; and David D. Martin, *Mergers and the Clayton Act* (Berkeley: University of California Press, 1959). Background on the Sherman Act is well covered in Hans B. Thorelli, *The Federal Antitrust Policy* (Baltimore: Johns Hopkins University Press, 1955); William L. Letwin, *Law and Economic Policy in America* (New York: Random House, 1965); and Arthur P. Dudden, "Men against Monopoly: The Prelude to Trust-Busting," *Journal of the History of Ideas,* XVIII (October 1957), 587–593.

The analytical literature on trade regulation policies by economists and lawyers is voluminous; much of it has been cited in the notes to this book. The starting point for the interested reader should be Paul J. McNulty, "Economic Theory and the Meaning of Competition," *Quarterly Journal of Economics,* LXXXII (November 1968), 639–656. Debate has raged over trade regulation policy generally, as well as over individual statutes and decisions. On one side stands the literature highly critical of trade regulation policy, of which the most extreme example is D. T. Armentano, *The Myths of Antitrust* (New Rochelle, N.Y.: Arlington House, 1972). The reader should also consult John S. McGee, *In Defense of Industrial Concentration* (New York: Praeger, 1971), and two collections of articles: Yale Brozen, ed., *The Competitive Economy* (Morristown, N.J.: General Learning Press, 1975), and J. Fred Weston and Stanley Ornstein, eds., *The Impact of Large Firms on the U.S. Economy* (Lexington, Mass.: Heath, 1973). The most forceful works in praise of the trade regulation laws are John M. Blair, *Economic Concentration* (New York:

Harcourt Brace Jovanovich, 1972), and George W. Stocking, *Workable Competition and Antitrust Policy* (Nashville: Vanderbilt University Press, 1961). A moderate outlook may be found in Carl Kaysen and Donald F. Turner, *Antitrust Policy* (Cambridge: Harvard University Press, 1959).

The major studies of specific policy areas include, on the Robinson-Patman Act, Corwin D. Edwards, *The Price Discrimination Law* (Washington, D.C.: Brookings Institution, 1959), and Frederick M. Rowe, *Price Discrimination Under the Robinson-Patman Act* (Boston: Little, Brown, 1962); on collusive practices, Almarin Phillips, *Market Structure, Organization, and Performance* (Cambridge: Harvard University Press, 1962); and on false and misleading advertising, George J. Alexander, *Honesty and Competition* (Syracuse: Syracuse University Press, 1967), and Richard Posner, *Regulation of Advertising by the F.T.C.* (Washington, D.C.: American Enterprise Institute for Public Policy Research, 1973). Once again, these books constitute only the tip of the iceberg, and the inquiring reader will discover a plethora of articles by scrutinizing the *Index of Legal Periodicals*.

Finally, a number of historians, economists, and political scientists have written provocative works on the problem of regulation generally. Outstanding examples include Theodore J. Lowi, *The End of Liberalism* (New York: Norton, 1969); Marver Bernstein, *Regulating Business by Independent Commission* (Princeton: Princeton University Press, 1955); Grant McConnell, *Private Power and American Democracy* (New York: Knopf, 1956); Henry J. Friendly, *The Federal Administrative Agencies* (Cambridge: Harvard University Press, 1962); and Emmette S. Redford, *The Regulatory Process* (Austin: University of Texas Press, 1969). Of the many books by political scientists on public policy making, I have found the most valuable to be James E. Anderson, *Public Policy Making* (New York: Praeger, 1975). Two indispensable review articles on theories of regulation are Thomas K. McCraw, "Regulation in America," *Business History Review*, XLIX (Summer 1975), 159–184, and Richard A. Posner, "Theories of Economic Regulation," *Bell Journal of Economics and Management Science*, V (Autumn 1974), 335–359.

Notes

Chapter 1

1. Adam Smith, *The Wealth of Nations* (1776; New York: Random House, 1937), p. 128.
2. Quoted in Ida M. Tarbell, *The Life of Elbert H. Gary* (New York: Appleton, 1925), p. 212.
3. Max Weber, *Economy and Society: An Outline of Interpretive Sociology,* 3 vols., ed. Guenther Roth and Claus Wittich, trans. E. Fischoff et al., 4th ed. (New York: Bedminster Press, 1968), I, 82, 83. Weber also observes that tradition and convention may regulate market freedom.
4. M. B. Carrott, "The Supreme Court and American Trade Associations, 1921–1925," *Business History Review,* XLIV (Autumn 1970), 320. See also W. H. Becker, "American Wholesale Hardware Trade Associations, 1870–1900," *Business History Review,* XLV (Summer 1971), 179–200.
5. Smith, *Wealth of Nations,* pp. 400, 401.
6. Details on railroads and rate regulation are provided in the following works: Gabriel Kolko, *Railroads and Regulation* (Princeton: Princeton University Press, 1965); Lee Benson, *Merchants, Farmers, and Railroads* (Cambridge: Harvard University Press, 1955); George H. Miller, *Railroads and the Granger Laws* (Madison: University of Wisconsin Press, 1971); M. G. Blackford, "Businessmen and the Regulation of Railroads and Public Utilities in California during the Progressive Era," *Business History Review,* XLIV (Autumn 1970), 307–319.
7. The most important of these works is Gabriel Kolko, *The Triumph of Conservatism* (New York: Free Press, 1963), especially pp. 1–10. See also Charles O. Jackson, *Food and Drug Legislation in the New Deal* (Princeton: Princeton University Press, 1970); Samuel P. Hays, *Conservation and the Gospel of Efficiency* (New York: Atheneum, 1969); and Norman Nordhauser, "Origins of Federal Oil Regulation in the 1920's," *Business History Review,* XLVII (Spring 1973), 54–71.
8. A good exposition of the traditional view of restrictive business legislation is Harold U. Faulkner, *The Decline of Laissez-Faire* (New York: Holt, Rinehart & Winston, 1951).
9. For two early examples see *Bureau of Statistics of the Book Paper Manufacturers,* 1 F.T.C. 38 (1917), and *Association of Flag Manufacturers of America,* 1 F.T.C. 55 (1918).
10. Robert F. Himmelberg, "Business, Antitrust Policy, and the Industrial

276 Notes

Board of the Department of Commerce, 1919," *Business History Review*, XLII (Spring 1968), 1–23.

11. See any text in price theory or industrial organization for the description of pure competition and monopoly markets. My characterization is based on Peter Asch, *Economic Theory and the Antitrust Dilemma* (New York: Wiley, 1970), pp. 9, 10. Even as an ideal, pure competition has been subjected to sharp criticism. See especially Joseph Schumpeter, *Capitalism, Socialism, and Democracy*, 3d ed. (New York: Harper & Row, 1950), pp. 84, 85, 104–106.

12. The starting point for the interested reader is Edward H. Chamberlin, *The Theory of Monopolistic Competition*, 8th ed. (1933; Cambridge: Harvard University Press, 1962), from which an enormous literature grew. For a trenchant critique of the assumptions see John S. McGee, *In Defense of Industrial Concentration* (New York: Praeger, 1971).

13. On the dynamics of competition see Saul Nelson and Walter Keim, *Price Behavior and Business Policy*, TNEC Monograph no. 1 (Washington, D.C.: Government Printing Office, 1941), pt. 1.

14. Ibid., p. 60.

15. "Originally the guarantee found an excuse for itself in that it was the exclusive promise of one company and so formed a sales argument for the salesmen handling that line. Now, when practically every manufacturer makes the same promise, it does not even offer a talking point against rival makes" (*Electrical Merchandising*, December 1936, p. 22).

16. Weber, *Economy and Society*, I, 335–336.

17. Ernest Freund, *Standards of American Legislation* (Chicago: University of Chicago Press, 1917), pp. 137 and 248.

18. Thorstein Veblen, *The Theory of Business Enterprise* (1904; New York: New American Library, Mentor ed., 1932), p. 12; see chap. 2 generally. See also Robert A. Martina, *Standardization Activities of National Technical and Trade Organizations*, U.S. Department of Commerce, National Bureau of Standards, Misc. Pub. no. M169 (Washington, D.C.: Government Printing Office, 1941), p. 1, and Charles E. Wilson, "Report of the Policy Committee on Standards," *Industrial Standardization*, July 1945, p. 145.

19. See, for example, Kolko, *Triumph of Conservatism*, pp. 98–110, and the statement of purpose of the National Canners Association cited in Samuel Kaidanovsky, *Consumer Standards*, TNEC Monograph no. 24 (Washington, D.C.: Government Printing Office, 1941), p. 205. See also Nelson and Keim, *Price Behavior*, p. 106.

20. Kaidanovsky, *Consumer Standards*, p. 199 (and pp. 196–210 generally). See also Charles Albert Pearce, *Trade Association Survey*, TNEC Monograph no. 18 (Washington, D.C.: Government Printing Office, 1941), pp. 309–319.

21. See Jessie V. Coles, *Standards and Labels for Consumer Goods* (New York: Ronald Press, 1949), pp. 293, 294.

22. See Grant McConnell, *Private Power and American Democracy* (New York: Knopf, 1966), pp. 64–69, and Kaidanovsky, *Consumer Standards*, pp. 201–209.

23. See generally Federal Trade Commission, *Control of Unfair Competitive Practices through Trade Practice Conference Procedure of the Federal Trade Commission*, TNEC Monograph no. 34 (Washington, D.C.: Government Printing Office, 1941); Susan Wagner, *The Federal Trade Commission* (New York: Praeger, 1971), pp. 49–51; and Kaidanovsky, *Consumer Standards*, p. 206.

24. Nelson and Keim, *Price Behavior*, p. 98.

25. Alfred D. Chandler, in "The Structure of American Industry in the

Twentieth Century: A Historical Overview," *Business History Review,* XLIII (Autumn 1969), 280–281, argues that the Sherman Act has had a minimal effect on economic structure and concentration.

26. U.S. Senate, 50th Cong., 2d sess., January 25, 1889, *Congressional Record,* XX, 1167.

27. U.S. Senate, 51st Cong., 1st sess., March 21, 1890, *Congressional Record,* XXI, 2461.

28. U.S. House of Representatives, 50th Cong., 2d sess., February 18, 1890, *Congressional Record,* XX, 1458. See also U.S. Senate, 50th Cong., 2d sess., March 21 and 27, 1890, ibid., pp. 2457–2460 and 2729; U.S. House of Representatives, 50th Cong., 2d sess., June 11 and 20, 1890, ibid., pp. 5960 and 6313; Robert H. Bork, "Legislative Intent and the Policy of the Sherman Act," *Journal of Law and Economics,* IX (October 1966), 39–48.

29. U.S. Senate, 51st Cong., 1st sess., March 21, 1890, *Congressional Record,* XXI, 2456; and William L. Letwin, *Law and Economic Policy in America* (New York: Random House, 1965), p. 33.

30. Smith, *Wealth of Nations,* p. 61. In contrast, many academic economists at the time of the Sherman Act attempted to discredit the free-competition views of Smith and to advance the view that some monopolies and combinations were beneficial in that they promoted stability. See Letwin, *Law and Economic Policy,* pp. 71–77.

31. Hans B. Thorelli, *The Federal Antitrust Policy* (Baltimore: Johns Hopkins University Press, 1955), pp. 9–163, especially pp. 15–17, 28, 41, 45, 47, 49.

32. U.S. Senate, 51st Cong., 1st sess., April 8, 1890, *Congressional Record,* XXI, 3151.

33. Donald Dewey, *Monopoly in Economics and Law* (Chicago: Rand McNally, 1959), pp. 142–143; Arthur P. Dudden, "Men against Monopoly: The Prelude to Trust-Busting," *Journal of the History of Ideas,* XVIII (October 1957), 588; and Thorelli, *Federal Antitrust Policy,* pp. 144, 150, 151, 157, 166.

34. Thorelli, *Federal Antitrust Policy,* p. 12.

35. Summarized in William Breit and Kenneth Elzinga, "The Instruments of Antitrust Enforcement," in *The Antitrust Dilemma,* ed. James A. Dalton and Stanford Levin (Lexington, Mass.: Heath, 1973), p. 102.

Chapter 2

1. Harold U. Faulkner, *The Decline of Laissez-Faire* (New York: Holt, Rinehart & Winston, 1951), p. 184.

2. See Gabriel Kolko, *The Triumph of Conservatism* (New York: Free Press, 1963), pp. 1–10.

3. Robert H. Wiebe, *Businessmen and Reform* (Cambridge: Harvard University Press, 1962), pp. 139–141; and Robert H. Wiebe, "Business Disunity and the Progressive Movement, 1901–1914," *Mississippi Valley Historical Review,* XLIV (March 1958), 664–685.

4. Alfred Lief, ed., *The Social and Economic Views of Mr. Justice Brandeis* (New York: Vanguard Press, 1930), p. 398.

5. Arthur S. Link, *Wilson: The New Freedom* (Princeton: Princeton University Press, 1956), p. 427.

6. See Edward C. Cox, Robert C. Fellmeth, and John E. Schulz, *"The Nader Report" on the Federal Trade Commission* (New York: Richard W.

Baron, 1969); and American Bar Association, *Report of the ABA Commission to Study the Federal Trade Commission* (Chicago, 1969).

7. The most graphic account of the absolute growth of the modern business corporation during the relevant period and a little beyond is Alfred D. Chandler and Stephen Salsbury, *Pierre S. du Pont and the Making of the Modern Corporation* (New York: Harper & Row, 1971).

8. Kolko, *Triumph of Conservatism*, pp. 26, 27.

9. U.S. Senate, 63rd Cong., 2d sess., July 24, 1914, *Congressional Record*, LI, 12619–12620; and Kolko, *Triumph of Conservatism*, pp. 26–66.

10. Kolko, *Triumph of Conservatism*, pp. 42–54.

11. U.S. Department of Commerce and Labor, Bureau of Corporations, *The Beef Industry* (Washington, D.C.: Government Printing Office, 1905), pp. 33–35, 83, 269.

12. U.S. Department of Commerce and Labor, Bureau of Corporations, *The Steel Industry*, (Washington, D.C.: Government Printing Office, 1911), pt. 1, pp. xxiii and 330–339. For further details see Gertrude G. Schroeder, *The Growth of Major Steel Companies, 1900–1950* (Baltimore: Johns Hopkins University Press, 1953).

13. U.S. Department of Commerce and Labor, Bureau of Corporations, *The International Harvester Co.* (Washington, D.C.: Government Printing Office, 1913), pp. 20–23, 26–28, 180–184.

14. Bureau of Corporations, *Steel Industry*, pt. 1, pp. iii–x.

15. Bureau of Corporations, *International Harvester Co.*, pp. xv–xxiii.

16. U.S. Department of Commerce and Labor, Bureau of Corporations, *The Transportation of Petroleum* (Washington, D.C.: Government Printing Office, 1906). For a convincing argument—well after the fact—that Standard Oil did not engage in predatory price cutting, see John S. McGee, "Predatory Price Cutting: The Standard Oil (N.J.) Case," *Journal of Law and Economics,* I (April 1958), 137–169.

17. John B. Clark and John M. Clark, *The Control of Trusts* (New York: Macmillan, 1912).

18. James Weinstein, *The Corporate Ideal in the Liberal State* (Boston: Beacon Press, 1968), p. 88.

19. Clark and Clark, *Control of Trusts,* p. 21.

20. Ibid., p. 77. See also pp. 9–35 and 96–102.

21. Arthur B. Darling, ed., *The Public Papers of Francis G. Newlands* (Boston: Houghton Mifflin, 1932), I, 418.

22. Clark and Clark, *Control of Trusts,* pp. 103, 104, 114–117, 168, 170–174, 182, 190.

23. Kolko, *Triumph of Conservatism*, pp. 173–175; and Melvin I. Urofsky, *Big Steel and the Wilson Administration* (Columbus: Ohio State University Press, 1969), pp. 56–59.

24. Louis Galambos, *Competition and Cooperation* (Baltimore: Johns Hopkins University Press, 1966), p. 50; Theodore J. Lowi, *The End of Liberalism* (New York: Norton, 1969), pp. 36, 37, 117, 118; and Grant McConnell, *Private Power and American Democracy* (New York: Knopf, 1966), pp. 57–58.

25. Link, *Wilson,* pp. 436–438, 441; Belle C. La Follette and Fola La Follette, *Robert M. La Follette* (New York: Macmillan, 1953), p. 487; and Gerald Leinwand, "A History of the United States Federal Bureau of Corporations" (unpublished Ph.D. dissertation, New York University, 1962), chap. 10.

26. Wiebe, *Businessmen and Reform,* p. 140.

27. U.S. Senate, 63rd Cong., 2d sess., July 13, 1914, *Congressional Record,* LI, 12025; see also pp. 12030 and 11233.

28. Ibid., July 16, 1914, p. 12208.

29. The leading study of the Bureau is Leinwand, "Bureau of Corporations."

30. Darling, ed., *Public Papers,* I, 407; see also p. 427.

31. Kolko, *Triumph of Conservatism,* pp. 175, 326; Wiebe, *Businessmen and Reform,* p. 138; Darling, ed., *Public Papers,* I, 418, 432. A brief legislative history of the F.T.C. Act may be found in James C. Lang, "The Legislative History of the Federal Trade Commission Act," *Washburn Law Journal,* XIII (Winter 1974), 6–25.

32. Gerard C. Henderson, *The Federal Trade Commission* (1924; New York: Agathon Press, 1968), p. 21; U.S. House of Representatives, Committee on Interstate and Foreign Commerce, 63rd Cong., 2d sess., 1914, *Interstate Trade Commission, Hearings;* and U.S. Senate, 63rd Cong., 2d sess., July 3, 1914, *Congressional Record,* LI, 11593.

33. *Interstate Trade Commission, Hearings,* p. 442.

34. U.S. Senate, 63rd Cong., 2d sess., June 25, 1914, *Congressional Record,* LI, 11081.

35. Ibid., p. 11084.

36. Weinstein, *Corporate Ideal,* pp. 8, 11, 86–89; and Kolko, *Triumph of Conservatism,* p. 176.

37. U.S. Senate, 63rd Cong., 2d sess., May 22, 1914, *Congressional Record,* LI, 9059.

38. One part of the 1938 Wheeler-Lea Amendment, Section 5(g), made orders final after "the expiration of the time allowed for filing a petition of review"; 5 U.S.C.A. 45(G). More recently, changes were instituted by the 1975 Magnuson-Moss Act.

39. Link, *Wilson,* pp. 413, 417, 418, 423.

40. Ibid., p. 427; see also p. 425.

41. Ibid., pp. 434–439.

42. U.S. Senate, 63rd Cong., 2d sess., January 20, 1914, *Congressional Record,* LI, 1962, 1963.

43. Ibid., p. 1963.

44. Ibid., May 19, 1914, p. 8842.

45. Ibid., pp. 8849–8850.

46. Ibid., p. 8850.

47. George Rublee, "The Original Plan and Early History of the Federal Trade Commission," *Proceedings of the Academy of Political Science,* XI, no. 4 (1926), 666 and 668; *Who Was Who in America* (Chicago: Marquis, 1960), III, 76; Link, *Wilson,* p. 438; Martin J. Sklar, "Woodrow Wilson and Liberalism," in *For a New America,* ed. James Weinstein and David Eakins (New York: Random House, 1970), pp. 60–62. See also U.S. Senate, 63rd Cong., 2d sess., July 2, 1914, *Congressional Record,* LI, 11537, 11538; and ibid., September 8, 1914, pp. 14787–14788.

48. Rublee, "Original Plan," p. 669.

49. U.S. Senate, 63rd Cong., 2d sess., September 8, 1914, *Congressional Record,* LI, 14788; Lief, ed., *Social and Economic Views,* pp. 399–400. But compare Bruce Wyman, "Unfair Competition by Monopolistic Corporations," *Annals of the American Academy of Political and Social Science,* XLII (July 1912), 69.

50. U.S. Senate, 63rd Cong., 2d sess., June 25, 1914, *Congressional Record,* LI, 11104; June 26, 1914, p. 11189; July 31, 1914, p. 13048.

51. Gilbert H. Montague, "Unfair Methods of Competition," *Yale Law Review*, XXV (1915–1916), 20–41.

52. Eugene R. Baker and Daniel J. Baum, "Section 5 of the Federal Trade Commission Act: A Continuing Process of Redefinition," *Villanova Law Review*, VI (Summer 1962), 560.

53. U.S. Senate, 63rd Cong., 2d sess., July 15, 1914, *Congressional Record*, LI, 12154.

54. Under common law the claim of competitive privilege was not permitted to override the fact that conduct was generally tortious; punching a competitor in the mouth was as much a battery as punching a neighbor in the mouth. See Milton Handler, *Cases and Materials on Trade Regulation* (Chicago: Foundation Press, 1937), pp. 540–550.

55. *Southern* v. *How*, 79 Eng. Rep. 1243 (1618).

56. Cited in U.S. Department of Commerce, Bureau of Corporations, *Trust Laws and Unfair Competition* (Washington, D.C.: Government Printing Office, 1915), p. 306.

57. James A. Fayne, "The Federal Trade Commission," *American Political Science Review*, IX (February 1915), 62–63.

58. William Dudley Foulke, "An Interstate Trade Commission," *Journal of Political Economy*, XX (April 1912), 407, 409, 410.

59. Montague, "Unfair Methods," pp. 29–30.

60. U.S. Senate, 63rd Cong., 2d sess., June 25, 1914, *Congressional Record*, LI, 11084, 11108; ibid., July 15, 1914, p. 12136.

61. Ibid., July 13, 1914, p. 12030.

62. *Standard Oil Co.* v. *United States*, 221 U.S. 1, 43 (1911); and *United States* v. *American Tobacco Co.*, 221 U.S. 106, 160 (1911).

63. Darling, ed., *Public Papers*, II, 6.

64. U.S. Senate, 63rd Cong., 2d sess., June 26, 1914, *Congressional Record*, LI, 11189.

65. Ibid., June 27, 1914, p. 11232.

66. Ibid., June 26, 1914, p. 11186.

67. Ibid., July 31, 1914, p. 13048; June 27, 1914, p. 11232; July 3, 1914, pp. 11593, 11601. (Emphasis supplied.)

68. Ibid., June 25, 1914, p. 11103.

69. Ibid., July 13, 1914, p. 12024.

70. Ibid., July 15, 1914, p. 12146 (emphasis supplied).

71. Ibid., June 25, 1914, p. 11104.

72. Ibid., July 16, 1914, p. 12213.

73. Ibid., July 2, 1914, pp. 11540–11541.

74. Robert H. Bork and Ward S. Bowman, "The Crisis in Antitrust," *Columbia Law Review*, LXV (March 1965), 369.

75. U.S. Senate, 63rd Cong., 2d sess., July 16, 1914, *Congressional Record*, LI, 12248.

76. William H. S. Stevens, *Unfair Competition* (Chicago: University of Chicago Press, 1917), p. 7; see also pp. 5 and 8.

77. U.S. Senate, 63rd Cong., 2d sess., June 25, 1914, *Congressional Record*, LI, 11086.

78. Ibid., July 13, 1914, p. 12030; September 28, 1914, p. 15829.

79. Henderson, *Federal Trade Commission*, pp. 25–33; David D. Martin, *Mergers and the Clayton Act* (Berkeley: University of California Press, 1959), pp. 20–56; Baker and Baum, "Section 5," pp. 537–538.

80. U.S. Senate, 63rd Cong., 2d sess., August 26, 1914, *Congressional Record*, LI, 14258.

81. Darling, ed., *Public Papers*, II, 13.

82. U.S. House of Representatives, 63rd Cong., 2d sess., May 22, 1914, *Congressional Record*, LI, 9083.

83. Ibid., p. 9084.

84. Ibid., p. 9070.

85. Ibid., May 25, 1914, p. 9197.

86. Ibid., May 22, 1914, p. 9072; May 26, 1914, p. 9256.

87. Ibid., May 22, 1914, p. 9083.

88. Not until 1950 did Congress amend Section 7 to embrace acquisitions of assets as well as of stock; see Martin, *Mergers*, pp. 221–253.

89. U.S. House of Representatives, 63rd Cong., 2d sess., May 26, 1914, *Congressional Record*, LI, 9257.

90. U.S. Senate, 63rd Cong., 2d sess., August 31, 1914, *Congressional Record*, LI, 16149. See also *United States* v. *Union Pacific Railroad Co.*, 226 U.S. 61, 88 (1912).

Chapter 3

1. Gerard C. Henderson, *The Federal Trade Commission* (1924; New York: Agathon Press, 1968), pp. 85–89; and Edward Cowan, "F.T.C. Honing Antitrust Axes," *New York Times*, Business Section, March 19, 1975.

2. Statement by F.T.C. Chairman Lewis Engman, in U.S. House of Representatives, 93rd Cong., 2d sess., Committee on Appropriations, *Agriculture, Environmental and Consumer Protection Appropriations for 1975, Hearings*, pp. 683–684.

3. Statement by Engman in *F.T.C. News Summary*, no. 2, 1974.

4. American Bar Association, *Report of the ABA Commission to Study the Federal Trade Commission* (Chicago, 1969), p. 39; and see p. 9. See also Edward C. Cox, Robert C. Fellmeth, and John E. Schulz, *"The Nader Report" on the Federal Trade Commission* (New York: Richard W. Baron, 1969), pp. 37–95.

5. U.S. House of Representatives, 93rd Cong., 2d sess., 1975, Committee on Interstate and Foreign Commerce, *Staff Report: The Federal Trade Commission*, 1974, pp. 1, 2, 8, 12.

6. Cox et al., "Nader Report," p. 130.

7. My impression, based on eight years as an attorney with the F.T.C., both in the field and at headquarters, is that most staff members are perfectly capable of coping with the tasks they are expected to perform.

8. See Henry J. Friendly, *The Federal Administrative Agencies* (Cambridge: Harvard University Press, 1962), pp. 19–24; and Thomas G. Blaisdell, Jr., *The Federal Trade Commission* (1932; New York: AMS Press, 1967), pp. 290–291.

9. Kenneth Culp Davis, *Discretionary Justice* (Baton Rouge: Louisiana State University Press, 1969), p. 4.

10. See David Easton, *A Systems Analysis of Political Life* (New York: Wiley, 1965), pp. 351–352.

11. Alfred D. Chandler, "The Structure of American Industry in the Twentieth Century: A Historical Overview," *Business History Review*, XLIII (Autumn 1969), 280. Contrast this careful study with the petulant attack on

antitrust enforcement in Mark Green, *The Closed Enterprise System* (New York: Grossman, 1972).

12. See Helen W. Soleau and Donnamarie Carr, *Digest of the Federal Trade Commission's Antimonopoly Cases* (Washington, D.C.: Federal Trade Commission, n.d.).

13. Marver Bernstein, *Regulating Business by Independent Commission* (Princeton: Princeton University Press, 1955).

14. See, for example, G. Cullom Davis, "The Transformation of the Federal Trade Commission, 1914–1929," *Mississippi Valley Historical Review*, XLIX (December 1962), 437–455.

15. See *United States Steel Corp.*, 8 F.T.C. 1 (1924), and George W. Stocking, *Basing Point Pricing and Regional Development* (Chapel Hill: University of North Carolina Press, 1954).

16. *Federal Trade Commission* v. *Eastman Kodak Co.*, 274 U.S. 619 (1927). See also Carl McFarland, *Judicial Control of the Federal Trade Commission* (Cambridge: Harvard University Press, 1933), pp. 68–70.

17. *Federal Trade Commission* v. *Beech-Nut Packing Co.*, 257 U.S. 441 (1922).

18. Details are provided in Federal Trade Commission, *Control of Unfair Competitive Practices through Trade Practice Conference Procedure of the Federal Trade Commission*, TNEC Monograph no. 34 (Washington, D.C.: Government Printing Office, 1941). On Hoover's philosophy, see Grant McConnell, *Private Power and American Democracy* (New York: Knopf, 1966), pp. 64–68.

19. Cited in Blaisdell, *Federal Trade Commission*, p. 93.

20. U.S. House of Representatives, 92d Cong., 2d sess., 1973, Committee on Appropriations, *Agriculture, Environmental and Consumer Protection Appropriations for 1973, Hearings*, pt. 4, p. 429.

21. See E. W. Hawley, *The New Deal and the Problem of Monopoly* (Princeton: Princeton University Press, 1966), pp. 72, 82, 84, 94–95, 108–109, 117.

22. The F.T.C. investigation, published in 84 volumes plus supplements and exhibits, is entitled *Utility Corporations* (Senate Doc. 92, 1928–1935). See F.T.C., *Summary Report on Economic, Financial, and Corporate Phases of Holding and Operating Companies of Electric and Gas Utilities*, Senate Doc. 92, pt. 73-A, 1935. On the history of the Public Utility Holding Company Act, see Philip Funigiello, *Toward a National Power Policy* (Pittsburgh: University of Pittsburgh Press, 1973).

23. Frank Fetter, *The Masquerade of Monopoly* (New York: Harcourt, Brace, 1931).

24. Full details are provided in Federal Trade Commission, *The Basing Point Problem* (Washington, D.C.: Government Printing Office, 1941), pp. 31–78. A good brief description of the system is contained in Samuel M. Loescher, *Imperfect Collusion in the Cement Industry* (Cambridge: Harvard University Press, 1959), pp. 5–9.

25. Federal Trade Commission, *Price Bases Inquiry: The Basing Point Formula and Cement Prices* (Washington, D.C.: Government Printing Office, 1932), p. xiii.

26. Federal Trade Commission, *Report to the President with Respect to the Basing Point System in the Iron and Steel Industry* (Washington, D.C.: Government Printing Office, 1935), p. 35.

27. *Schechter Corporation* v. *United States*, 295 U.S. 495 (1935).

28. Corwin Edwards, *The Price Discrimination Law* (Washington, D.C.: Brookings Institution, 1959), pp. 363–364.

29. *Federal Trade Commission v. Cement Institute*, 333 U.S. 683 (1948).

30. The story is well told in Earl Latham, *The Group Basis of Politics* (Ithaca: Cornell University Press, 1952), chaps. 2–5.

31. Federal Trade Commission, *Advisory Opinion Digests* (Washington, D.C.: Government Printing Office, 1969), pp. 1–6.

32. Green, *Closed Enterprise System*, pp. 382–383.

33. Richard Posner, "The Federal Trade Commission," *University of Chicago Law Review*, XXXIV (Fall 1969), 69. Posner's experience, and my own, is confirmed by F.T.C. staff members who have served with the agency over a long period and have had a substantial amount of experience in dealing with letters and applications of complaint.

34. Federal Trade Commission, *Annual Report of the Federal Trade Commission, 1915* (Washington, D.C.: Government Printing Office, 1915), p. 12.

35. Federal Trade Commission, *Annual Report of the Federal Trade Commission, 1916* (Washington, D.C.: Government Printing Office, 1916), p. 5. See also Henderson, *Federal Trade Commission*, pp. 49–50.

36. U.S. Senate, 74th Cong., 1st sess., 1936, Committee on Interstate Commerce, *To Amend the Federal Trade Commission Act, Hearings*, pp. 82 and 88. (Emphasis supplied.)

37. Federal Trade Commission, *Annual Report of the Federal Trade Commission, 1956* (Washington, D.C.: Government Printing Office, 1956), p. 21.

38. *F.T.C. News Summary*, no. 27, 1957.

39. American Bar Association, *Report*, p. 40.

40. Ibid., p. 37. Approximately two-thirds of the complaints received by the Antitrust Division, whose jurisdiction substantially overlaps that of the F.T.C., come from businessmen seeking protection against competitors, groups of competitors, or suppliers; see James E. Anderson, "The Politics of Antitrust Administration," in *Politics and Economic Policy Making*, ed. James E. Anderson (Reading, Mass.: Addison-Wesley, 1970), p. 239.

41. Leo Bogart, *Strategy in Advertising* (New York: Harcourt, Brace & World, 1967), p. 2.

42. An underlying assumption of administration, whether public or private, in a modern capitalist society is that the prevailing mode of thought and operation is, in Weberian terms, instrumentally rational. For, as Weber shows, a modern capitalist society that was not instrumentally rational could not function. See Max Weber, *Economy and Society: An Outline of Interpretive Sociology*, 3 vols., ed. Guenther Roth and Claus Wittich, trans. E. Fischoff et al., 4th ed. (New York: Bedminster Press, 1968), I, 24, 25, 63–205.

43. Frederick M. Rowe, "The Federal Trade Commission's Administration of the Antiprice Discrimination Law," *Columbia Law Review*, LXIV (March 1964), 430.

44. U.S. Senate, 85th Cong., 1st sess., 1958, *Administered Prices: Steel*, S. Rept. 1387, pp. 78–93. For an extended theoretical discussion, see Gardiner C. Means, *Pricing Power and the Public Interest* (New York: Harper & Row, 1962), pp. 16–46.

45. Means, *Pricing Power*, pp. 29–34; Corwin D. Edwards, *Maintaining Competition* (New York: McGraw-Hill, 1949). I am not seeking either to confirm or to deny the theory of administered prices as an explanation of inflation, though there is considerable evidence that, because of efficiencies passed on to consumers, "administered price" industries have displayed a slower rate of

price increase than many others. My point relates rather to styles of conduct in oligopolistic industries on the one hand and highly unconcentrated industries on the other. See A. A. Thompson, "Absolute Firm Size, Administered Prices, and Inflation," *Economic Inquiry,* XII (June 1974), 240–254; and Gardiner C. Means, "The Administered Price Thesis Confirmed," *American Economic Review,* LXII (June 1972), 292–306.

46. Ralph Cassidy, Jr., *Price Warfare in Business Competition* (East Lansing: Michigan State University, Bureau of Business and Economic Research, 1963), pp. 51–52; and U.S. Department of Agriculture, Economic Research Service, *Price Wars in City Milk Markets* (Washington, D.C.: Government Printing Office, 1966), pp. 86, 87.

47. Federal Trade Commission, *Annual Report of the Federal Trade Commission, 1959* (Washington, D.C.: Government Printing Office, 1959), p. 4.

48. Paul Rand Dixon, "Robinson-Patman Is Not Dead—Merely Dormant" (address delivered before the National Retail Merchants Association, May 21, 1975), pp. 1–4.

49. 15 U.S.C.A., 45(b).

50. Federal Trade Commission, *Trade Regulation Rule Including a Statement of Its Basis and Purpose: The Failure to Post Minimum Octane Numbers on Gasoline Dispensing Pumps Constitutes an Unfair Trade Practice and Unfair Method of Competition* (December 16, 1971), p. iv.

51. *National Petroleum Refiners Association* v. *Federal Trade Commission* (C.C.A., D.C., 1973), 1973–1 Trade Cases, para. 74, 575, p. 94517.

52. U.S. House of Representatives, 93rd Cong., 2d sess., Committee on Appropriations, *Agriculture, Environmental and Consumer Protection Appropriations for 1975, Hearings,* pt. 6, p. 665.

53. Ibid., Committee on Interstate and Foreign Commerce, *Staff Report: The Federal Trade Commission, 1974,* p. 1.

54. Ibid., p. 14.

Chapter 4

1. See, for example, "F.T.C.'s Tougher Tactics for Regulating Business," *Business Week,* May 19, 1975, p. 66, a typical expression of this view.

2. Robert H. Bork and Ward S. Bowman, "The Crisis in Antitrust," *Columbia Law Review,* LXV (March 1965), 366–367. See also Thomas E. Kauper, "The 'Warren Court' and the Antitrust Laws: Of Economics, Populism, and Cynicism," *Michigan Law Review,* LXVII (December 1968), 269–288.

3. *Timken Roller Bearing Co.,* 58 F.T.C. 98 (1961); set aside in 299 F. 2d 839 (C.C.A., 6, 1962).

4. *Beltone Hearing Aid Co.,* 52 F.T.C. 830 (1961); *Otarion, Inc.,* 53 F.T.C. 780 (1961).

5. U.S. Senate, 87th Cong., 2d sess., 1962, Committee on the Judiciary, *The Price of Hearing Aids,* S. Rept. 2216, pp. 5–7; and *Beltone Hearing Aid Co.,* 52 F.T.C. 836 (1961).

6. *Outboard Marine & Manufacturing Co.,* 52 F.T.C. 1553 (1956).

7. *Mytinger & Casselberry,* 57 F.T.C. 717 (1960).

8. For example, in *International Shoe Co.,* 54 F.T.C. 1120 (1958), the company showed that it had furnished supervisory and special services to retailers, the benefits of which it did not want to share with competitors.

9. *Photostat Corporation,* 56 F.T.C. 300 (1959); on tie-in arrangements generally, see Eugene M. Singer, "Market Power and Tying Arrangements,"

Antitrust Bulletin, VIII (July–August 1963), 653–657; and Ward S. Bowman, "Tying Arrangements and the Leverage Problem," *Yale Law Journal,* LXVII (November 1957), 19–36.

10. *Photostat Corporation.*

11. *Sav-A-Stop, Inc.,* 55 F.T.C. 1807 (1959).

12. *Asheville Tobacco Board of Trade,* 54 F.T.C. 1043 (1960), and *Wallace Tobacco Board of Trade,* 62 F.T.C. 733 (1963).

13. *Goodyear Tire & Rubber Co. and Atlantic Refining Co.,* 58 F.T.C. 309 (1961); *Firestone Tire & Rubber Co. and Shell Oil Co.,* 58 F.T.C. 371, 1199 (1961); *B. F. Goodrich Co. and Texaco Inc.,* 62 F.T.C. 1172 (1963). The Supreme Court upheld the F.T.C. in *Atlantic Refining Co.* v. *F.T.C.,* 381 U.S. 357 (1965), and *F.T.C.* v. *Texaco, Inc.,* 393 U.S. 223 (1968), emphasizing that the disparity in bargaining power between refiner and service station implied coercion to accept the tied TBA products.

14. *Brown Shoe Co.,* 62 F.T.C. 679 (1963), later affirmed by the Supreme Court in 384 U.S. 316 (1966).

15. *Procter & Gamble Co.,* 56 F.T.C. 1623 (1960).

16. *Sandura Co.,* 61 F.T.C. 756 (1962).

17. Ibid., p. 809. Details on the industry are provided in Robert F. Lanzilotti, *The Hard Surface Floor Covering Industry* (Pullman: State College of Washington Press, 1955).

18. *Luria Brothers & Co.,* 62 F.T.C. 243, (1963); affirmed in 389 F. 2d 847 (C.C.A., 3, 1968).

19. For a fuller development of this argument, see Ward S. Bowman, *Patent and Antitrust Law* (Chicago: University of Chicago Press, 1973), pp. 54–61.

20. Lee Preston, "Restrictive Distribution Arrangements: Economic Analysis and Public Policy Standards," *Law and Contemporary Problems,* XXX (Summer 1965), 511–512.

21. See, for example, *Tyson's Corner Regional Shopping Center,* F.T.C. Dkt. 8886 (1974); *Gimbel Brothers Inc.,* Dkt. 8885 (1974); and *House Co.,* file no. 7210067 (1975).

22. See, for example, *Georgia Pacific,* file no. 6910085 (1973); *Occidental Petroleum,* file no. 6910092 (1974); and *Diamond Shamrock Co.,* file no. 7110035 (1974).

23. Bowman, *Patent and Antitrust Law,* p. 61. See also D. T. Armentano, *The Myths of Antitrust* (New Rochelle, N.Y.: Arlington House, 1972), pp. 198–230, for a discussion of restrictive practice cases brought privately and by the Department of Justice.

24. The leading cases announcing the per se principles include *United States* v. *Trenton Potteries Co.,* 273 U.S. 392 (1927); *United States* v. *Socony-Vacuum Oil Co.,* 310 U.S. 150 (1940); and *Timken Roller Bearing Co.* v. *United States,* 341 U.S. 593 (1950).

25. Almarin Phillips, *Market Structure, Organization, and Performance* (Cambridge: Harvard University Press, 1962), p. 73. See also George J. Stigler and James K. Kindahl, *The Behavior of Industrial Prices* (New York: National Bureau of Economic Research, 1970), pp. 92–93; and R. B. Heflebower, "Conscious Parallelism and Administered Prices," in Almarin Phillips, ed., *Perspectives on Antitrust Policy* (Princeton: Princeton University Press, 1965), pp. 88–116. An analysis of the relationship between cases of criminal price fixing and industry concentration has shown that 94 percent of the cases brought in 1955–1965 involved firms in the 85 percent of industries in which the four largest firms account for less than 60 percent of the industry's sales;

see James M. Clabault and John F. Burton, *Sherman Act Indictments, 1955–1965* (New York: Federal Legal Publications, 1966), p. 130.

26. See Armentano, *Myths of Antitrust*, pp. 132–137.

27. This is Arthur A. Thompson's conclusion in his careful empirical study "Absolute Firm Size, Administered Prices, and Inflation," *Economic Inquiry*, XII (June 1974), 240–254. K. E. A. De Silva reaches a similar conclusion for the case of Canada in "Industrial Concentration and Price Changes in Canadian Manufacturing Industries, 1961–1967," *Quarterly Review of Economics and Business*," XI (Spring 1971), 80–84. But compare Gardiner C. Means, "The Administered Price Thesis Confirmed," *American Economic Review*, LXII, (June 1972), 292–306.

28. See, for example, Samuel M. Loescher, *Imperfect Collusion in the Cement Industry* (Cambridge: Harvard University Press, 1959). After the F.T.C.'s victory in the Cement Institute case, the industry reverted to a freight absorption system that resulted in identical prices to delivery points.

29. *Westinghouse Electric Corp.*, 60 F.T.C. 1272 (1962), appears to be the only case brought by the F.T.C. that has involved identical bidding.

30. See *Cordova District Fisheries Union*, 52 F.T.C. 66, 731 (1956); *Puget Sound Salmon Canners, Inc.*, 53 F.T.C. 342 (1956); and *Queen Anne's County Clam Association*, 57 F.T.C. 281 (1960). The latter case involved the clam diggers of Queen Anne's County, Maryland, whose gross annual sales amounted to between $1.5 and 2 million. Cases involving fishing cooperatives are discussed in detail in Stanley Hack, *Legal Aspects of Small Business Use of Cooperative Arrangements* (Madison: University of Wisconsin Press, 1964), pp. 35–38.

31. See E. W. Hawley, *The New Deal and the Problem of Monopoly* (Princeton: Princeton University Press, 1966), pp. 360–362; and Earl Latham, *The Group Basis of Politics* (Ithaca: Cornell University Press, 1952), pp. 71–72.

32. George P. Lamb and Sumner S. Kittelle, *Trade Association Law and Practice* (Boston: Little, Brown, 1956), p. 73.

33. *American Cyanamid Co.*, 63 F.T.C. 1747 (1963); affirmed in 401 F. 2d 574 (C.C.A. 6, 1968).

34. For example, *Safeway Stores, Inc.* v. *Federal Trade Commission*, 366 F. 2d 795 (C.C.A. 9, 1966).

35. *Dr. Miles Medical Co.* v. *Park & Sons Co.*, 220 U.S. 373 (1911).

36. On Brandeis, see Alfred Lief, ed., *The Social and Economic Views of Mr. Justice Brandeis* (New York: Vanguard Press, 1930), pp. 398–400. See U.S. Senate, 63rd Cong., 2d sess., September 8, 1914, *Congressional Record*, LI, 14788, for a fair trade bill drafted by Rublee.

37. Hawley, *New Deal*, pp. 254–258, and Joseph C. Palamountain, *The Politics of Distribution* (Cambridge: Harvard University Press, 1955), pp. 92–106, 235–243.

38. For details see S. C. Hollander, "United States of America," in *Resale Price Maintenance*, ed. B. S. Yamey (Chicago: Aldine, 1966), pp. 65–100, and the materials cited therein; and F. Marion Fletcher, *Market Restraints in the Retail Drug Industry* (Philadelphia: University of Pennsylvania Press, 1967), pp. 54–68. After reviewing the literature on resale price maintenance, Hollander concludes that "the results clearly have been undesirable from the point of view of consumers and the economy as a whole" (p. 100). In the face of an accelerating inflation rate in the mid-1970s, several states have recently nullified their fair trade laws.

39. See, for example, *American Tobacco Co.*, 1 F.T.C. 539 (1918), and *Hammerhill Paper Co.*, file no. 7310051 (1974).

40. *Federal Trade Commission* v. *Beech-Nut Packing Co.*, 257 U.S. 441 (1922).

41. See, for example, *Harper & Brothers*, 52 F.T.C. 1017 (1956).

42. *Doubleday & Co., Inc.*, 52 F.T.C. 169, 181 (1955).

43. See, for example, *Schick, Inc.*, 55 F.T.C. 665 (1958). Charges of discrimination in price and advertising allowances were also brought in these cases.

44. Hearings are held periodically, both in the Senate and in the House, on bills that would enable manufacturers to establish national prices at which wholesalers and retailers may resell branded products. Associations of dealers in electric razors and similar goods have consistently supported these bills. In the words of the House Interstate and Foreign Commerce Committee, "Over the years, this legislation has consistently been supported by numerous trade associations and organizations representing a large segment of wholesalers and retailers including druggists, jewelers, electric appliance dealers" (U.S. House of Representatives, 88th Cong., 1st sess., 1963, *Quality Stabilization Act*, H. Rept. 566, p. 3).

45. *Sun Oil Co.*, 55 F.T.C. 955 (1959); *Sun Oil Co.*, 63 F.T.C. 1371 (1963); and *Atlantic Refining Co.*, 63 F.T.C. 1407 (1963).

46. See, for example, *Central Linen Service*, 64 F.T.C. 1307 (1964), and *H. J. Heinz*, 52 F.T.C. 1607 (1956).

47. See, for example, "Small Business: The Maddening Struggle to Survive," *Business Week*, June 30, 1975, pp. 95–102.

Chapter 5

1. See Frederick M. Rowe, *Price Discrimination under the Robinson-Patman Act* (Boston: Little, Brown, 1962), p. 3.

2. Joseph C. Palamountain, *The Politics of Distribution* (Cambridge: Harvard University Press, 1955), pp. 5–10.

3. Ibid., pp. 58–254.

4. Ibid., pp. 58–90; see also the materials cited therein. The investigation established that approximately 85 percent of the difference between chains' and nonchains' selling prices resulted from the chains' lower operating expenses. Even this figure was an underestimate, for the F.T.C. did not ascertain the extent to which quantity discounts corresponded to cost savings. See M. A. Adelman, *A & P: A Study in Price-Cost Behavior and Public Policy* (Cambridge: Harvard University Press, 1959), p. 152.

5. Cited in Carl H. Fulda, "Food Distribution in the United States: The Struggle between Independents and Chains," *University of Pennsylvania Law Review*, XCIX (June 1951), 1051.

6. Ibid., p. 1082.

7. Palamountain, *Politics of Distribution*, pp. 188–234, 260, 261.

8. U.S. House of Representatives, 74th Cong., 1st sess., 1935, Committee on the Judiciary, *To Amend the Clayton Act, Hearings*, p. 1.

9. U.S. House of Representatives, 74th Cong., 2d sess., 1935, *Prohibition of Price Discriminations*, H. Rept. 2287, p. 4.

10. Ibid., pt. 2, p. 6.

11. Rowe, *Price Discrimination*, pp. 330–420; and Corwin D. Edwards, *The Price Discrimination Law* (Washington, D.C.: Brookings Institution, 1959), pp. 131–207.

12. Rowe, *Price Discrimination,* pp. 421–451; and Edwards, *Price Discrimination Law,* pp. 486–517.

13. E. W. Hawley, *The New Deal and the Problem of Monopoly* (Princeton: Princeton University Press, 1966), pp. 254–258; Palamountain, *Politics of Distribution,* pp. 235–254; and F. Marion Fletcher, *Market Restraints in the Retail Drug Industry* (Philadelphia: University of Pennsylvania Press, 1967), pp. 54–57.

14. Hawley, *New Deal,* pp. 259–266; Fulda, "Food Distribution," pp. 1116–1121; and S. C. Hollander, "United States of America," in *Resale Price Maintenance,* ed. B. S. Yamey (Chicago: Aldine, 1966), pp. 73–74.

15. Brian Dixon, *Price Discrimination and Marketing Management* (Ann Arbor: University of Michigan, Bureau of Business Research, 1960), p. 84.

16. Adelman, *A & P,* pp. 153–160.

17. See Alan Stone, "Coordination in Government: The F.T.C. and the Robinson-Patman Act," *Business and Government Review,* XI (July–August 1970), 29.

18. Mayo Thompson, "Antitrust, the F.T.C., and Consumer Prices: A Funny Thing Happened on the Way to the Supreme Court," address before the Federal Bar Association, February 6, 1975, p. 11.

19. Ibid., pp. 9–10.

20. U.S. House of Representatives, 92d Cong., 2d sess., 1973, Committee on Appropriations, *Agriculture, Environmental and Consumer Protection Appropriations for 1973, Hearings,* pt. 4, pp. 427, 428.

21. On support for this law see "New Life for Robinson-Patman," *Business Week,* August 11, 1975, p. 71.

22. *Federal Trade Commission* v. *Anheuser-Busch,* 363 U.S. 536, 549 (1960). The economic definition is different; in economic terms, price discrimination "occurs whenever and to the extent that there are price differences for the same product or service sold by a single seller, and not accounted for by cost differences or by changes in the level of demand; or when two or more buyers of the same goods and services are charged the same price despite differences in the cost of serving them" (U.S. Attorney General's National Committee to Study the Antitrust Laws, *Report* [Washington, D.C.: Government Printing Office, 1955], pp. 333–334). Hence in many instances pricing policies are economically discriminatory without being legally discriminatory.

23. See Albert E. Sawyer, *Business Aspects of Pricing under the Robinson-Patman Act* (Boston: Little, Brown, 1963), pp. 89–112.

24. Jules Backman, "An Economist Looks at the Robinson-Patman Act," *A.B.A. Antitrust Section Report,* XVII (1960), 355–356.

25. Edward H. Levi, "The Robinson-Patman Act—Is it in the Public Interest?" *A.B.A. Antitrust Section Report,* VIII (1952–1953), 61.

26. *Federal Trade Commission* v. *Morton Salt Co.,* 334 U.S. 37 (1948).

27. *Utah Pie Co.* v. *Continental Baking Co.,* 386 U.S. 685 (1967).

28. Levi, "Robinson-Patman Act," pp. 61–62.

29. Ibid., p. 62.

30. U.S. Senate, 87th Cong., 2d sess., 1963, Subcommittee on Antitrust and Monopoly, Committee on the Judiciary, *Concentration Ratios in Manufacturing Industry, 1958,* pt. 1, pp. 107–113.

31. Ibid., p. 11. The figures were much the same in 1963; see U.S. Senate, 89th Cong., 2d sess., 1966, Subcommittee on Antitrust and Monopoly, Committee on the Judiciary, *Concentration Ratios in Manufacturing Industry, 1963,* pt. 1, p. 139. By 1970 the share held by the four largest firms had declined to

20 percent; see Federal Trade Commission, *Economic Report on the Dairy Industry* (Washington, D.C.: Government Printing Office, 1973), p. 152.

32. U.S. National Commission on Food Marketing, *Organization and Competition in Food Retailing* (Washington, D.C.: Government Printing Office, 1966), pp. 34, 280–281.

33. Ibid., pp. 10, 41, 43; Ralph Cassidy, Jr., *Competition and Price Making in Food Retailing* (New York: Ronald Press, 1962), pp. 68–114; and Rom J. Markin, *The Supermarket: An Analysis of Growth, Development, and Change* (Pullman: Washington State University Press, 1963), pp. 36–56. A detailed survey of the drawing power of food stores concluded that "as the level of product offering at the retail site increases, the drawing power increases" (Bernard J. La Londe, *Differentials in Supermarket Drawing Power* [East Lansing: Michigan State University, Bureau of Business and Economic Research, 1962), p. 47.

34. *Hruby Distributing Co.,* 61 F.T.C. 1437, 1446 (1962). On price diversity, see Paul E. Nelson and Lee E. Preston, *Price Merchandising in Food Retailing: A Case Study* (Berkeley: University of California, Institute of Business and Economic Research, 1966), p. 99.

35. *Foremost Dairies, Inc.,* 62 F.T.C. 1344 (1963).

36. A. D. H. Kaplan, Joel B. Dirlam, and Robert F. Lanzilotti, *Pricing in Big Business* (Washington, D.C.: Brookings Institution, 1958), p. 284.

37. *Sun Oil Co.,* 55 F.T.C. 955 (1959) and 391 U.S. 505 (1963); *American Oil Co.,* 60 F.T.C. 1786 (1962) and 325 F. 2d 101 (C.C.A., 7, 1963).

38. Ralph Cassidy, Jr., *Price Making and Price Behavior in the Petroleum Industry* (New Haven: Yale University Press, 1954), pp. 262–276. Melvin G. de Chazeau and Alfred E. Kahn, *Integration and Competition in the Petroleum Industry* (New Haven: Yale University Press, 1959), pp. 456, 457, show that the stations that initiate price wars are ordinarily independents who purchase their supplies from independent refiners.

39. A full catalog of restraints is contained in Stanley C. Hollander, *Restraints upon Retail Competition* (East Lansing: Michigan State University, Bureau of Business and Economic Research, 1965).

40. *Sunshine Biscuit Co.,* 58 F.T.C. 674 (1961); reversed in 306 F. 2d 48 (C.C.A., 7, 1962). The Commission announced that it did not consider itself bound by this reversal, since it represented the views of only one circuit.

41. *Tri-Valley Packing Association,* 60 F.T.C. 1134 (1962).

42. *General Foods Corp.,* 52 F.T.C. 798 (1958).

43. Cassidy, *Competition and Price Making,* pp. 128–132, 162–167; Markin, *Supermarket,* pp. 65–70; and William H. Kaven, "Impact of Private Label Ice Cream on Industry Structure and Conduct" (unpublished Ph.D. dissertation, Cornell University, 1966), pp. 103–107. Kaven concludes that "market determination of wholesale prices of private label ice cream and resultant reduction of private label wholesale prices have, in effect, influenced manufacturers to consolidate into larger and more efficient manufacturing plants that have reduced production costs" (p. 175).

44. *Borden Company,* 62 F.T.C. 130 (1963), affirmed 383 U.S. 637 (1966).

45. Frederick M. Rowe, *The Price Discrimination Law* (Boston: Little, Brown, 1962), pp. 161–162.

46. John S. McGee, "Some Economic Issues in Robinson-Patman Land," *Law and Contemporary Problems,* XXX (Summer 1965), 547–548.

47. See, for example, *Arkansas City Co.,* 54 F.T.C. 246 (1957); *Southern Oxygen Co.,* 54 F.T.C. 1237 (1958); *Amalgamated Sugar Co.,* 54 F.T.C. 943

(1958); *Sav-A-Stop, Inc.,* 55 F.T.C. 1807 (1959); and *Kelly Creamery Co.,* 57 F.T.C. 1460 (1960).

48. *Maryland Baking Co.,* 52 F.T.C. 1679 (1956); affirmed and modified in 243 F. 2d 716 (C.C.A., 4, 1957) and 53 F.T.C. 1106 (1957). See the discussion in Edwards, *Price Discrimination Law,* pp. 447–448.

49. *Forster Manufacturing Co.,* 62 F.T.C. 852 (1963).

50. Relatively few cases have been brought under Section 2(f) because of the substantial evidentiary requirements imposed on the Commission by the courts. See Rowe, *Price Discrimination Law,* chap. 14.

51. Charles W. Davisson, *The Marketing of Automotive Parts* (Ann Arbor: University of Michigan, Bureau of Business Research, 1954), pp. 3–22; and U.S. Senate, 90th Cong., 2d sess., 1968, Committee on the Judiciary, Subcommittee on Antitrust and Monopoly, *Automotive Repair Industry, Hearings,* pp. 5–19, 133–138. The scope of the parts problem is indicated by the fact that the standard parts manual has more than 100,000 entries.

52. Davisson, *Marketing of Automotive Parts,* pp. 22–25; and *Automotive Repair Industry, Hearings,* pp. 7, 8.

53. *Automotive Repair Industry, Hearings,* pp. 9–11. William Leonard, professor of economics at Hofstra University and an expert on the automotive parts industry, told the Senate subcommittee that competition among service outlets is intense and dealer pressure to increase margins severe because of the vigorous competition of mass merchandisers who purchase directly from manufacturers.

54. Davisson, *Marketing of Automotive Parts,* pp. 26–41, 104–105, 113, 127.

55. Ibid., pp. 769–775.

56. *Airtex Products, Inc.,* 55 F.T.C. 1754 (1959); *American Ball Bearing Co.,* 57 F.T.C. 1259 (1960); and *Thompson Products, Inc.,* 55 F.T.C. 1252 (1959).

57. Examples include *Alhambra Motor Parts,* 57 F.T.C. 1007 (1960); *Automotive Jobbers, Inc.,* 60 F.T.C. 19 (1962); and *National Parts Warehouse,* 63 F.T.C. 1692 (1963).

58. William Fellner, *Competition among the Few* (1949; New York: Augustus M. Kelley, 1960), p. 185. Fellner goes on to point out, however (pp. 187–188), that in oligopolistic industries relative loss will almost necessarily result from competition rather than coordination (or, as he puts it, quasi-agreements) in innovation, product variation, and advertising. Hence there is an inducement to extend quasi-agreements to these areas. Only if some competitive change can have a decisive impact on rivals is there a relative gain in nonprice competition. See also Fritz Machlup, *The Economics of Sellers' Competition* (Baltimore: Johns Hopkins University Press, 1952), pp. 408–411 and 449–456.

59. See, for example, *Walter Holding Co.,* 61 F.T.C. 413 (1962); *Tom C. Lange,* 61 F.T.C. 263 (1962); and *Dixie-Central Produce Co.,* 61 F.T.C. 67 (1962).

60. The F.T.C. reports that slightly more than half of all restraint-of-trade cases brought by it in the food-processing industry between 1950 and 1965 were brokerage matters. Of the 158 cases brought under Section 2(c) during this period, 82 were against members of the citrus fruit industry and 28 were against members of the northwestern salmon fishing industry. Almost all were against small firms. See Federal Trade Commission, *The Structure of Food Manufacturing* (Washington, D.C.: Government Printing Office, 1966), p. 176.

61. *Daniel H. Sobo,* 53 F.T.C. 783 (1957).

62. Palamountain, *Politics of Distribution*, pp. 193–194.

63. Cited in Rowe, *Price Discrimination Law*, p. 33.

64. William H. Fisher, III, "Sections 2(d) and (e) of the Robinson-Patman Act: Babel Revisited," *Vanderbilt Law Review*, XI (March 1958), 466–467.

65. Cited in Harold B. Meyers, "The Roots of the F.T.C.'s Confusion," in *The Regulated Businessman*, ed. John A. Larson (New York: Holt, Rinehart & Winston, 1966), pp. 137–138.

66. The F.T.C. has also brought successful actions against recipients of discriminatory allowances under Section 5 of the F.T.C. Act.

67. Hawley, *New Deal*, pp. 60, 100, 251, 253; and Fulda, "Food Distribution," pp. 1089–1090.

68. Donald Dewey, *Monopoly in Economics and Law* (Chicago: Rand McNally, 1959), p. 196.

69. For an indictment of such discretion, see Theodore J. Lowi, *The End of Liberalism* (New York: Norton, 1969), pp. 287–297.

Chapter 6

1. *Swift & Co.*, 5 F.T.C. 143 (1922).

2. *Eastman Kodak Co.*, 7 F.T.C. 434 (1924).

3. *Federal Trade Commission* v. *Eastman Kodak Co.*, 274 U.S. 619, 623 (1927).

4. *Annual Report of the Federal Trade Commission, 1927* (Washington, D.C.: Government Printing Office, 1927), p. 67.

5. *Jacob Siegel Co.* v. *Federal Trade Commission*, 327 U.S. 608, 612–613 (1946). See also *Herzfeld* v. *Federal Trade Commission*, 140 F. 2d 207, 209 (C.C.A., 2, 1944).

6. *Federal Trade Commission* v. *Ruberoid Co.*, 343 U.S. 470, 473 (1952).

7. *Federal Trade Commission* v. *Brown Shoe Co., Inc.*, 384 U.S. 316, 321 (1966).

8. *L. G. Balfour Co.* v. *Federal Trade Commission*, 442 F. 2d 1 (C.C.A., 7, 1971). See also *Federal Trade Commission* v. *Dean Foods*, 384 U.S. 597, 606 N. 4 (1966).

9. See, for example, *United States* v. *Union Pacific Railroad Co.*, 226 U.S. 61 (1912); *United States* v. *Lehigh Valley Railroad Co.*, 254 U.S. 255 (1920); and *United States* v. *Southern Pacific Co.*, 259 U.S. 214 (1922).

10. See *Federal Trade Commission* v. *Western Meat Co.*, 272 U.S. 554 (1926).

11. Federal Trade Commission, *Report on Corporate Mergers* (Washington, D.C.: Government Printing Office, 1955), pp. 154–156; see also David Martin, *Mergers and the Clayton Act* (Berkeley: University of California Press, 1959), pp. 254–260.

12. The Senate report on the bill stated that the amendment's purpose was to "cope with monopolistic tendencies in their incipiency and well before they have attained such effects as would justify a Sherman Act proceeding" (quoted in Martin, *Mergers*, p. 251).

13. Federal Trade Commission, *Report on the Merger Movement* (Washington, D.C.: Government Printing Office, 1948), p. 68.

14. George Stigler, *Five Lectures on Economic Problems* (New York: Macmillan, 1950), Appendix, pp. 63–65.

15. J. Fred Weston, *The Role of Mergers in the Growth of Large Firms* (Berkeley and Los Angeles: University of California Press, 1961), pp. 102–

28. Demsetz, "Two Systems," p. 179.

29. Arthur A. Thompson, "Absolute Firm Size, Administered Prices, and Inflation," *Economic Enquiry*, XII (June 1974), 240–254.

30. Weiss, "Concentration-Profits Relationship," p. 233.

31. Reported in "Are Some Key Industries Pushing Up Inflation?" *Business Week*, October 6, 1975, p. 48.

32. William F. Baxter, "Wall Street and William Jennings Bryan," *New Republic*, August 16, 1969, p. 14. Henry G. Manne, "Mergers and the Market for Corporate Control," *Journal of Political Economy*, LXXIII (April 1965), 119, notes that mergers are of importance in protecting noncontrolling shareholders and are in any event more desirable than the increased number of bankruptcies that would ensue if mergers were totally prohibited. See also J. Fred Weston and Stanley Ornstein, "Trends and Causes of Concentration: A Survey," in *Impact of Large Firms*, ed. Weston and Ornstein, p. 18.

33. See James B. Quinn, "Technological Competition: Europe v. U.S.," *Harvard Business Review*, XLIV (July–August 1966), 113.

34. Bock and Farkas, *Concentration and Productivity*, pp. 4–5.

35. Weston and Ornstein, "Trends and Causes," pp. 19–20.

36. Peter Asch, *Economic Theory and the Antitrust Dilemma* (New York: Wiley, 1970), p. 293.

37. Weston, *Role of Mergers*, p. 104.

38. Lewis Beman, "What We Learned from the Great Merger Frenzy," *Fortune*, April 1973, p. 73. But see also Ralph Nelson, *Merger Movements in American Industry, 1895–1956* (Princeton: Princeton University Press, 1959). Nelson rejects the theory that consolidation movements are due exclusively to their promoters' desire for quick turnover profits. Nevertheless, the data compel Nelson to conclude (pp. 99, 119) that during periods of high merger activity, capital market conditions, especially as reflected in the changing prices of stocks, have been far more important than industrial conditions in causing mergers.

39. H. Igor Ansoff et al., *Acquisition Behavior of U.S. Manufacturing Firms, 1946–1965* (Nashville: Vanderbilt University Press, 1971), pp. 26–30.

40. *Studies by the Staff of the Cabinet Committee on Price Stability* (Washington, D.C.: Government Printing Office, 1969), p. 45.

41. Betty Bock, *Statistical Games and the "200 Largest" Industrials: 1954 and 1968* (New York: National Industrial Conference Board, 1970), p. 10.

42. Weston and Ornstein, "Trends and Causes," pp. 4–6.

43. Alfred D. Chandler, "The Structure of American Industry in the Twentieth Century: A Historical Overview," *Business History Review*, XLIII (Autumn 1969), 280–281.

44. Michael Gort and Thomas F. Hogarty, "New Evidence on Mergers," *Journal of Law and Economics*, XIII (April 1970), 183. See also Weston and Ornstein, "Trends and Causes," p. 13; and Lawrence G. Goldberg, "Effects of Conglomerate Mergers on Competition," *Journal of Law and Economics*, XVI (April 1973), 139–140.

45. Federal Trade Commission, *Conglomerate Merger Performance* (Washington, D.C.: Government Printing Office, 1972), pp. 132–133; Goldberg, "Effect of Conglomerate Mergers," pp. 149–157; and Lawrence G. Goldberg, "Conglomerate Mergers and Concentration Ratios," *Review of Economics and Statistics*, LVII (August 1974), 303–309.

46. See Gort and Hogarty, "New Evidence," pp. 173–174, and Federal

Trade Commission, *Conglomerate Merger Performance,* pp. 59–60. See also Ansoff et al., *Acquisition Behavior,* pp. 12–14.

47. Beman, "What We Learned," p. 70.

48. See, for example, Richard O. Zerbe, "Antitrust Cases as a Guide to Directions in Antitrust Research and Policy," in *The Antitrust Dilemma,* ed. James A. Dalton and Stanford Levin (Lexington, Mass.: Heath, 1973), pp. 71–74.

49. Norman R. Collins and Lee R. Preston, *Concentration and Price-Cost Margins in Manufacturing Industries* (Berkeley: University of California Press, 1968), p. 6.

50. See U.S. Senate, 88th Cong., 1st sess., 1963, Committee on the Judiciary, *Administered Prices, Hearings,* pt. 29, p. 17973.

51. Ralph Cassidy, Jr., *Competition and Price Making in Food Retailing* (New York: Ronald Press, 1962), p. 53.

52. See particularly Willard Arant, "Competition of the Few among the Many," *Quarterly Journal of Economics,* LXX (August 1956): 327–345; and Richard Ruggles, "The Nature of Price Flexibility and the Determinants of Relative Price Changes in the Economy," in National Bureau Committee for Economic Research, *Business Concentration and Price Policy* (Princeton: Princeton University Press, 1955), pp. 441–495.

53. Ruggles, "Nature of Price Flexibility," pp. 486–487.

54. John Perry Miller, "Measures of Monopoly Power and Concentration: Their Economic Significance," in Universities National Bureau Committee for Economic Research, p. 134.

55. Kenneth Elzinga, "The Antimerger Law: Pyrrhic Victories," *Journal of Law and Economics,* XII (April 1969), 43–78.

56. Mark Green, *The Closed Enterprise System* (New York: Grossman, 1972), pp. 337–362.

57. Federal Trade Commission, *Statistical Report on Mergers and Acquisitions* (Washington, D.C.: Government Printing Office, 1973), p. 58.

58. *United States* v. *Philadelphia National Bank,* 374 U.S. 321 (1963).

59. *United States* v. *Von's Grocery Co.,* 86 S. Ct. 1478 (1966).

60. *United States* v. *General Dynamics,* 415 U.S. 486 (1974).

61. *Diamond Crystal Salt Co.,* 56 F.T.C. 818 (1960), and *A. G. Spalding & Bros.,* 56 F.T.C. 1155 (1962); affirmed in 301 F. 2d 583 (C.C.A., 3, 1962).

62. George J. Stigler, "The Economic Effects of the Antitrust Laws," *Journal of Law and Economics,* IX (October 1966), 232. See also Carl Eis, "The 1919–1930 Merger Movement in American Industry," *Journal of Law and Economics,* IX (October 1966), p. 296.

63. Harold C. Livesay and Patrick G. Porter, "Vertical Integration in American Manufacturing, 1899–1948," *Journal of Economic History,* XXIX (September 1969), 495–496 (emphasis supplied).

64. The leading case is *Brown Shoe Co.* v. *United States,* 370 U.S. 294 (1962), which is criticized devastatingly in John L. Peterman, "The Brown Shoe Case," *Journal of Law and Economics,* XVIII (April 1975), 81–146. The leading F.T.C. case is *Union Carbide Corp.,* 59 F.T.C. 614, 1479 (1961).

65. Joel Dean and Warren Gustus, "Vertical Integration and Section 7," *New York University Law Review,* XL (October 1965), 702.

66. Sam Peltzman, "Issues in Vertical Integration Policy," in *Public Policy toward Mergers,* ed. Fred Weston and Sam Peltzman (Pacific Palisades, Calif.: Goodyear, 1969), pp. 167–176.

67. *Lehigh Portland Cement Co.,* 80 F.T.C. 922, 926 (1972).

68. William J. Boyd, "Vertical Integration in the Cement and Concrete Industry" (address presented before the National Sand and Gravel Association and the National Ready Mixed Concrete Association, January 28, 1970), p. 10.

69. Bruce T. Allen, "Vertical Integration and Market Foreclosure: The Case of Cement and Concrete," *Journal of Law and Economics,* XIV (April 1971), 273. My discussion relies heavily on Allen's article.

70. See, for example, "Behind the Breakup in Big Business Mergers," *U.S. News and World Report,* July 27, 1970, p. 45, which reports that while 323 corporations sold divisions or production lines in the first half of 1969, the number for the comparable period in 1970 jumped to 606 (an increase of 88 percent). See also "Why Mergers Have Dropped with a Thud," *U.S. News and World Report,* April 14, 1975, p. 75.

71. *Procter & Gamble Co.,* 63 F.T.C. 1465 (1963); affirmed in 386 U.S. 568 (1967).

72. David M. Blank, "Television Advertising: The Great Discount Illusion or Tony-pandy Revisited," *Journal of Business,* XLI (January 1968), 10–38; and John L. Peterman, "The Clorox Case and the Television Rate Structure," *Journal of Law and Economics,* XI (October 1968), 321–432.

73. *Reynolds Metals Co.,* 63 F.T.C. 2040 (1960).

74. *Consolidated Foods Co.,* 62 F.T.C. 929 (1963); affirmed in 380 U.S. 592 (1965). See also James H. Lorie and Paul Halpern, "Conglomerates: the Rhetoric and the Evidence," *Journal of Law and Economics,* XIII (April 1970), 150–153.

75. See John C. Narver, *Conglomerate Mergers and Market Competition* (Berkeley: University of California Press, 1967), pp. 104–117, 124.

76. Donald F. Turner, "Conglomerate Mergers and Section 7 of the Clayton Act," *Harvard Law Review,* LXXVIII (May 1965), 1352–1353.

77. *Foremost Dairies, Inc.,* 60 F.T.C. 944 (1962).

78. Arant, "Competition of the Few," pp. 332–338; Roger Sherman and Thomas D. Willett, "Potential Entrants Discourage Entry," *Journal of Political Economy,* LXXV (August 1967), 400–403.

79. U.S. Senate, 90th Cong., 1st sess., 1967, Select Committee on Small Business, *Planning, Regulation and Competition, Hearings,* p. 8.

80. Complaint, *Kellogg Company et al.,* F.T.C. Dkt. 8883 (1972).

81. "The F.T.C. Declares a War on Oligopoly," *Business Week,* January 29 1972, p. 24.

82. Complaint, *Exxon Corporation et al.,* F.T.C. Dkt. 8934 (1973).

83. "Kellogg: Target for Today," *Forbes,* June 1, 1973, p. 24.

84. Sheldon Zalaznick, "The Fight for a Place at the Breakfast Table," *Fortune,* December 1967, pp. 128–130, 186, 191–192.

85. Ibid.

86. See the testimony of J. Fred Weston in U.S. Senate, 93rd Cong., 1st sess., 1973, Committee on the Judiciary, *Industrial Reorganization Act, Hearings,* pt. 1, p. 235.

Chapter 7

1. U.S. House of Representatives, 63rd Cong., 2d sess., 1914, Committee on the Judiciary, *Trust Legislation, Hearings,* p. 1765.

2. The Supreme Court's reasoning is given in *McLean* v. *Fleming,* 96 U.S. 245 (1887).

3. U.S. Senate, 63rd Cong., 2d sess., June 25, 1914, *Congressional Record,* LI, 11105.

4. Ibid., p. 11109.

5. Federal Trade Commission, *Memorandum on Unfair Competition at the Common Law* (Washington: Government Printing Office, 1916), passim; and U.S. Department of Commerce, Bureau of Corporations, *Trust Laws and Unfair Competition* (Washington, Government Printing Office, 1916), pp. 323–327, 332–389, 431–455.

6. Gerard Henderson's study of the F.T.C.'s first decade, *The Federal Trade Commission* (1924; New York: Agathon Press, 1968), concludes (p. 166) that "a fraud which merely injures the person defrauded, without affecting or tending to affect a competitor, appears to be beyond the Commission's jurisdiction."

7. In 1928 and 1929, 85 percent of orders entered by the Commission concerned deceptive advertising and related practices. See "Scope of the Jurisdiction of the Federal Trade Commission over False and Misleading Advertising," *Yale Law Review,* XL (May 1931), 617.

8. See S. Chesterfield Oppenheim, *Unfair Trade Practices* (St. Paul, Minn.: West, 1950), p. 425n.

9. *Lumley* v. *Gye,* 118 Eng. Rep. 749 (1853).

10. *Beekman* v. *Marsters,* 195 Mass. 205 (1907); and *H. Friedberg, Inc.* v. *McClary,* 173 Ky. 579 (1917).

11. See *Temperton* v. *Russell,* 1 Queen's Bench Decisions 715 (1893), in which interference with a prospective contract was held to be tortious.

12. Henderson, *Federal Trade Commission,* p. 171. The case referred to is *Phillips Brothers & Co.,* 4 F.T.C. 297 (1922).

13. Henderson, *Federal Trade Commission,* pp. 179, 181.

14. Ibid., pp. 181, 189–193. And see "Scope of the Jurisdiction," p. 622; this editorial comment also observes (p. 617) that in 1915 the Associated Advertising Clubs sought F.T.C. assistance in combating certain kinds of deception.

15. See *Raladam Co.* v. *Federal Trade Commission,* 42 F. 2d 430 (C.C.A., 6, 1930); affirmed in 283 U.S. 643 (1931).

16. *Federal Trade Commission* v. *Raladam Co.,* 316 U.S. 149 (1942).

17. U.S. House of Representatives, 75th Cong., 1st sess., 1937, *Extension of Federal Trade Commission's Authority over Unfair Acts and Practices and False Advertising of Food, Drugs, Devices and Cosmetics,* H. Rept. 1613 to accompany S. 1077, p. 3. See also Huston Thompson, "Highlights in the Evaluation of the Federal Trade Commission," *George Washington Law Review,* 8 (January–February, 1940), 278–279.

18. Henderson, *Federal Trade Commission,* p. 166.

19. U.S. House of Representatives, 74th Cong., 2d sess., 1936, Committee on Interstate and Foreign Commerce, *Federal Trade Commission Act, Hearings,* p. 50.

20. Ibid., p. 78.

21. "Federal Trade Commission—False and Misleading Advertising," *Michigan Law Review,* XXXI (April 1933), 817; and "A Revised Federal Trade Commission Act—The Wheeler-Lea Amendment," *University of Pennsylvania Law Review,* LXXXVI (May 1938), 759.

22. This discussion relies heavily upon Charles O. Jackson, *Food and Drug Legislation in the New Deal* (Princeton: Princeton University Press, 1970).

23. Jackson, *Food and Drug Legislation,* pp. 27–29; and James H. Young, *The Medical Messiahs* (Princeton: Princeton University Press, 1967), pp. 164–166.

24. Jackson, *Food and Drug Legislation*, p. 124; and "Fourth Food and Drug Fight," *Business Week*, January 16, 1937, pp. 38, 40.

25. Jackson, *Food and Drug Legislation*, pp. 79–80.

26. Ibid., p. 176; "22,000 Food Folk Meet," *Business Week*, January 30, 1937, p. 17; and "Who Shall Control Advertising," *Business Week*, April 3, 1937, pp. 42, 44. Another issue of *Business Week* (March 13, 1937) reported that "some trade groups are even rendering underground aid and comfort to the trade commission in its fight for advertising control" ("Drug Bill Past Senate," pp. 15–16).

27. "Ready for Drug Bill Solution," *Business Week*, June 12, 1937, pp. 25–26.

28. *Annual Report of the Federal Trade Commission, 1935* (Washington, D.C.: Government Printing Office, 1935), pp. 14–15. A detailed legislative history of the Wheeler-Lea Act is contained in Charles Wesley Dunn, *Wheeler-Lea Act* (New York: Stechert, 1938).

29. U.S. Senate, 75th Cong., 3d sess., January 12, 1938, *Congressional Record*, XXCIII, 391, 392.

30. Ibid., p. 413.

31. U.S. Senate, 74th Cong., 2d sess., 1936, Committee on Interstate Commerce, *To Amend the Federal Trade Commission Act, Hearings*, pp. 88, 101–103; U.S. House of Representatives, 75th Cong., 1st sess., 1937, Committee on Interstate and Foreign Commerce, *To Amend the Federal Trade Act, Hearings*, p. 74; and Jackson, *Food and Drug Legislation*, pp. 79, 90, 123.

32. U.S. Senate, *To Amend the Federal Trade Commission Act, Hearings*, p. 88.

33. Jackson, *Food and Drug Legislation*, p. 81.

34. U.S. House of Representatives, 75th Cong., 3d sess., January 12, 1938, *Congressional Record*, XXCIII, 418.

35. See U.S. Senate, 74th Cong., 2d sess., May 14, 1936, *Congressional Record*, XXC, 6589.

36. House of Representatives, *Extension of Federal Trade Commission's Authority*, p. 21.

37. Ibid., p. 24.

38. Ibid.

39. Ibid., pp. 23–24.

40. Jackson, *Food and Drug Legislation*, pp. 171–174.

41. U.S. House of Representatives, 75th Cong., 3d sess., January 12, 1938, *Congressional Record*, XXCIII, 392. See the argument made in response by Congressman Edward Kenney, pointing out that a cease-and-desist order would not deter potential offenders. He observed, prophetically, that a devious businessman who is found disseminating false advertising can easily change his advertising (ibid., pp. 394, 400, 406, 408).

42. U.S. Senate, 74th Cong., 2d sess., 1936, *Amendments to the Federal Trade Commission Act*, Senate Rept. 1705, p. 1.

43. U.S. House of Representatives, 75th Cong., 3d sess., January 12, 1938, *Congressional Record*, XXCIII, 392.

44. After the Wheeler-Lea Amendment was enacted, Congressman Lea still opposed a new drug bill that would govern labeling; but a tragedy that cost many lives, as a result of consumption of an unsafe drug, so aroused popular opinion that a weak drug bill was enacted (Jackson, *Food and Drug Legislation*, pp. 151–174, 176–200).

45. Richard Posner, *Regulation of Advertising by the F.T.C.* (Washing-

ton, D.C.: American Enterprise Institute for Public Policy Research, 1973), p. 5.

46. The distinctions derive from Michael R. Darby and Edi Karny, "Free Competition and the Optimal Amount of Fraud," *Journal of Law and Economics*, XIII (April 1973), 69.

47. Posner, *Regulation of Advertising*, p. 5.

48. Tom Dillon, "What Is Deceptive Advertising?" *Journal of Advertising Research*, XIII (October 1973), 10.

49. Posner, *Regulation of Advertising*, p. 6.

50. See *Advertising Age*, August 26, 1974.

51. For varying estimates, see Edwin H. Sutherland, *White Collar Crime* (New York: Holt, Rinehart & Winston, 1949), and Raymond Baumhart, S. J., *Ethics in Business* (New York: Holt, Rinehart & Winston, 1968).

52. American Bar Association, *Report of the ABA Commission to Study the Federal Trade Commission* (Chicago, 1969), p. 39.

53. U.S. Senate, 88th Cong., 1st sess., 1963, Special Committee on Aging, *Frauds and Quackery Affecting the Older Citizen, Hearings*, p. 132.

54. Ibid., pp. 153, 168; and ibid., 2d sess., 1964, Special Committee on Aging, *Health Frauds and Quackery, Hearings*, pp. 130, 237.

55. U.S. House of Representatives, 85th Cong., 2d sess., 1958, *False and Misleading Advertising (Weight Reducing Remedies)*, H. Rept. 2553, p. 22; and ibid., *False and Misleading Advertising (Prescription Tranquilizing Drugs)*, H. Rept. 2688, pp. 4–15, 18, 19.

56. U.S. Senate, 88th Cong., 2d sess., Special Committee on Aging, *Health Frauds and Quackery, Hearings*, p. 132; and Edward C. Cox, Robert C. Fellmeth, and John E. Schulz, *"The Nader Report" on the Federal Trade Commission* (New York: Richard W. Baron, 1969).

57. See U.S. Senate, 91st Cong., 1st and 2d sess., 1971, Committee on Commerce, *Consumer Protection, Hearings*, p. 14.

58. Cox, Fellmeth, and Schulz, *"Nader Report,"* pp. 37–95.

59. American Bar Association, *Report*, p. 39.

60. Speech delivered by Chairman Miles Kirkpatrick before a meeting of international advertising executives; see "F.T.C. Chief Attacks Ads as Insulting," *Washington Post*, January 9, 1971, p. D6.

61. See, for example, George J. Alexander, *Honesty and Competition* (Syracuse, N.Y.: Syracuse University Press, 1967), pp. 106–111.

62. U.S. House of Representatives, 91st Cong., 2d sess., 1970, Committee on Interstate and Foreign Commerce, *Class Action and Other Consumer Protection Procedures, Hearings*, p. 65.

63. Ibid., *Staff Report: The Federal Trade Commission, 1974*, p. 19.

64. *Ocean Spray Cranberries, Inc.*, 80 F.T.C. 975 (1972).

65. Ibid., p. 983.

66. *Boise Tire Co.*, file no. 7323087 (1973).

67. *Sugar Information, Inc.*, 81 F.T.C. 711 (1973).

68. *Firestone Tire and Rubber Co.*, 81 F.T.C. 398 (1972); and *Steven Rizzi*, F.T.C. Dkt. 8937 (1975).

69. *Firestone*, pp. 467–471.

70. M. Keith Hunt, "Effects of Corrective Advertising," *Journal of Advertising Research*, XIII (October 1973), 15–22. On refusal to order corrective advertisements for punitive purposes, see *Sir Carpet Inc.*, F.T.C. Dkt. 8891 (1974).

71. *Pay Less Drug Stores Northwest, Inc.*, 82 F.T.C. 1473 (1973).

72. *Heater* v. *Federal Trade Commission,* C.C.H. Trade Reg. Reporter, para. 75, 244 (C.C.A., 9, 1974).

73. *Pfizer Inc.,* 81 F.T.C. 23, 63 (1972).

74. *K-Mart Enterprises, Inc.,* file no. 7423155 (1974).

75. "Madison Avenue's Response to Its Critics," *Business Week,* June 10, 1972, p. 51.

76. Posner, *Regulation of Advertising,* p. 25.

77. For an interesting study of the contribution of advertising expenditures to the increases in sales of various products, see J. O. Peckham, "Guidelines for Marketing," *Nielsen Researcher,* XXIII, no. 2 (1965), 3–13. See also Leo Bogart, *Strategy in Advertising* (New York: Harcourt, Brace & World, 1967), pp. 78–79.

78. Bogart, *Strategy,* p. 7.

Chapter 8

1. *Federal Trade Commission* v. *Standard Education Soc.,* 86 F. 2d 692, 696 (C.C.A., 2, 1936).

2. *Federal Trade Commission* v. *Standard Education Soc.,* 302 U.S. 112, 116 (1937).

3. George J. Alexander, *Honesty and Competition* (Syracuse, N.Y.: Syracuse University Press, 1967), p. 8.

4. *Rhodes Pharmacal Co., Inc.* v. *Federal Trade Commission,* 208 F. 2d 382, 387 (C.C.A., 7, 1953); and *Giant Food Inc.* v. *Federal Trade Commission,* 322 F. 2d 977 (1963). See also Dorothy Cohen, "The Concept of Unfairness as It Relates to Advertising Legislation," *Journal of Marketing,* XXXVIII (July 1974), 9–11.

5. *Federal Trade Commission* v. *Colgate-Palmolive,* 380 U.S. 374 (1965).

6. See *Bristol-Myers Co.,* 46 F.T.C. 162 (1949).

7. See *Sewell* v. *Federal Trade Commission,* 240 F. 2d 228 (C.C.A., 9, 1956); reversed 353 U.S. 969 (1957).

8. American Bar Association, *Report of the ABA Commission to Study the Federal Trade Commission* (Chicago, 1969), p. 40.

9. Ibid., pp. 27, 49; and Edward C. Cox, Robert C. Fellmeth, and John E. Schulz, *"The Nader Report" on the Federal Trade Commission* (New York: Richard W. Baron), pp. 20–33.

10. Legislative details are discussed in *E. F. Drew & Co., Inc.,* 51 F.T.C. 1056 (1955).

11. See *The Blanton Co.,* 53 F.T.C. 580 (1956); *Food Town Inc.,* 51 F.T.C. 671 (1956); and *The Grand Union Co.,* 56 F.T.C. 1483 (1960).

12. *Arrow Metal Products Corp.,* 53 F.T.C. 721 (1957); *Chatham Research Laboratories,* 56 F.T.C. 1196 (1960); *Clinford Comb and Novelty Co., Inc.,* 53 F.T.C. 604 (1956); *Vulcanized Rubber and Plastics Co.,* 53 F.T.C. 920 (1957); *Dominion Briquettes & Chemicals Ltd.,* 59 F.T.C. 175 (1961); *E. Leask,* 56 F.T.C. 946 (1961); *Franklin Shockey Co.,* 56 F.T.C. 303 (1959); *Garay & Co., Inc.,* 57 F.T.C. 497 (1960); *Harker China Co.,* 62 F.T.C. 1382 (1963); *John Flynn & Sons, Inc.,* 60 F.T.C. 652 (1962); *Onyx Art Creations, Inc.,* 59 F.T.C. 792 (1961); and *Pearls by Deltah,* 62 F.T.C. 659 (1963).

13. See *Bussell, Inc.,* 60 F.T.C. 133 (1962); and *Glamore, Inc.,* 60 F.T.C. 227 (1962).

14. *Knickerbocker Case Corp.,* 58 F.T.C. 805 (1961).

15. *Keith M. Merrick Co.,* 57 F.T.C. 1255 (1960); *Better Rhinestone*

Jewelry Corp., 63 F.T.C. 1304 (1963); *Sheffield Merchandise Inc.,* 56 F.T.C. 988 (1960); *Hawthorne Watch Co.,* 54 F.T.C. 1670 (1958); *Barclay Home Products Inc.,* 52 F.T.C. 879 (1956); *Capra Gem Co.,* 63 F.T.C. 1912 (1963); *Esquire Manufacturing Co., Inc.,* 57 F.T.C. 1451 (1960); *A & L Seamon,* 55 F.T.C. 233 (1958); *F. H. Leather Products,* 56 F.T.C. 1174 (1960); and *Abbey Brush Corp.,* 53 F.T.C. 816 (1957).

16. *Capra Gem Co.,* 63 F.T.C. 1912, 1923 (1963).

17. *Abbey Brush Corp.,* 53 F.T.C. 816 (1957).

18. See, for example, *Budco, Inc.,* 57 F.T.C. 652 (1958); *Theta-Electronics, Inc.,* 57 F.T.C. 877 (1960); *Televideo Corp. of America,* 57 F.T.C. 1199 (1960).

19. Among the twelve orders entered in 1956–1964 are *Double Eagle Refining Co.,* 54 F.T.C. 1035 (1958); *Hugh Penn Oil Co., Inc.,* 53 F.T.C. 256 (1956); and *Royal Oil Corp.,* 54 F.T.C. 1292 (1958). See also *Saliper Refining Co.,* 54 F.T.C. 1026 (1958).

20. See, for example, *Wayne Oil Tank & Pump Co.,* 1 F.T.C. 259 (1918), and Gerard C. Henderson, *The Federal Trade Commission* (1924; New York: Agathon Press, 1968), pp. 212–213.

21. Disparaging claims are of two types. The first involves claims that rival products are harmful; see, for example, *Eversharp, Inc.,* 57 F.T.C. 841 (1960); *Lanolin Plus, Inc.,* 54 F.T.C. 446 (1957); *Saladmaster Sales,* 53 F.T.C. 874 (1957); and *Timed Energy,* 55 F.T.C. 300 (1958). The other category deprecates rival products and alleges superiority for the manufacturer's product. See *The Harwald Co.,* 59 F.T.C. 1302 (1961); *L. R. Gatley Co.,* 60 F.T.C. 1642 (1962); and *Prince Macaroni Manufacturing Co.,* 56 F.T.C. 362 (1959).

22. *Carter Products, Inc.,* 60 F.T.C. 782 (1962). See also note 5 above.

23. *MCP Foods Inc.,* 82 F.T.C. 1207 (1973); *Ford Motor Co.,* file no. 7223122 (1974); *Atlantic Hosiery Mills,* file no. 7423133 (1974); *Carnation Co.,* file no. 7423073 (1974); and *Fedders Corp.,* F.T.C. Dkt. 8932 (1975).

24. *Advertising Age,* May 26, 1975, p. 1.

25. Information based on U.S. House of Representatives, Committee on Interstate and Foreign Commerce, 93rd Cong., 2d sess., 1975, *Staff Report: The Federal Trade Commission, 1974,* p. 19, and interviews with agency personnel in 1975.

26. Richard Posner, *Regulation of Advertising by the F.T.C.* (Washington, D.C.: American Enterprise Institute for Public Policy Research, 1973), p. 28.

27. Ibid., p. 27.

28. See the summary in Alexander, *Honesty and Competition,* pp. 156–159. Representative cases include *Acme Sparkler & Specialty Co.,* 58 F.T.C. 1111 (1961); *Comptone Co., Ltd.,* 57 F.T.C. 960 (1961); *Courtesan, Inc.,* 57 F.T.C. 794 (1960); *The Englishtown Corp.,* 56 F.T.C. 672 (1959); and *Manco Watch Strap Co., Inc.,* 60 F.T.C. 495 (1962).

29. Examples of this type of case are *Sydnee, Inc.,* 54 F.T.C. 139 (1957), and *Harsam Distributors, Inc.,* 54 F.T.C. 1212 (1957).

30. See *Savoy Watch Co., Inc.,* 63 F.T.C. 473 (1963); *Silvercraft Co., Inc.,* 54 F.T.C. 972 (1958); and *A. E. Lewis & Co.,* 54 F.T.C. 1141 (1958).

31. See Alexander, *Honesty and Competition,* pp. 178–194. Typical cases include *A. J. Hollander & Co., Inc.,* 60 F.T.C. 10 (1962); *Cole Steel Equipment Co., Inc.,* 55 F.T.C. 505 (1958); *Pioneers, Inc.,* 57 F.T.C. 552 (1960); *Stacey-Warner Corp.,* 56 F.T.C. 20 (1959); *United States Safety Service Co.,* 55 F.T.C. 453 (1958); and *Beatrice Foods Co., Inc.,* 81 F.T.C. 830 (1972).

32. See Henderson, *Federal Trade Commission*, pp. 226–227. See *Dexter Thread Mills*, 53 F.T.C. 59 (1956); *Standard Mills, Inc.*, 63 F.T.C. 978 (1963); *Lafayette Brass Manufacturing Co., Inc.*, 57 F.T.C. 704 (1960); and *Juvenile Furniture Manufacturing Co.*, 63 F.T.C. 325 (1963).

33. *Redi-Brew Corp.*, file no. 7323111 (1975); *J. D. Gramm, Inc.*, 82 F.T.C. 1019 (1973); *Reiser Co., Inc.*, 61 F.T.C. 1378 (1962); *Chemical Compounds, Inc.*, 59 F.T.C. 1354 (1961); *M. Lober & Associates Co.*, 59 F.T.C. 375 (1961); *Champion Products Inc.*, 55 F.T.C. 142 (1958); *Comstock Chemical Co., Inc.*, 56 F.T.C. 33 (1959); *Dormeyer Corp.*, 60 F.T.C. 1116 (1962); *Lincoln Luggage Co., Inc.*, 60 F.T.C. 601 (1962); *Celtic Construction Co., Inc.*, 59 F.T.C. 352 (1961); and *Art National Manufacturers Distribution Co., Inc.*, 58 F.T.C. 719 (1961).

34. F. Marion Fletcher, *Market Restraints in the Retail Drug Industry* (Philadelphia: University of Pennsylvania Press, 1967), pp. 224–239. See also Lester G. Telser, "Advertising and Competition," *Journal of Political Economy*, LXXII (December 1964), 537–562.

35. See *Giant Food, Inc.*, 61 F.T.C. 326, 333, 351 (1962); and *George's Radio and Television Co., Inc.*, 60 F.T.C. 179 (1962). The F.T.C. employs the same theory in cases involving such similar terms as "manufacturer's list," "original list," and "comparative list value." See *Enterprise Stores*, 61 F.T.C. 930 (1962), and *Job Lot Trading Co.*, 62 F.T.C. 1198 (1963).

36. See *Lasky Enterprises, Inc.*, 56 F.T.C. 1303 (1960); *Reichardt Furniture Co.*, 56 F.T.C. 1023 (1960); *Royal Tile Co. of North Philadelphia*, 59 F.T.C. 406 (1961); *Fertig's Fifth Avenue, Inc.*, 58 F.T.C. 973 (1961).

37. See *National Drug Plan, Inc.*, 59 F.T.C. 170 (1961); *Home Furniture, Inc.*, 61 F.T.C. 1457 (1962).

38. *Earl Scheib, Inc.*, 63 F.T.C. 1049 (1963); see also *Seekonk Freezer Meats, Inc.*, 82 F.T.C. 1019 (1973). A variant is "distress" prices; see *Paul Bruseloff*, 82 F.T.C. 1090 (1973).

39. *The Orloff Co., Inc.*, 52 F.T.C. 709 (1956).

40. Examples are *Coro, Inc.*, 63 F.T.C. 1164 (1963); *Morris Lober & Associates*, 55 F.T.C. 209 (1958); and *Sans & Streiffe Inc.*, 63 F.T.C. 138 (1963).

41. *The Regina Corp.*, 61 F.T.C. 983 (1962).

42. *Mary Carter Paint Co.*, 60 F.T.C. 1786 (1962). See also *The Garland Co.*, 61 F.T.C. 1552 (1962), and *Robbin Products*, 62 F.T.C. 1461 (1963).

43. American Bar Association, *Report*, p. 40.

44. See *Tashof v. Federal Trade Commission*, 437 F. 2d 707 (C.C.A., D.C., 1970), in which salesmen's manuals giving instructions on how to employ bait-and-switch tactics were introduced; and *Consumer Products of America v. Federal Trade Commission*, 400 F. 2d 930 (C.C.A., 3, 1968), in which it was shown that encyclopedia salesmen received no commissions on sales of a low-priced advertised set of books.

45. Posner, *Regulation of Advertising*, pp. 19, 20.

46. See, for example, *People v. Glubo*, 5 N.Y. 2d 461 (1959).

47. *National Carpet Service Co.*, 82 F.T.C. 1354, 1363 (1973).

48. See F.T.C., *Trade Regulation Rule for the Prevention of Unfair and Deceptive Advertising and Labeling of Cigarettes in Relation to the Health Hazards of Smoking* (June 22, 1964), p. 1. Details on the cigarette controversy are provided in A. Lee Fritschler, *Smoking and Politics* (New York: Appleton-Century-Croft, 1969).

49. Cigarette Rule, pp. 100–101.

50. "Defending the Weed," *Wall Street Journal*, January 24, 1972, p. 1.

51. F.T.C., *Trade Regulation Rule Relating to . . . Quick Freeze Aerosol Spray Products* (May 21, 1969).

52. *Hayr Chemical Co., Inc.*, 52 F.T.C. 1091 (1956); *Drake Laboratories, Inc.*, 53 F.T.C. 1063 (1957); and *The Marcy Co.*, 55 F.T.C. 1622 (1959).

53. *Orlando of Calabria, Inc.*, file no. 7523107 (1975); *Hair Replacement Research Center, Inc.*, file no. 7523109 (1975); and *Hair Replacement Centers of Flushing, Inc.*, file no. 7523108 (1975).

54. For example, *Klear Vision Contact Lens Specialists, Inc.*, 54 F.T.C. 1678 (1958); *Kenmore Optical Co.*, 57 F.T.C. 628 (1960); and *Dunshaw, Inc.*, 58 F.T.C. 637 (1961).

55. *Lens Craft R & D Co.*, file no. 7223122 (1974).

56. See, for example, *The Health Guild*, 56 F.T.C. 140 (1959); *Omega Chemical Co., Inc.*, 54 F.T.C. 1461 (1958); *Ru-Ex Inc.*, 59 F.T.C. 839 (1961); and *O-Jib-Wa Medicine Co.*, 53 F.T.C. 1205 (1957). A temporary injunction was entered against Travel King, Inc., in 1974.

57. *Le-Blanc Medicine Co.*, 52 F.T.C. 607 (1956).

58. *Colgate-Palmolive Co.*, 58 F.T.C. 422 (1961).

59. *Carter Products, Inc.*, 53 F.T.C. 307 (1956). See also American Bar Association, *Report*, pp. 28–32.

60. *Benton & Bowles, Inc.*, 82 F.T.C. 1444 (1973); *Thomas J. Lipton, Inc.*, 82 F.T.C. 1493 (1973); and *Standard Brands, Inc.*, 82 F.T.C. 1176 (1973).

61. *Essex Varnish Co.*, 1 F.T.C. 138 (1918); *National Binding Machine Co.*, 1 F.T.C. 44 (1917); *Standard Car Equipment Co.*, 1 F.T.C. 144 (1918); and *Muenzen Specialty Co.*, 1 F.T.C. 30 (1917).

62. *State v. Russell, Inc.*, 101 Utah 89 (1941).

63. *Federal Trade Commission v. Keppel*, 291 U.S. 304 (1934).

64. Examples include *Allison's Co.*, 54 F.T.C. 1727 (1958); *Dandy Products Co., Inc.*, 62 F.T.C. 1413 (1963); and *Western Star Mill Co.*, 52 F.T.C. 1294 (1956).

65. For discussion of the applicable law and principles, see *Silverman* v. *Federal Trade Commission*, 145 F. 2d 751 (1944), and *Rothschild* v. *Federal Trade Commission*, 200 F. 2d 39 (1952).

66. *United States Retail Credit Association, Inc.*, 57 F.T.C. 1510 (1960), and *U.S. Association of Credit Bureaus, Inc.*, 58 F.T.C. 1044 (1961).

67. U.S. Senate, 90th Cong., 2d sess., 1968, Committee on Commerce, *Door-to-Door Sales Regulation, Hearings*, pp. 54, 130, 174; and Cox, Fellmeth, and Schulz, "Nader Report," p. 32.

68. *Federal Trade Commission v. Sperry and Hutchinson Co.*, 92 S. Ct. 898, 905 (1972).

69. Federal Trade Commission, *Trade Regulation Rule . . . Retail Food Store Advertising and Marketing Practices* (July 12, 1971).

70. Examples are *Adell Chemical Co.*, 54 F.T.C. 1801 (1958); *Allchem Manufacturing Co., Inc.*, 56 F.T.C. 480 (1959); *James B. Tompkins*, 63 F.T.C. 1644 (1963); and *Master Mechanic Manufacturing Co.*, 59 F.T.C. 792 (1961).

71. *Philip Morris, Inc.*, 82 F.T.C. 16 (1973), and *FMC Corp.*, F.T.C. Dkt. 8961 (1975).

72. See Alexander, *Honesty and Competition*, pp. 21–22; and Vance Packard, *The Hidden Persuaders* (New York: David McKay, 1957).

Chapter 9

1. Max Weber, *Gesammelte Politische Schriften*, as quoted in Georg Lukacs, *History and Class Consciousness* (Cambridge: MIT Press, 1971), p. 96.

2. Theodore J. Lowi, *The End of Liberalism* (New York: Norton, 1969).

3. The first Meat Inspection Act is a good example. See Gabriel Kolko, *The Triumph of Conservatism* (New York: Free Press, 1963), pp. 98–108.

4. U.S. House of Representatives, 76th Cong., 3d sess., August 30, 1940, *Congressional Record*, XXXCVI, 11310–11311. See also the remarks of Congressman Herbert O'Connor in support of the bill, ibid., p. 11323, and U.S. House of Representatives, 76th Cong., 1st sess., 1939, *Wool Fabrics Labeling Bill*, H. Rept. 907, pp. 6–7.

5. U.S. House of Representatives, 76th Cong., 1st sess., 1939, *Wool Fabrics Labeling Bill*, p. 1.

6. Ibid., pp. 2–3.

7. U.S. Senate, 76th Cong., 3d sess., October 2, 1940, *Congressional Record*, XXXCVI, 13022. See also Congressman Lyle Boren's remarks, U.S. House of Representatives, 76th Cong., 3d sess., August 30, 1940, ibid., p. 11318.

8. U.S. House of Representatives, 76th Cong., 3d sess., August 30, 1940, ibid., pp. 11328 and 11337; U.S. Senate, 76th Cong., 3d sess., September 12 and October 2, 1940, ibid., pp. 11986 and 13006–13111.

9. U.S. House of Representatives, 76th Cong., 3d sess., August 30, 1940, ibid., pp. 11319–11320; U.S. Senate, 76th Cong., 3d sess., September 12 and October 3, 1940, ibid., pp. 11973, 6044A, 6053A. See also "Require Wool Labels," *Business Week*, September 7, 1940, p. 15.

10. "Require Wool Labels," p. 17; U.S. Senate, 76th Cong., 3d sess., October 1, 1940, *Congressional Record*, XXCVI, 12935–12937; ibid., October 2, 1940, p. 13020.

11. U.S. House of Representatives, 76th Cong., 3d sess., August 30, 1940, *Congressional Record*, XXCVI, 11331. See also "Wool Act Protested," *Business Week*, October 12, 1940, p. 46. Senator Thomas quoted an editorial in the *Sheep and Goat Raisers*, a trade magazine, to the same effect. The trade magazine expected that a bill similar to the Wool Act would eliminate the use of reused wool in the manufacture of clothing and increase the sale of virgin wool to "an enormous extent" (U.S. Senate, 76th Cong., 3d sess., October 2, 1940, *Congressional Record*, XXXCVI, 13023).

12. U.S. Senate, 76th Cong., 3d sess., August 30, 1940, *Congressional Record*, XXCVI, 11310, 11314, 11331. In 1938 imports of woolen rags amounted to 794,436 pounds, valued at $262,201. The duty then was 18 cents per pound. In January 1939, in accordance with the trade agreement with Great Britain, the duty was reduced to 9 cents, and 1939 imports amounted to 8,417,818 pounds valued at $2,321,943 (ibid., p. 11334). See also *Wool Fabrics Labeling Bill*, p. 6.

13. American Bar Association, *Report of the ABA Commission to Study the Federal Trade Commission* (Chicago, 1969), pp. 46, 47.

14. See, for example, *A & G Hat & Cap Mfg. Co., Inc.*, 57 F.T.C. 576 (1960); *Reo Garment Inc.*, 57 F.T.C. 584 (1960); *Axelrod & Son*, 57 F.T.C. 597 (1960); and *Barnard Hosiery Co., Inc.*, 57 F.T.C. 681 (1960).

15. Examples are *Alpine Quilting Co., Inc.*, 57 F.T.C. 1204 (1960), and *Gladstone Textile Corp.*, 57 F.T.C. 1495 (1960).

16. *Cluny Juniors,* 57 F.T.C. 998 (1960), and *Dixie Army Surplus Store,* 61 F.T.C. 266 (1962), illustrate this point.

17. *Elliott Knitwear, Inc.,* 54 F.T.C. 1398, 1430 (1958). See also *Fox Knapp Manufacturing Co.,* 59 F.T.C. 1428 (1961).

18. "Cotton, Wool, Silk, and Man-Made Fibers Production," *World Almanac,* 1970, p. 145; and Jesse W. Markham, *Competition in the Rayon Industry* (Cambridge: Harvard University Press, 1952), pp. 31–36.

19. Identification of the manufacturer or distributor is not required in advertising.

20. Victor R. Fuchs, *The Economics of the Fur Industry* (New York: Columbia University Press, 1957), p. 80.

21. U.S. Senate, 81st Cong., 1st sess., 1949, Committee on Interstate and Foreign Commerce, *Fur Labeling, Hearings,* p. 13.

22. Ibid., p. 14.

23. Ibid., pp. 23, 30. Congressman Joseph O'Hara (U.S. House of Representatives, 82nd Cong., 1st sess., June 18, 1951, *Congressional Record,* XCVII, 6693), pointing out that "there is a practice of taking cheap furs and giving it a fancy name," advocated a uniform system of fur naming. See also U.S. House of Representatives, 82nd Cong., 1st sess., 1951, *Fur Labeling,* H. Rept. 546, p. 2; and U.S. Senate, 82nd Cong., 1st sess., 1951, *Fur Labeling,* S. Rept. 78, pp. 1–3, 6.

24. Fuchs, *Economics of the Fur Industry,* pp. 18–19.

25. Ibid., p. 150. Fuchs notes that, as originally introduced, the act required each skin or piece of skin to be separately marked with the country of origin, both before and after processing. Such a requirement would have constituted a serious and costly impediment for importers. The desire of domestic fur farmers and their customers to restrict imports of foreign furs is also noted in "I. J. Fox Pushes Branded Furs," *Business Week,* November 20, 1948, p. 88.

26. *Fur Labeling,* H. Rept. 546, p. 2, notes that the domestic industry bred "high grade" fur animals and hence required protection from cheap imports. Also see *Fur Labeling,* S. Rept. 78, pp. 1–2.

27. The F.T.C.'s letter is reprinted in *Fur Labeling,* S. Rept. 78, p. 6.

28. U.S. Senate, *Fur Labeling, Hearings,* pp. 59, 71, 73–82, 94–97, 161. Some retailers also opposed the bill, not on substantive grounds but because of the bookkeeping burdens the act would impose.

29. Ibid., pp. 94–97.

30. *Annual Report of the Federal Trade Commission, 1972* (Washington, D.C.: Government Printing Office, 1972), p. 21. See also Richard Posner, *Regulation of Advertising by the F.T.C.* (Washington, D.C.: American Enterprise Institute for Public Policy Research, 1973), p. 27.

31. Congressional Quarterly Service, *Congress and the Nation, 1945–1964* (Washington, 1965), p. 1167.

32. U.S. House of Representatives, 83d Cong., 1st sess., 1953, Committee on Interstate and Foreign Commerce, *Flammable Fabrics Act, Hearings,* pp. 136–137.

33. Ibid., p. 92; see also pp. 37, 48, 66, 92.

34. A typical order is *Nichimen Co., Inc.,* 64 F.T.C. 330 (1964).

35. Ralph Nader, "The Great American Gyp," in *Consumerism,* ed. David Aaker and George Day (New York: Free Press, 1971), p. 30.

36. *Annual Report of the F.T.C.,* 1972, p. 23.

37. U.S. Senate, 89th Cong., 1st sess., 1963, Committee on Commerce, *Problems of the Domestic Textile Industry: Third Supplementary Report,* p. 14.

38. U.S. House of Representatives, 85th Cong., 1st sess., 1957, Committee on Interstate and Foreign Commerce, *Textile Fiber Products Identification Act, Hearings,* p. 40; see also pp. 19–20.

39. Ibid., p. 24; and U.S. House of Representatives, 85th Cong., 1st sess., August 14, 1957, *Congressional Record,* LIII, 14746–14748.

40. *Textile Fiber Products, Hearings,* p. 22. See also U.S. Senate, 85th Cong., 2d sess., 1958, Committee on Interstate and Foreign Commerce, *Textile Labeling Legislation, Hearings,* p. 22; and Congressman Smith's remarks of August 14, 1957, in *Congressional Record,* LIII, 14751.

41. House, *Textile Fiber Products, Hearings,* p. 210.

42. Senate, *Textile Labeling, Hearings,* p. 123.

43. U.S. House of Representatives, 85th Cong., 1st sess., August 14, 1957, *Congressional Record,* LIII, 14751; see also pp. 14748, 14752.

44. Ibid., p. 14750; House of Representatives, 85th Cong., 1st sess., August 14, 1957, *Congressional Record,* LIII, 14750. *Textile Fiber Products, Hearings,* pp. 111, 136, 208–211; and Senate, *Textile Labeling, Hearings,* pp. 212, 273.

45. Susan Wagner, *The Federal Trade Commission* (New York: Praeger, 1971), p. 165.

46. American Bar Association, *Report,* p. 48.

47. Congressional Quarterly Service, *Congress and the Nation* (Washington, D.C., 1969), II, 96.

Chapter 10

1. Colston E. Warne, "Is It Time to Re-evaluate the Consumer Activities of the Federal Government?" *Journal of Consumer Affairs,* Summer 1967, p. 25.

2. A useful review of the growth of consumerism is Mark Nadel, *The Politics of Consumer Protection* (Indianapolis: Bobbs-Merrill, 1971). I have drawn on Nadel's work but my analysis differs from his in several respects.

3. Ralph Nader, *Unsafe at Any Speed* (New York: Simon & Schuster, 1965).

4. See the analysis in Paul H. Weaver, "Liberals and the Presidency," *Commentary,* October 1975, p. 51.

5. On the growth of advertising expenditures, see Jules Backman, *Advertising and Competition* (New York: New York University Press, 1967), p. 189.

6. Walter McQuade, "Why Nobody's Happy about Appliances," *Fortune,* May 1972, p. 182.

7. Stephen Greyser and Stephen Diamond, "Business Is Adapting to Consumerism," *Harvard Business Review,* LII (September 1974), 58.

8. *Public Papers of the Presidents of the United States: Richard M. Nixon* (Washington, D.C.: Office of the Federal Register, 1969), p. 884.

9. See the survey data in "America's Growing Antibusiness Mood," *Business Week,* June 17, 1972, pp. 100–103.

10. "Business Responds to Consumerism," *Business Week,* September 6, 1969, p. 102.

11. Ibid.; and see "Madison Avenue's Response to Its Critics," *Business Week,* June 10, 1972, p. 50.

12. See U.S. Senate, 85th Cong., 2d sess., 1958, Committee on the Judiciary, Subcommittee on Antitrust and Monopoly, *Administered Prices: Automobiles, Report,* pp. 121–123.

13. See *The Papercraft Corp.,* 63 F.T.C. 1965 (1963); *Superior Insulating*

Tape Co., 61 F.T.C. 416 (1960); and *Dell Publishing Co.,* 54 F.T.C. 1623 (1958).

14. Jessie V. Coles, *Standards and Labels for Consumer Goods* (New York: Ronald Press, 1949), p. 421.

15. John M. Gaus and Leon Wolcott, *Public Administration and the United States Department of Agriculture* (Chicago: Public Administration Service, 1940), p. 176; and U.S. House of Representatives, 89th Cong., 2d sess., 1966, Committee on Interstate and Foreign Commerce, *Fair Packaging and Labeling, Hearings,* pt. 1, pp. 308–309.

16. "War for the Packaging Dollar," *Dun's Review,* December 1964, pp. 89–96.

17. Nadel, *Politics of Consumer Protection,* p. 40.

18. "Consumer Interests," *Weekly Compilation of Presidential Documents,* II (1966), 424, 428.

19. Jeremy Main, "Industry Still Has Something to Learn about Congress," *Fortune,* February 1967, p. 128.

20. *Fair Packaging and Labeling, Hearings,* pt. 1, pp. 295, 305, 308–309; pt. 2, pp. 880, 882; Congressional Quarterly Service, *Congress and the Nation* (Washington, D.C., 1969), II, 793.

21. *Fair Packaging and Labeling, Hearings,* pt. 1, pp. 31–33, 43–45.

22. Main, "Industry Still Has Something to Learn," pp. 128–129, 191–192, 194.

23. U.S. House of Representatives, 89th Cong., 2d sess., October 3, 1966, *Congressional Record* LXII, 24837.

24. U.S. House of Representatives, 91st Cong., 2d sess., 1970, Committee on Interstate and Foreign Commerce, *Class Action and Other Consumer Protection Procedures,* p. 300.

25. See U.S. Federal Trade Commission, "Regulations under Section 5(c) of the Fair Packaging and Labeling Act," *Federal Register,* XXXVI, 12284–12288 (June 21, 1971).

26. *F.T.C. News Summary,* no. 3, 1974.

27. The only packaging case in the first six months of 1973, for example, was *Activitoys, Ltd.,* 82 F.T.C. 1264 (1973).

28. *Congressional Record,* CXIV (1968), 1422.

29. "Consumer Interests," *Weekly Compilation of Presidential Documents,* II (1966), 424.

30. See Theodore Volckhausen, "Trends in Lending," *Banking,* November 1968, p. 68; and Homer Kripke, "Gesture and Reality in Consumer Credit Reform," in *Consumerism,* ed. David Aaker and George Day, 2d ed. (New York: Free Press, 1974), p. 221.

31. Details are provided in Homer Kripke, "Consumer Credit Regulation," *Columbia Law Review,* LXVIII (March 1968), 456–457.

32. U.S. House of Representatives, 90th Cong., 1st sess., 1967, Committee on Banking and Currency, Subcommittee on Consumer Affairs, *Consumer Credit Protection Act, Hearings,* p. 124.

33. Ibid., pp. 348–349; and Congressional Quarterly Service, *Congress and the Nation,* II, 809.

34. *Consumer Credit Protection Act, Hearings,* pp. 347–353.

35. "Lenders Doubt that the Truth Will Hurt," *Business Week,* June 30, 1968, p. 130.

36. *Consumer Credit Protection Act, Hearings,* pp. 210–228.

37. See, for example, ibid., pt. 2, pp. 705–712.

38. "Lenders Doubt"; and *Congressional Record,* LXIV (1968), 1438.
39. F. Angell, "Some Effects of Truth in Lending Legislation," *Journal of Business,* XLIV (January 1971), 78–81.
40. Kripke, "Gesture and Reality," pp. 220–221.
41. Richard Posner, *Regulation of Advertising by the F.T.C.* (Washington, D.C.: American Enterprise Institute for Public Policy Research, 1973), p. 25; and Kripke, "Gesture and Reality," pp. 219–220.
42. See, for example, *Sharpe's Appliance Store, Inc.,* 82 F.T.C. 1 (1973).
43. *Annual Report of the Federal Trade Commission, 1972* (Washington, D.C.: Government Printing Office, 1972), p. 19.
44. Betty Furness, former special assistant to the President for consumer affairs, quoted in Kripke, "Gesture and Reality," p. 224.
45. See, for example, *B. W. Cooke,* 9 F.T.C. 283 (1925); *E. P. James,* 1 F.T.C. 380 (1919); and *Akron Tire Co.,* 2 F.T.C. 119 (1919).
46. *Baldwin Bracelet Corp.,* 61 F.T.C. 1345 (1962); *Clinton Watch Co.,* 57 F.T.C. 222 (1960), affirmed in 291 F. 2d 838 (C.C.A., 7, 1961).
47. McQuade, "Why Nobody's Happy," p. 182.
48. Ibid., p. 180. See also the statement of Congressman John Dingell in U.S. House of Representatives, 92d Cong., 1st sess., 1971, Committee on Interstate and Foreign Commerce, *Consumer Warranty Protection, Hearings,* p. 98.
49. U.S. House of Representatives, 93rd Cong., 2d sess., 1974, *Consumer Product Warranties and Federal Trade Commission Improvements Act,* H. Rept. 1107, pp. 25–26.
50. Ibid., p. 26; and *Consumer Warranty Protection, Hearings,* pp. 211–213.
51. Every state except Louisiana has adopted the Uniform Commercial Code on Warranties. See Sections 2/312–317, 2/714–715, and 2/718–719 of the code.
52. U.S. House of Representatives, 93d Cong., 1st sess., 1973, Committee on Interstate and Foreign Commerce, *Consumer Warranty Protection: 1973, Hearings,* pp. 166–168; and 92nd Cong., 1st sess., 1971, *Consumer Warranty Protection, Hearings,* pp. 179–180.
53. *Consumer Warranty Protection: 1973, Hearings,* pp. 280, 340–341.
54. *Consumer Warranty Protection, Hearings,* p. 148.
55. Ibid., p. 297.
56. U.S. Senate, 93rd Cong., 1st sess., 1973, *Magnuson-Moss Warranty– Federal Trade Commission Improvement Act,* S. Rept. 151, p. 6.
57. Milton Friedman, "Barking Cats," *Newsweek,* February 19, 1973, p. 70.

Chapter 11

1. Two recent good reviews of theories of regulation are Thomas K. McGraw, "Regulation in America," *Business History Review,* XLIX (Summer 1975), 159–184, and Richard A. Posner, "Theories of Economic Regulation," *Bell Journal of Economics and Management Science,* 5 (Autumn 1974), 335–359. The modern classic on economic regulation is Alfred E. Kahn, *The Economics of Regulation,* 2 vols. (New York: Wiley, 1970–1971).
2. Alfred D. Chandler, "The Structure of American Industry in the Twentieth Century: A Historical Overview," *Business History Review,* XLIII (Autumn 1969), 460–461.
3. See Sam Peltzman, "An Evaluation of Consumer Protection Legislation: The 1962 Drug Amendments," *Journal of Political Economy,* LXXXI (September–October 1973), 1049–1091; and J. M. Jadlow, "Price Competition and

the Efficacy of Prescription Drugs," *Nebraska Journal of Economics and Business*, XI (Autumn, 1972), 121–133. The burden of William M. Capron, ed., *Technological Change in Regulated Industries* (Washington, D.C.: Brookings Institution, 1971), is that technological development in highly regulated industries falls far short of even a reasonable target for public policy, let alone of the ideal.

4. Paul MacAvoy, "The Effectiveness of the Federal Power Commission," *Bell Journal of Economics and Management Science*, I (Spring 1970), 113–128; and Paul MacAvoy, "The Regulation Induced Shortage of Natural Gas," *Journal of Law and Economics*, XIV (April 1971), 167–199.

5. James S. Earley, in "Marginal Policies of Excellently Managed Firms," *American Economic Review*, XLVI (March 1956), 44–71, and in *American Economic Review Papers and Proceedings*, XLVII (May 1957), 330–335, has verified empirically that these are the overriding goals of business firms.

6. "Goodyear Chief Hits Regulation," *New York Times*, November 11, 1975, p. 45; and "Fortune's Directory of the 500 Largest Industrial Corporations," *Fortune*, May 1975, pp. 208–238.

7. See E. J. Mishan, *The Costs of Economic Growth* (London: Penguin, 1967), pp. 147–151.

8. For details see U.S. Senate, 87th Cong., 1st sess., 1961, Committee on the Judiciary, Subcommittee on Antitrust and Monopoly, *Administered Prices: Drugs*, S. Rept. 448.

9. A superb essay summarizing the literature on externalities is E. J. Mishan, "The Postwar Literature on Externalities: An Interpretative Essay," *Journal of Economic Literature*, XIII (March 1971), 1–28.

10. Neil Chamberlain, *The Limits of Corporate Responsibility* (New York: Basic Books, 1973), pp. 5–6. See also Christopher D. Stone, *Where the Law Ends* (New York: Harper & Row, 1975), pp. 88–92.

11. Robert Heilbroner et al., *In the Name of Profits* (New York: Doubleday, 1972), p. 210.

12. For details see "The Silent Crisis in R & D," *Business Week*, March 8, 1976, p. 90.

13. The classic statement of the conflict between capitalism and private virtue remains Bernard Mandeville, *The Fable of the Bees* (1714; Baltimore: Penguin, 1970).

Index

ECONOMIC REGULATION
AND THE PUBLIC INTEREST

Designed by R. E. Rosenbaum.
Composed by York Composition Company, Inc.,
in 10 point Linotype Times Roman, 2 points leaded,
with display lines in monotype Perpetua.
Printed letterpress from type by York Composition Company
on Warren's Number 66 text, 50 pound basis.
Bound by John H. Dekker & Sons, Inc.
in Holliston book cloth
and stamped in All Purpose foil.

Library of Congress Cataloging in Publication Data
(For library cataloging purposes only)

Stone, Alan, 1931–
   Economic regulation and the public interest.

   Includes index.
   Bibliography: p.
   1. United States. Federal Trade Commission. I. Title.
HD2775.F92 1977   353.008'26   76-25645
ISBN 0-8014-1066-5

103. Weston concludes (p. 102) that "if all firms had been established at some arbitrary starting point, say 1903, and internal growth of the amounts which they actually experienced had been their only method of growth, present concentration levels would be virtually unchanged."

16. Henry A. Einhorn, "Competition in American Industry, 1939–1958," *Journal of Political Economy,* LXXIV (October 1966), 507; G. Warren Nutter and Henry A. Einhorn, *Enterprise Monopoly in the United States: 1899–1958* (New York: Columbia University Press, 1969), pp. 81–93.

17. John Lintner and J. Keith Butters, "Effects of Mergers on Industrial Concentration, 1940–1946," *Review of Economics and Statistics,* XXXII (February 1950), 30–48; see also Martin, *Mergers,* p. 233.

18. U.S. Senate, 80th Cong., 1st sess., 1947, Committee on the Judiciary, *Amending Sections 7 and 11 of the Clayton Act, Hearings,* p. 7.

19. An excellent summary of oligopoly theories is contained in Leonard W. Weiss, "The Concentration-Profits Relationship and Antitrust," in *Industrial Concentration: The New Learning,* ed. Harvey J. Goldschmid et al. (Boston: Little, Brown, 1974), pp. 188–193.

20. See Augustin Cournot, *The Mathematical Principles of the Theory of Wealth* (1838; Homewood, Ill.: Richard D. Irwin, 1963); William Fellner, *Competition among the Few* (New York: Knopf, 1949), pp. 77–86; and Edward H. Chamberlin, *The Theory of Monopolistic Competition,* 8th ed. (Cambridge: Harvard University Press, 1962), chap. 5, pt. 4.

21. See John M. Vernon, *Market Structure and Industrial Performance* (Boston: Allyn & Bacon, 1972), chaps. 3–6.

22. Joe S. Bain, "Relation of Profit Rate to Industry Concentration: American Manufacturing, 1936–1940," *Quarterly Journal of Economics,* LXV (August 1951), 293–324.

23. Yale Brozen, "Bain's Concentration and Rates of Return Revisited," *Journal of Law and Economics,* XIV (October 1971), 366. See also Yale Brozen, "The Antitrust Task Force Deconcentration Recommendation," *Journal of Law and Economics,* XIII (October 1970), 279–292.

24. Stanley Ornstein, "Concentration and Profits," in *The Impact of Large Firms on the U.S. Economy,* ed. J. Fred Weston and Stanley I. Ornstein (Lexington, Mass.: Heath, 1973), p. 101.

25. Harold Demsetz, "Two Systems of Belief about Monopoly," in *Industrial Concentration,* ed. Goldschmid, p. 179.

26. Harold Demsetz, "Industry Structure, Market Rivalry, and Public Policy," in *Industrial Concentration,* ed. Goldschmid, pp. 80–81; and Yale Brozen, "Concentration and Profits: Does Concentration Matter?" in ibid., pp. 69–70.

27. Betty Bock and Jack Farkas, *Concentration and Productivity* (New York: National Industrial Conference Board, 1969), pp. 4–5. See also Caleb A. Smith, "Survey of the Empirical Evidence of Economies of Scale," in *Business Concentration and Price Policy,* National Bureau Committee for Economic Research (Princeton: Princeton University Press, 1955), p. 229. Industry studies that support the Bock-Farkas thesis include Charles E. Edwards, *Dynamics of the United States Automobile Industry* (Columbia: University of South Carolina Press, 1965), and John S. McGee, "Economies of Size in Auto Body Manufacture," *Journal of Law and Economics,* XVI (October 1973), 239–274. But contrast Federal Trade Commission, *Economic Report on the Influence of Market Structure on the Profit Performance of Food Manufacturing Industries* (Washington, D.C.: Government Printing Office, 1969), p. 7.